Decolonizing University Teaching and Learning

Also available from Bloomsbury

Assessment for Social Justice: Perspectives and Practices within Higher Education by Jan McArthur
Changing Higher Education for a Changing World edited by Claire Callender, William Locke, Simon Marginson
Community-Based Transformational Learning: An Interdisciplinary Inquiry into Student Experiences and Challenges edited by Christian Winterbottom, Jody S. Nicholson, F. Dan Richard
Experiments in Decolonizing the University: Towards an Ecology of Study by Hans Schildermans
Exploring Consensual Leadership in Higher Education: Co-operation, Collaboration and Partnership edited by Lynne Gornall, Brychan Thomas, and Lucy Sweetman
Leadership for Sustainability in Higher Education by Janet Haddock-Fraser, Peter Rands, Stephen Scoffham
Negotiating Learning and Identity in Higher Education: Access, Persistence and Retention edited by Bongi Bangeni and Rochelle Kapp
Reflective Teaching in Higher Education by Paul Ashwin, David Boud, Susanna Calkins, Kelly Coate, Fiona Hallett, Greg Light, Kathy Luckett, Jan McArthur, Iain MacLaren, Monica McLean, Velda McCune, Katarina Mårtensson, Michelle Tooher
Socially Just Pedagogies: Posthumanist, Feminist and Materialist Perspectives in Higher Education edited by Vivienne Bozalek, Rosi Braidotti, Tamara Shefer and Michalinos Zembylas
The Roma in European Higher Education: Recasting Identities, Re-imagining Futures edited by Louise Morley, Andrzej Mirga, Nadir Redzepi
Transforming University Education: A Manifesto by Paul Ashwin

Decolonizing University Teaching and Learning

An Entry Model for Grappling with Complexities

D. Tran

BLOOMSBURY ACADEMIC
LONDON • NEW YORK • OXFORD • NEW DELHI • SYDNEY

BLOOMSBURY ACADEMIC
Bloomsbury Publishing Plc
50 Bedford Square, London, WC1B 3DP, UK
1385 Broadway, New York, NY 10018, USA
29 Earlsfort Terrace, Dublin 2, Ireland

BLOOMSBURY, BLOOMSBURY ACADEMIC and the Diana logo are trademarks of Bloomsbury Publishing Plc

First published in Great Britain 2021
This paperback edition published 2023

Copyright © D. Tran and Contributors, 2021

D. Tran and Contributors have asserted their right under the Copyright, Designs and Patents Act, 1988, to be identified as Author of this work.

For legal purposes the Acknowledgments on p. xii constitute an extension of this copyright page.

Cover image © Maxwell Monivongsa Gemmill and Alastair Gemmill

All rights reserved. No part of this publication may be reproduced or transmitted in any form or by any means, electronic or mechanical, including photocopying, recording, or any information storage or retrieval system, without prior permission in writing from the publishers.

Bloomsbury Publishing Plc does not have any control over, or responsibility for, any third-party websites referred to or in this book. All internet addresses given in this book were correct at the time of going to press. The author and publisher regret any inconvenience caused if addresses have changed or sites have ceased to exist, but can accept no responsibility for any such changes.

A catalogue record for this book is available from the British Library.

A catalog record for this book is available from the Library of Congress.

Library of Congress Cataloging-in-Publication Data
Names: Tran, D., author.
Title: Decolonizing university teaching and learning: an entry model for grappling with complexities / D. Tran.
Description: London, UK; New York, NY: Bloomsbury Academic, 2021. | Includes bibliographical references and index. |
Identifiers: LCCN 2020055550 (print) | LCCN 2020055551 (ebook) | ISBN 9781350160019 (hardback) | ISBN 9781350160026 (ebook) | ISBN 9781350160033 (epub)
Subjects: LCSH: Education, Higher–Social aspects. | Education, Higher–Aims and objectives. | Education, Higher–Curricula. | Culturally relevant pedagogy.
Classification: LCC LC191.9 .T73 2021 (print) | LCC LC191.9 (ebook) | DDC 378--dc23
LC record available at https://lccn.loc.gov/2020055550
LC ebook record available at https://lccn.loc.gov/2020055551

ISBN: HB: 978-1-3501-6001-9
PB: 978-1-3502-1676-1
ePDF: 978-1-3501-6002-6
eBook: 978-1-3501-6003-3

Typeset by Deanta Global Publishing Services, Chennai, India

To find out more about our authors and books visit www.bloomsbury.com and sign up for our newsletters.

Dedicated to Reaksmey Lim

Contents

List of Figures	viii
Preface	ix
Acknowledgments	xii
Introduction	1
1 What Does It Mean to Decolonize Teaching and Learning?	7
2 What Is Good Development?: *With Contributions from Nelly Kibirige and Bernadine Idowu-Onibokun*	23
3 The TRAAC Model	49
4 Bringing Together Materials for a Decolonized Curriculum: *With Contributions from Jason Arday and Joanne Dunham*	63
5 Moving Away from Passive Inclusivity	87
6 Staff and Student Perceptions: *With Contributions from Ryan Carty, Rahma Elmahdi, and Emilie Fairnington*	101
7 Delivery and Power Dynamics	125
8 Implementing the TRAAC Model across Disciplines: *With Contributions from Paul Breen, Anthony Cullen, Rahma Elmahdi, Peter Jones, Savvas Michael, and Dawn Reilly*	135
Conclusion	163
References	171
Notes on Contributors	205
Index	209

Figure

1 The TRAAC Model (Teaching Approach, Relationship, Activity and Assessment, and Content): An Entry Point For Challenging Conversations about Decolonizing   50

Preface

While there has been a rapid rise in interest surrounding decolonizing work in recent years, decolonizing work has been engaged with for generations. The issues discussed in this book are therefore not new. Today's climate of growing commitment to address inequalities we owe to the early efforts of those before us who dedicated their lives to bring issues of equality of education and decolonizing to the forefront of debate and those who have continued to keep this work as a constant priority. Is "decolonizing" a topic, subject, movement, process, or an agenda? This book employs all of these terms to describe decolonizing, as it is all of these things, sometimes more of one than others depending on the context being discussed. When decolonizing is approached as a general topic, it can cover an array of issues and histories. The subject of decolonizing teaching and learning within this book is focused on the relationship between curriculum, pedagogy, staff, and students. Student-led campaigns calling for universities to be decolonized have led to the subject becoming a movement for change. Through developing and implementing appropriate interventions, steps can be taken to progress the decolonizing agenda, which works toward creating a more equal university environment and experience. This book is intended for colleagues who are interested in decolonizing teaching and learning and those who are unsure about what it involves and what its impact could be.

Before delving into a detailed consideration of decolonizing teaching and learning, it is helpful to outline the context and purpose of this book, simultaneously considering the scope and limitations of the text. At the time of writing, the world was reeling from the first wave of deaths caused by the Covid-19 pandemic. During the outbreak, media attention was drawn to the disproportionate number of Black, Asian, and Minority Ethnic (BAME) victims. The same year saw racial inequalities pushed further to the forefront of global news as high-profile deaths of unarmed Black Americans as a result of police brutality led to worldwide calls to tackle systemic racism. Though these events and crises were happening outside of the higher education (HE) sector, they have significantly influenced growing calls for universities to review existing practices and structures in order to develop anti-racist teaching and learning environments.

These recent events helped to reinvigorate the Rhodes Must Fall campaign at Oxford University and have in many ways drawn more attention to the decolonizing agenda and what HE institutions are doing to engage in decolonizing work. Reference to "decolonizing universities" and "decolonizing the curriculum" has been on the increase within the HE sector internationally as staff and students express growing support for the movement by critically examining the ongoing impacts and manifestations of colonial histories within universities. Raising the profile of the topic can play a role in developing the culture of an institution. However, there have also been arguments that criticize the value and efforts to decolonize the institution, teaching, and learning. At times, the topic is treated as supplementary to other commonplace university agendas.

This book considers apprehensions about decolonizing and offers a summary of key arguments within existing critical discussion on its meaning and value. The text does not claim to reference all related literature and work focused on decolonizing, but it does engage with a growing body of literature and explores this emerging area of research through mindful considerations of ranging positions, perspectives, and contexts. The contextually based and complex discussions concerning decolonization means one cannot be guided through the process in a particular way. Therefore, while the book discusses central challenges to the decolonizing process and ruminates on practical suggestions for how these may be grappled with, the text is not intended to be read as a handbook for decolonizing teaching and learning, nor is it an anthropologically oriented text. The book draws on Critical Race Theory (CRT), and during these times where calls for progress regarding equality have been magnified, the text may be used to navigate a different space when attempting to progress discussions on decolonizing.

The focus of the book is HE teaching and learning within the UK context, mirrored in the UK-based institutions under consideration across all the contributions. The use of the UK term BAME, which stands for Black, Asian, and Minority Ethnic, in this book is not intended to homogenize groups of people. When referencing literature and studies that take place in different contexts, terms such as "Aboriginal," "Indigenous," and "People of Color" are also employed. This points to the way the Teaching, Relationship, Activity and Assessment, and Content (TRAAC) model asks users to engage with global academic contributions. However, as noted in the recent "#BAMEOver—A Statement for the UK" (2020), it is vital to problematize the use of labels and to recognize identities of "people who are ethnically and culturally diverse, and who experience racism in our society."

Rather than offering up answers or resolutions, this book aims to highlight the benefits of decolonizing teaching and learning for all students and staff. Participating in the process of reflection and reflexivity is a vital part of engaging in conversations to do with decolonizing, and this can be very challenging. This book makes no promises but offers up the TRAAC model as an entry point for challenging conversations. By framing the chapters of the book around the topic headings in the segments of the model, the text may in some ways be understood as a user guide for TRAAC—but this is not to say that the book is a user guide for decolonizing teaching and learning. By bringing together questions raised within existing scholarly discussions on decolonizing teaching and learning, the TRAAC model provides some meaningful prompts to help instigate deeper reflections of and conversations around decolonizing by way of supporting colleagues to start a productive dialogue. Through these critically reflective and reflexive conversations, action-oriented discussions can simultaneously take place.

Acknowledgments

The value of this book lies in the contributions from authors based across a number of universities: Jason Arday, Ryan Carty, Anthony Cullen, Bernadine Idowu-Onibokun, Peter Jones, Nelly Kibirige, Paul Breen, Joanne Dunham, Rahma Elmahdi, Emilie Fairnington, Savvas Michael, and Dawn Reilly. I thank the contributors wholeheartedly for their personal stories, shared experiences, reflections, and authentic conversations which touch upon core areas of consideration relating to decolonizing teaching and learning. I thank my family and friends for their support, understanding, and patience while the coming together of this book has taken a significant place in my mind and heart. I thank critical friends, including Reza Gholami, Rashi Rohatgi, and James Wisdom, who have cast their knowledgeable eyes over proposals, sample chapters, and/or entire drafts—I am grateful for your time, feedback, and unwavering encouragement throughout the writing process. Thank you also to Alison Baker for providing professional guidance during this journey.

Introduction

When exploring the subject of decolonizing, scholars have placed emphasis on different issues depending on the context under consideration. This affects what labels may be used to refer to involved parties such as "colonizer," "colonized," "settler," "Aboriginal," and "Indigenous." As the contextual focus of this book is the higher education (HE) sector, the core parties involved are "students" and "staff." "Students" refers to students of all levels of study across subject areas in HE. Staff refers to all university employees whose work relates to teaching and/or supporting learning including academic, professional services, and technical colleagues. Rather than looking into how efforts to decolonize have impacted a particular area of research, the book references scholarship that explores decolonizing across a range of disciplines to consider how it is understood and engaged with as both a subject and a process by staff and students. While the topic of decolonizing is connected to discussions relating to inclusivity, the BAME awarding gap, and access and participation, to subsume decolonizing under these areas risks failing to acknowledge and respond to its particular areas of concern. The book situates the decolonizing process as an extension of inclusivity work and calls for it to be addressed as a prioritized agenda.

What connects all the chapters together is the TRAAC model. Each chapter focuses on one or more segments of TRAAC: Teaching Approach, Relationship, Activity and Assessment, and Content. The model does not frame the discussion of decolonizing but helps to link themes that are threaded through interconnecting discussions. An authentic exploration of the subject requires space for the discussion to grow and develop outside of a structure. Decolonizing is an emotive topic that can spark an array of reactions among individuals engaging with its term and related arguments. It can be difficult to translate the agenda into practical interventions and measurable outputs. This challenge leads to resistance to engage in the decolonizing process. There is also growing pressure among universities to show active engagement in the decolonizing process and to evidence their impact, but the process cannot be rushed. The purpose of TRAAC is to help start the process of confronting issues related to decolonizing teaching and learning through a developmental dialogue. This is mirrored in the tone in which this book is written.

Chapter 1, "What Does It Mean to Decolonize Teaching and Learning?," outlines the recent renewed interest in critical discussion concerning the decolonizing movement within the HE sector. This includes a summary of influential campaigns and core arguments relating to efforts to decolonize the university. These point to the continuation of colonial legacies being prominent in HE through the maintenance of colonial structures within the academy. The discussions lead into those of decolonizing teaching and learning, where focus turns to curriculum and pedagogy. The process of decolonizing involves questioning the tendency to favor Western perspectives and materials. Decolonizing reviews the privileging of Western thinking and explores the impact this can have on professional development, student experience, and the growth of a university. The chapter discusses apprehensions concerning the topic and uses critical race theory as a theoretical framework for highlighting the value of engaging with the questions surrounding decolonizing teaching and learning.

Chapter 2, "What Is Good Development?," begins by considering the difference between continuing professional development and what may be called "good development." Putting forth a set of suggested principles for good development, the chapter then explores how engaging in the process of decolonizing can be a form of good development due to its focus on the positive impact and development of others over the individual. Decolonizing teaching and learning is summarized as a valuable developmental activity for all staff involved in teaching and supporting learning. While critical attention on the subject has renewed in recent years, the risk that accompanies such topicality is that it may be perceived as a passing trend. Consequently, there is the danger that the agenda may not receive the responsiveness needed from senior managers and staff throughout an institution.

Growing engagement with the topic can have a significant impact on enhancing teaching practice, student engagement and belonging, and learning experiences. Chapter 2 also includes contributions from Nelly Kibirige and Bernadine Idowu-Onibokun. Nelly engages with the TRAAC model from a personal perspective, responding to the questions raised within the model from the position of a student, mother, and Students' Union president at London South Bank University. Bernadine concentrates on the activity and assessment segment of TRAAC to encourage reflection and discussion among a focus group of students from different disciplines. The contributions underline the need to engage with students as core university stakeholders in a developmental dialogue. The conversation around decolonizing should involve participants across HE institutions and student voices should be central in these discussions.

Chapter 3, "The TRAAC Model," explains the purpose and structure of TRAAC (Teaching Approach, Relationship, Activities and Assessment, Content). Each segment of the model focuses on an area(s) of teaching and learning and has three corresponding questions that can be used to support reflection and planning for curriculum design and teaching approaches. Though the questions in the TRAAC model may initially seem rather general, each one is unpacked in detail later in the chapter. The model may be used developmentally by an individual or as part of a group discussion. The purpose is to provide an accessible model that can be used to support reflexivity, reflection, discussion, and forward planning. The questions raised in TRAAC will not be new to teaching practitioners. The sections of the model refer to areas of teaching and learning that are likely linked in some way or other to formal review processes. It is hoped that employed holistically, the questions raised can help to act as an entry point for deeper critical reflection in regard to decolonizing teaching and learning.

As Archer (2010: 2) notes, "reflection and reflexivity have fuzzy borders and can shift from one to the other." Archer also comments, "The distinguishing feature of reflexivity is that it has the self-referential characteristic of 'bending-back' some thought upon the self, such that it takes the form of *subject-object-subject*" (2010). Dewey and Schön are influential figures in the consideration of reflection. Dewey's "detailed analysis of reflection rests in interpretive interests, in 'making sense of the world' in the process of effective education" (Moon 2004: 15). Dewey believed that reflection could help elucidate a situation "in which there is experienced obscurity, doubt, conflict, disturbance of some sort into a situation that is clear, settled, harmonious" (Dewey 1933: 100–1 cited in Redmond 2006: 9). For Dewey, the process of reflection is followed by actions to help one move forward. These ideas influenced the work of Schön. Lyons (2010: 15) describes how Schön paid attention to the way professionals "exhibit a kind of knowing-in-practice, and they can reveal a kind of capacity to reflect on their knowing in the midst of action." Schön (1983: 280) says, "we are most likely to initiate reflection-in-action when we are stuck or seriously dissatisfied with our performance." Engaging in Dewey's and Schön's ideas on reflection allows for exploration of the areas in the TRAAC model to become more relevant, personal, and developmental.

Referring to the segments of "Content" and "Activities and Assessment" of the TRAAC model, Chapter 4, "Bringing Together Materials for a Decolonized

Curriculum," begins by discussing the different ways academics understand and approach "curriculum." Attention then turns to what are typically considered to be important key questions when planning a curriculum and contrasts this with areas that may lack attention, and which can affect student engagement and feelings of belonging. The chapter then emphasizes the importance of valuing student voices when developing a decolonized curriculum. There is growing work being carried out across the sector to decolonize reading collections to provide more inclusive reading lists. But decolonizing means looking at all areas of teaching and learning where equality, diversity, and inclusion can be enhanced.

Contributions from Jason Arday and Joanne Dunham extend the chapter's discussions on decolonizing the curriculum. Jason's contribution problematizes the Eurocentric canon and calls for structural, cultural, and organizational change to break the monopoly and diversify curricula. Joanne's contribution raises awareness of how libraries can play a significant role in helping with decolonizing teaching and learning and engages with the TRAAC model from a library context. Both contributions highlight the need to push past passive inclusivity and explore new ways of enhancing levels of student belonging in our materials.

Chapter 5, "Moving Away from Passive Inclusivity," focuses on the "Contents" and "Activities and Assessment" segments of the TRAAC model. It discusses how the decolonizing agenda aims to move away from passive inclusivity and surface-level changes when reviewing curriculum design and delivery. It then explores the extent to which the relationship between researcher, participant(s), and methodology can form a decolonized space for research to be carried out. The chapter then reviews teaching practices that can affect levels of student belonging and strategies that can be employed to enhance levels of belonging. Discussion of the use of English as the primary language of instruction in the majority of UK HE classrooms is also touched on by way of looking at the relationship between language and student experience in light of the decolonizing agenda. The chapter then considers the role that technology can play in the process of decolonizing before discussing ways in which the culture of assessment can influence student perceptions of a program and the discipline more widely.

Chapter 6, "Staff and Student Perceptions," looks at the "Relationship" segment of TRAAC to consider the ways in which staff perceptions of students can influence classroom interactions. Unconscious bias can lead to the treatment of particular student groups differently. By considering how unconscious bias can impact teaching and learning, the chapter explores the ways in which individual motivations, belief systems, and experiences feed into the decisions we make in the classroom. Our thoughts, speech, and actions can all be influenced by unconscious bias. Greater awareness of its influence means it can be reflected upon and responded to. Doing so helps to prevent biases from negatively impacting the students' learning experience.

Similarly, the way in which students perceive their teacher may affect levels of trust, engagement, and interest in a particular session, course, or program. The power of seeing diversity among staff can influence a student's sense of belonging and their accessibility to role models who they feel are relatable. The chapter includes contributions from Ryan Carty, Rahma Elmahdi, and Emilie Fairington. All are personal reflections on their individual experiences within HE and explore how relationships inside and outside of the classroom are affected by assumptions and unconscious bias. Ryan's contribution emphasizes the impact which varying levels of inclusivity can have on the student experience. Rahma's contribution underlines the role which reflection and reflexivity can play in supporting one's personal development. Emilie's reflection considers issues relating to equality in education and sport.

Chapter 7, "Delivery and Power Dynamics," focuses on the segments "Teaching Approaches" and "Relationships" of the TRAAC model. The chapter begins by exploring power in the classroom: how it can be created and negotiated. Attention also falls on the topic of trust in the classroom: how it may be located in terms of a spectrum and the ways in which trust can be given, received, and shared. Although there are a number of growing courses and programs offered online or through blended delivery, traditional modes of face-to-face teaching still hold value. This chapter considers different teaching approaches and the challenges that come with them. Focus then turns to how the language of delivery can affect the classroom environment and how being mindful of the ways in which messages are communicated can impact levels of student belonging and participation.

The penultimate chapter, "Implementing the TRAAC Model Across Disciplines," is made up of case studies. The chapter consists of contributions from Paul Breen, Anthony Cullen, Rahma Elmahdi, Peter Jones, Savvas Michael, and Dawn Reilly. Paul focuses on implementing the model in an Academic English context, looking at how the relationship between language, culture, teaching, and learning can be negotiated. Anthony applies the segments of the TRAAC model to the context of Public Law. Rahma teaches medical students and focuses on the TRAAC model's questions on content and learning activities to consider the adoption of a social constructivist perspective to decolonize teaching and learning. Peter's contribution explores student diversity in mass participation universities and discusses decolonizing and declassifying learning and teaching in sociology. By using the TRAAC model to frame discussion, Savvas considers the awarding gap between BAME and white students within the field of law and interrogates the possible reasons for the under representation of BAME solicitors. Dawn's contribution focuses on the area of accounting and summarizes how the TRAAC model was used to reflect and refresh a particular module to enhance levels of inclusivity in an effort to take steps toward decolonizing teaching and learning on a program.

The contributions are from colleagues reflecting on experiences that are based across a number of institutions and departments. This points to how decolonizing HE teaching and learning is not limited to one area of work but is a process that requires attention and commitment across a university to make meaningful change. The authors range across disciplines, looking at different issues relating to the subject of decolonizing. Reflecting on personal experiences, staff and student relationships, subject-specific challenges, and wider issues within HE, each contribution across the book is grounded in its employment of the TRAAC model as a mode of entry into discussing particular issues around decolonizing teaching and learning. Across chapters, contributions are followed by a summary which focuses on shared themes and issues raised. This is not intended to homogenize individual experiences but draws attention to shared experiences and concerns.

The last chapter, "Conclusion," considers where the arguments may be heading regarding decolonizing learning and teaching, what this means for the future of learning and teaching in HE, and the ways in which work carried out to decolonize may be measured for success. There is a need to review the ongoing manifestations of colonial legacies such as structural issues and problematic hegemonic narratives which affect both student and staff experiences at university. Interrogating these narratives requires openness, authenticity, and courage to confront emotions and conversations that dislocate one's own position and mindset. It is vital that the university community as a whole is involved in the decolonizing dialogue to ensure that changes made are ones appropriate to the institution. There is no singular approach to decolonizing a university, curriculum, campus, or classroom. Rather, the challenges and actions are context specific.

1

What Does It Mean to Decolonize Teaching and Learning?

This chapter begins with an overview of the recent renewed interest in decolonizing within the higher education (HE) sector globally and particularly within the United Kingdom. It then moves on to an examination of the term and its associated meanings. The increasing use of the word "decolonizing" to cover a range of areas and activities means its detail can sometimes be lost or unappreciated. The chapter puts forth an understanding of decolonization as an extension of discussions concerning inclusivity, as a process which confronts issues concerning colonial manifestations in current institutional structures, curriculum, and pedagogy. Focus then turns to the relationship between race and education before outlining the way critical race theory can be used as a lens which connects issues that are central to the critical discussion of decolonizing teaching and learning.

The Recent Rise of Decolonizing Curricula: Rhodes Must Fall

The current university learning environment is one with strong ties to a colonial history. "University as we understand it today can be traced to a western genealogy" (Icaza and Vázquez 2018: 111). Calls to decolonize teaching and learning interrogate the extent to which universities in their current state are able to offer a learning environment that can be effectively engaged with by everyone. The tension between coloniality (Quijano 2000) and a growing push toward thoughtful change across all sections and layers of HE is captured in the campaigns and discussions on decolonizing teaching and learning.

South Africa has been at the forefront of decolonizing university campaigns. In March 2015 at the University of Cape Town (UCT) Activist Chumani Maxwele threw excrement on to the campus statue of Cecil Rhodes, a nineteenth-century imperialist. A short article for South African History Online (2015) reports, "Maxwele's protest, staged as a political performance, was in response to the lack of attention given to the symbols on campus that are physical reminders of White supremacy and Black subjugation and oppression that is rooted in South Africa." Rhodes's (1877) belief in a racial hierarchy, once confessing he thought "[the British] are the finest race in the world," meant that the statue was, for many, a constant reminder of past traumas and continuing racial inequalities in South Africa that go back further than apartheid. An interview with a senior researcher at UCT in 2018 made note of how "Rhodes' colonial architectural ideals are deeply embedded in the education system. Eventually, these conditions fuelled the students' demands for decolonized curricula and a transformed institutional culture" (Matebeni 2018).

Maxwele's demonstration quickly grew into a larger student protest with the #RhodesMustFall campaign, eventually leading to Rhodes's statue being dismantled a month later. Universities across South Africa could not ignore the growing calls for greater change toward a more equal and accessible education. Attention on student demonstrations was further powered by the #FeesMustFall protests (Fihlani 2019). Debates addressing the ongoing colonial legacies within universities have been widespread, with decolonizing efforts taking place in Canada, Australia, and America, to name some examples. Some of the action by students and faculty in America has led to the renaming of university buildings (Brooks 2017; Namakkal 2015; Simpson 2017). The same has happened at the University of Cape Town (Patel 2019).

Inspired by events at UCT, student activists at the University of Oxford in the UK led their own Rhodes Must Fall campaign, though the latter did not end with the removal of Rhodes's statue (Rawlinson 2016). There have been a number of other university campaigns that have also focused on addressing racial and educational inequalities. University College London (UCL) led the "Why Is My Curriculum White?" (WIMCW) campaign and produced a video in 2014 where students discuss their views on colonial legacies, whiteness, and decolonizing universities. The Students Union also led a "Decolonise UCL" (2017) campaign. The WIMCW campaign steered other UK universities to question their institutional structures and the heavy reliance on Western knowledge in course content and raise further questions about how to engage in the decolonizing process.

Examples of other institutions grappling with these issues include the Leeds University Union "Why Is My Curriculum White?" campaign (2015) and the Warwick Open Education Series (2015). The University of Sussex Students'

Union (2019) "Decolonize Sussex" campaign "aims to raise awareness of and challenge the complex and varied legacies of racism, imperialism and colonialism within all spheres of [the] university." Keele University (2019) set up a decolonizing curriculum network and published a manifesto online, and De Montfort University launched Decolonising DMU in November 2019. The School of Oriental and African Studies (SOAS) set up a Decolonizing SOAS working group and published a decolonizing curriculum toolkit online (2018). Work on race equality at the University of the Arts London (UAL) has heavily stemmed from long-standing efforts by Shades of Noir and student voices. "In 2009 Shades of Noir (SoN) was created by Aisha Richards. SoN is an independent program that supports 1. Curriculum design, 2. Pedagogies of social justice through representation, 3. Cultural currency, 4. Accessible knowledge" (Shades of Noir 2020). With an influential social media campaign UAL SO WHITE (2015), "'UAL so White' won the best national campaign of the year at NUS Black Students conference 2016" (Tajudeen 2016). In recent years at UAL a Decolonising the Arts Curriculum Zine (2018) and a Decolonising the Arts Institute (2020) have been launched. Such campaigns and sites across these universities are not the products of decolonized institutions but are markers of institutions engaged in the ongoing process of decolonizing.

Student-led campaigns draw attention to more than just statues on campus. They underline student dissatisfaction with the university curriculum, teaching, and learning environment. Efforts to decolonize teaching and learning consider how these areas and others can be reviewed to help enhance the university environment into one that is shaped by the needs and voices of the present rather than the past. Critical discussion on the hierarchy of *what* is studied and *how* within HE has long been debated, but the recent succession of student-led campaigns around decolonizing has meant that HE institutions must thoughtfully respond to these concerns by implementing necessary changes across all areas of the institution, or risk failing the lifeblood of the sector, the students themselves.

The work that has been carried out by universities across the country so far is evidence of the growing interest in decolonizing, an acknowledgment of continued inequalities that run deep within an institution and an effort to address these. However, in spite of the recognized campaigns and work that has been carried out, the impact these have had to change core practices and the culture of an institution has been limited. Decolonizing is a continuing process for long-lasting change, and current work reflects the early stage the sector is currently in regarding the decolonizing journey. Retaining this commitment and developing the resource and capacity for decolonizing work is vital if significant change is to occur.

Understanding Decolonizing Teaching and Learning

It is difficult to outline what decolonizing university teaching and learning means in one definition as it covers various intersecting issues and topics such as history, politics, culture, and, of course, education. But for Tuck and Yang (2012: 1), applying the term "decolonization" to an educational setting is problematized, "The easy adoption of decolonizing discourse by educational advocacy and scholarship, evidenced by the increasing number of calls to 'decolonize our schools,' or use 'decolonizing methods,' or, 'decolonize student thinking,' turns decolonization into a metaphor." It is a subject rooted in a number of interrelated topics, all of which should be treated sensitively.

Behari-Leak et al. (2017) also comment on the complexity of the term: "People want a precise definition. But it's not that simple. [. . .] An understanding of the process of 'decolonisation' lies more in its detail than its definition." Anjana Ragavan, taking part in a video talk on "Decolonising Higher Education," stresses the role which context plays in discussions of decolonizing, "the work that decoloniality is means that it has to be diversely understood and diversely framed depending on the context you are working with" (Abdi 2020: seventeenth minute). As Pirbhai-Illich, Pete, and Martin (2017: 4) appreciate, "we recognise that all attempts to know, and to cocreate new knowledge, are socially situated—as individuals our standpoints will necessarily limit what can be known and what we are permitted to know. It is through solidarity and critical intercultural dialogue that we are able to begin to imagine human relations differently."

In "Decolonizing the University," Gebrial (2018: 20) notes, "decolonization is about recognising the roots of contemporary racism in the multiple material, political, social and cultural processes of colonialism." Decolonizing teaching and learning involves reviewing the ways in which the past manifests itself in the present through the problematic structures being upheld. These need to be fully recognized before purposeful steps can be taken to move forward. This process involves questioning power dynamics, hegemonic narratives, and hierarchies that can impact on levels of belonging. Pete (2018: 174) states, "decolonization begins with naming colonial structures then moving to reframe, remake and reform them." Le Grange (2016: 6) speaks of decolonization as "decentring [Western knowledge] or perhaps deterritorialising it." In the setting of university classrooms, these practical learning spaces are where colonial structures can be echoed or transformed. For Le Grange, "The decolonised curriculum is based on the 4Rs central to an emergent Indigenous paradigm [. . .] relational accountability, respectful representation, reciprocal appropriation, and rights and regulation" (2016: 9).

For Fomunyam (2017: 6797), decolonization is a move "away from the political or traditional notion of decolonising which means the process of relinquishing control of a territory by the coloniser to the colonised, to the more rigorous intricacy of shedding away colonial legacies from the education system be it material or ideological." Expectations, goals, and the process to achieve the decolonizing agenda are further complicated by the origins of the institution itself. Abdi (2020: sixth minute) raises the question, "to what extent can we actually do that work [decolonizing in practice] within systems and within organisations that are not designed to do that work?" There is also the argument that the work to decolonize teaching and learning is only relevant to a few subject areas such as literature and history. But decolonizing considers aspects of teaching and learning that are central to all subject areas including teaching approaches, assessment, content, and the student learning experience.

The difficulty of discussing traumatic histories, ongoing legacies of the past, and hesitations toward efforts to engage in decolonizing teaching and learning has led to misunderstandings of and tensions around what decolonizing means and entails. Mgqwashu (2016), speaking of the South African context, notes the perspective "that decolonization equals an attack on white academics by black academics [. . .] requires unsettling." While emphasizing how the country's history created racial divisions that have become embedded in education, Mgqwashu (2016) goes on to explain that "Decolonization is not a project over which one racial group can claim sole custodianship." While acts associated with colonization are undertakings of power and dominance, the process of decolonization is not aimed at substituting one type of control with another. It involves opening up new ways of seeing, examining, and producing knowledge which challenges the privileging of Western-centrism that currently pervades HE.

Misunderstandings of the decolonizing agenda can lead to miscommunication, which can lead to conversations breaking down at the earliest of stages. Rather than focusing on explaining what decolonizing involves through a short definition, it is helpful to acknowledge its evolving nature. There is no defined end point for decolonizing as it is not fixed in nature. Decolonizing is an evolving process and current understandings of the term will likely develop and change over time too. The process of grappling with decolonizing does not begin with trying to forcefully pin it down into a singular mode of understanding. To respond to calls of decolonizing teaching and learning is to listen, reflect, explore, and review.

Ferguson et al. (2019: 3–4) note the following regarding decolonizing learning, "it's about considering multiple perspectives and making space to think carefully about what we value. Decolonizing learning helps us to recognize, understand, and challenge the ways in which our world is shaped by colonialism. It also prompts us to examine our professional practices." This may lead to discomfort and tension, but such feelings should be recognized as necessary steps toward positive change. The process of decolonizing may create internal conflict as well as external conflicting viewpoints. But as hooks stresses (Brosi and hooks 2012: 76), "The truth is that you cannot build community without conflict." "Decolonizing Learning opens up the most exciting, and the most unsettling, possibilities. This is a pedagogy that could produce radical changes in education, leading to learning that not only supports and develops communities but is also strongly rooted within them" (Ferguson et al. 2019: 7).

The fruition of these possibilities requires honest reflection and a commitment to being open to views and positions that may disorientate one's own. Lorde (1984: 3) emphasizes the need for "learning how to take our differences and make them strengths. For the master's tools will never dismantle the master's house. They may allow us temporarily to beat him at his own game, but they will never enable us to bring about genuine change." Although Lorde's statement is here made in reference to the need for acknowledgment of differences among women when discussing feminist theory and the requirement for a greater incorporation of voices from poor women, Black and third world women, and lesbians, the points raised can also be applied to the process of decolonizing teaching and learning. hooks (2003: 35) comments that "through the cultivation of awareness, through the decolonization of our minds, we have the tools to break with the dominator model of human social engagement and the will to imagine new and different ways that people might come together."

As Shay (2016) notes, "One of the concerns of the decolonizing movement, is how curriculum content is dominated by—to name some—white, male, western, capitalist, heterosexual, European worldviews. This means the content under-represents and undervalues the perspectives, experiences, epistemologies of those who do not fit into these mainstream categories." Consequently, "The causes related to women in the global South that capture Western fascination are often those whose discussion participates in justifying—or at least does not challenge—imperialist domination" (Khader 2019: 2). The tendency to favor Western knowledge and positioning is a common concern across many disciplines and has affected how decolonization is approached. Meda (2019: 3–4) summarizes, "[t]he first is a radical approach where Western knowledge is fully rejected. The second is an integrative approach which seeks to accommodate both Indigenous and Western knowledge." For Oladimeji (2018: 95–100), "Indigenous knowledge is local knowledge: knowledge that is unique to a given culture or society [. . .] Indigenous knowledge is not yet fully utilized in the educational development process."

Calls to decolonize teaching and learning should not be an attack on any group of peoples. Haffner (2018) similarly remarks, "decolonising reading lists is not about kicking out white scholars on the basis of their whiteness, but rather critically thinking about their arguments and assumptions and reading them alongside scholars that produce alternative knowledges from non-Western standpoints." To carry out a "find and replace" on all reading material published by a white author or that which favors Western contexts, approaches, and/or ideas would be as beneficial as passively diversifying a curriculum purely to fulfill the requirements of an inclusivity checkbox. This book employs the term "White" in line with Lander and Santoro, who note, "The term 'white' signifies those racialised as white and is not used to indicate homogeneity" (2017: 1020).

Inclusivity and Decolonizing—What's the Difference?

It is accepted that universities across the UK have made significant efforts to engage with the inclusivity agenda. Much has been written about inclusivity and it is an often-employed term within the sector. Definitions relating to inclusivity in HE emphasize inclusiveness for all student groups. Terms such as "equality," "diversity," and "internationalization" are familiar expressions when discussing inclusive curricula, pedagogies, and assessments (see, for example, Wray 2013; Thomas and May 2010). Morgan and Houghton (2011: 5) define an inclusive curriculum as "one that takes into account students' educational, cultural and social background and experience as well as the presence of any physical or sensory impairment and their mental well-being."

For Dei (2016: 36),

> The meaning of inclusion can be so liberalized as to imply merely adding to what already exists and in fact strengthening what exists through this process.

However, a more subversive take on inclusion is about beginning "anew" and to engage this through creating new tools, spaces/places with a new vision. Inclusion is not bringing people into what already exists; it is making a new space, a better space for everyone.

What both the inclusivity and decolonizing agendas share is the aim for all students to experience positive well-being and belonging at university. Decolonizing teaching and learning can be viewed as an extension of discussions concerning inclusivity. This is not to say that inclusivity is ineffective or to undervalue the work that has been and continues to be done within the area of inclusivity. Rather, it is to emphasize that decolonizing work is a necessary extension of inclusivity. Decolonizing interrogates how colonial legacies can manifest itself in different ways in HE spaces such as through institutional structures, teaching and learning practices, and relationships. The process of decolonizing confronts these issues, calling for an open and authentic developmental space for these to be explored and responded to.

To subsume the subject of decolonizing under the umbrella of an inclusivity or widening participation agenda risks detracting focus from the value which a critical exploration of the subject can have on university teaching and learning. The Higher Education Policy Institute (HEPI 2020) "published a new report with original testimony and practical guidance for UK universities on decolonising higher education." "Miseducation: decolonising curricula, culture and pedagogy in UK universities" by Mia Liyanage (2020: 9) "establishes that the decolonisation of UK universities is vital for the improvement of course curricula, pedagogical practice, staff wellbeing and the student experience." The first of five key recommendations in the report is "Get educated about decolonisation and end its conflation with equality, diversity and inclusion initiatives" (2020). The temptation to place decolonizing work under more common place agendas also suggests a hesitation to address the distinctness of the subject head on. Reframing these discussions in any way other than being direct about decolonizing may make for more comfortable meetings, but the outcome of this will be limited progress, as the conversations taking place would not be addressing the distinct concerns that decolonizing raises. To engage with the decolonizing agenda effectively, work must be carried out at both an institutional and individual level. As Felix and Friedberg (2019) comment, "Much as institutions may like to think the issue can be solved by working their way through a checklist of actions, decolonizing begins with individuals deconstructing themselves and looking inward to the roots of their own identity."

"Extending these discussions involves reflecting on our own position, perspectives and unconscious bias so that we can consider how these affect our relationships with students, the ways in which we approach teaching and curriculum design, and therefore the student learning experience" (Reilly and Tran 2019: 23). Such a personal activity can be temporarily dislocating, which may prevent some colleagues from wanting to participate. Reluctance to engage in this process may also derive from reservations of tackling a topic which has at the forefront a phrase associated with other weighty terms, those of "race," "politics," and "power" to name a few (Tran 2019: 1). If a person feels underconfident discussing these topics, has not previously been exposed to, or engaged with such challenging conversations, an instinctive reaction might be to avoid the subject of decolonizing altogether. But an avoidance of the subject will not resolve the issues.

The Equality Challenge Unit (2013: 1) defines unconscious bias as "a bias that we are unaware of, and which happens outside of our control [. . .] influenced by our background, cultural environment and personal experiences." Unconscious bias can occur in all aspects of life including the university classroom, among staff and students. A decolonizing lens can help draw attention to how unconscious bias can affect decision making, conversation, approaches in thinking, and social interactions within the classroom. The willingness to reflect, review, and respond, however, is an important step toward development. In an opinion piece for *The Guardian*, Gopal (2017) notes, "A decolonized curriculum would bring questions of class, caste, race, gender, ability and sexuality into dialogue with each other, instead of pretending that there is some kind of generic identity we all share. [. . .] Ultimately, to decolonize is to ask difficult questions of ourselves."

Race and Education

"It is now well accepted by social scientists, that the notions of 'race' and whiteness, in their social significance, are guided not so much by any biological foundation as by the social meanings that are ascribed to them" (Guess 2006: 653). Before focusing on the dynamics of race and education, the context in which this book was written is briefly outlined by way of highlighting how recent global events have reinvigorated campaigns calling for greater equality and decolonizing universities. In 2020 the world was experiencing the impacts of the Covid-19 pandemic caused by a new highly contagious and deadly respiratory coronavirus. The WHO (2020) provides a timeline of the outbreak, which started in December 2019 when "Wuhan Municipal Health Commission, China, reported a cluster of cases of pneumonia in Wuhan, Hubei Province. A novel coronavirus was eventually identified." During the outbreak, media attention was drawn to the disproportionate number of BAME victims (see, for example, BBC News England 2020; Massey and Makoni 2020). "Of the 3,883 critical patients registered in the UK on March 10 [2020], 33.6% were from BAME communities. This is despite BAME communities accounting for only 14% of the population" (Campbell 2020). Khan (2020) argues how "pre-existing ethnic inequalities have had an adverse impact on the number of BAME people affected by Covid-19."

By March 2020 nonessential shops were ordered to close and nonessential travel prohibited. "As the coronavirus spread, reports of xenophobic attacks on Asian students did too" (McKie 2020). Further aggravating the situation were "the potential impacts of misleading and biased media coverage on Chinese individuals' mental health" (Wen et al. 2020: 1). In an article by Lau (2020) on the rising xenophobia, a number of academics offer their views. One of these academics, Wu, comments, "The rise of attacks against 'Asian-looking people' is deeply rooted in the historical discrimination against Chinese and Asians in Western cultures and societies" (2020). By way of responding to this, Wen "suggested including diversity issues in the curriculum and opening lines of communication between students, faculty and administrations—efforts that would require cooperation from multiple stakeholders" (2020).

The same year saw racial inequalities pushed further to the forefront of global news as high-profile deaths of unarmed Black Americans as a result of police brutality led to worldwide calls to tackle systemic racism. Breonna Taylor, "a certified EMT who hoped to become a nurse, was shot to death by plainclothes police officers while asleep in her apartment in Louisville, Kentucky," on March 13, 2020 (Mahdawi 2020). On May 25, 2020, police officer Derek Chauvin knelt on the neck of George Floyd for nearly nine minutes in Minneapolis, ignoring the father's efforts to inform officers that he could not breathe, causing him to die only hours after. George Floyd's family members are quoted as describing him as a "devoted father" and "gentle giant" (Aljazeera 2020). Subsequent protests across the United States "flared up [. . .] as people demand[ed] justice and systemic change to end police brutality" (Aratani 2020). The protests also drew attention to the #BlackLivesMatter movement, "In 2013, three radical Black organizers—Alicia Garza, Patrisse Cullors, and Opal Tometi—created a Black-centered political will and movement building project called #BlackLivesMatter" (Black

Lives Matter: Her Story 2021)."Black Lives Matter Foundation, Inc is a global organization in the US, UK, and Canada, whose mission is to eradicate white supremacy and build local power to intervene in violence inflicted on Black communities by the state and vigilantes" (Black Lives Matter: About 2020).

Mass protests also took place in the UK in support of protests in America while simultaneously highlighting the connection between race and police action in the UK.

> [R]ecent statistics from the Home Office and Ministry of Justice show: In 2018-19, black people were more than nine times as likely to be stopped and searched by police as white people. [. . .] [T]hree times as likely to be arrested [. . . and] more than five times as likely to have forced used against them by police as white people. (Reality Check team 2020)

The protests calling for change revived the Rhodes Must Fall campaign at the University of Oxford, and across the UK statues became situated "at the centre of a cultural battle" (Ridgwell 2020). Worldwide protests saw a number of statues linked to slavery and colonialism being removed (BBC News 2020; Rea 2020; Wall 2020). Greater pressure has been placed on HE institutions to do more to create an anti-racist culture and interrogate their institutional structures.

Terminology of the attainment gap, attainment differentials, achievement gap, awarding gap, or opportunity gap, as it is sometimes referred to, continues to be problematized. Advance HE (2019) notes, "Traditionally the language of the attainment gap has focused on students' underachievement or lack of attainment, whereas it should focus on the institutional culture, curriculum and pedagogy." This is mirrored in the shift in terminology as a growing number of universities are favoring the term awarding gap to stress the responsibility of the institution to address the issue. The existence of the BAME awarding gap highlights how race does play a part in HE. A report by Universities UK and National Union of Students (2019: 1) underlines how "A student's race and ethnicity can significantly affect their degree outcomes. [. . . T]he gap between the likelihood of White students and students from [BAME] backgrounds getting a first- or upper-second-class degree is among the most stark—13% among 2017–18 graduates." Miller's review of the gap (2016: 20) highlights, "if BME students are being disadvantaged by their HE providers, this is in contravention of the legal obligations for universities and other public institutions as set out in the Equality Act 2010 and the Race Relations (Amendment) Act 2000."

Shying away from conversations that are directly about race may therefore be read as a choice to ignore this issue. "A change in culture is needed alongside a clear institutional message that issues of race are embedded within wider strategic goals" (Universities UK and National Union of Students 2019: 2). Efforts to address the awarding gap are often considered as part of university inclusivity agendas. Approaching the awarding gap through a decolonizing lens may help to review the issue on a deeper level. But this does not mean reducing efforts to a few interventions to help decolonize a curriculum and expecting this to result in a closed awarding gap. Decolonizing work looks to change the culture of a university by interrogating all aspects of an institution to enhance the teaching and learning environment for students and staff.

Delgado and Stefancic (2012: 3) offer an overview of the critical race theory movement, originating in the 1970s within the legal discipline, "a collection of activists and scholars interested in studying and transforming the relationship among race, racism and power." Over time, CRT has been explored across a range of subject areas "and has been taken up beyond the United States to include work in Europe, South America, Australia and Africa" (Rollock and Gillborn 2011: 5). As Leonardo (2013: 602) points out,

> CRT has staked a claim on a unique methodology that represents a mixture of existing historiographies, literary and narrative analyses and legal case studies, which is inseparable from its ideological commitments about the reality of race and racism. In other words, CRT offers a way of conducting research that speaks against current objectifications of race, not just a way of interpreting it.

Ladson-Billings and Tate (1995: 60) drew "parallels between the way critical race legal scholars understand their position vis-à-vis traditional legal scholarship and the ways critical race theory applied to education offers a way to rethink traditional educational scholarship." In light of decolonizing issues, McLaughlin and Whatman (2011: 369) state, "power and interests are connected, and a CRT analysis can point to sites within university curricula where, and describe how, systems of privilege need to change." For Joseph (2010: 11), applying CRT to decoloniality "means decolonising the university and the higher education landscape; not just the curriculum." Further exploring CRT in education, Dixson and Anderson (2018: 122) outline "fundamental ideas to assist scholars in operationalizing ideas from the legal literature into educational research and scholarship." Their "parallel 'boundaries' for CRT scholarship in education" (2018) are listed:

1. CRT in education argues that racial inequity in education is the logical outcome of a system of achievement premised on competition.

2. CRT in education examines the role of education policy and educational practices in the construction of racial inequity and the perpetuation of normative whiteness.
3. CRT in education rejects the dominant narrative about the inherent inferiority of people of color and the normative superiority of white people.
4. CRT in education rejects ahistoricism and examines the historical linkages between contemporary educational inequity and historical patterns of racial oppression.
5. CRT in education engages in intersectional analyses that recognize the ways that race is mediated by and interacts with other identity markers (i.e., gender, class, sexuality, linguistic background, and citizenship status).
6. CRT in education agitates and advocates for meaningful outcomes that redress racial inequity. CRT does not merely document disparities. (2018)

Referring to these "parallel boundaries" for CRT during discussions on decolonizing HE teaching and learning is not to force the subject into a preexisting set of criteria. These boundaries do, however, help to point to the interconnected issues of historical oppression, racial inequality, and educational inequality that need to be explored when engaging with the subject of decolonizing. It is worthwhile to comment on how Dixson and Anderson's "parallel boundaries" may correspond to decolonizing teaching and learning.

1. "CRT in education argues that racial inequity in education is the logical outcome of a system of achievement premised on competition" (Dixson and Anderson 2018: 122): The competitive environment within universities accumulates with final exams and summative assessments, all grades going towards the final degree outcome. With only a first or upper second class being considered a "good degree" among many graduate employers, the sense of competition is heightened. When taking into consideration the awarding gap, this competitive atmosphere becomes fraught with further tensions as BAME students are less likely to achieve a "top degree." Through a decolonizing lens, HE teaching and learning is explored to consider why and how this education system generally seems to favor white over BAME students.
2. "CRT in education examines the role of education policy and educational practices in the construction of racial inequity and the perpetuation of normative whiteness" (Dixson and Anderson 2018): Lorde (1984: 117) explores the "privilege of whiteness" and Harris (1995: 290) notes,

"Whiteness as property has carried and produced a heavy legacy. [. . .] It has blinded society to the systems of domination that work against so many by retaining an unvarying focus on vestiges of systemic racialized privilege which subordinates those perceived as a particularized few— the Others." Frankenberg (1993: 1 cited in DiAngelo 2011: 56) defines whiteness as "a location of structural advantage, of race privilege. Second, it is a 'standpoint,' a place from which White people look at [them]selves, at others, and at society. Third, 'Whiteness' refers to a set of cultural practices that are usually unmarked and unnamed." Relating Frankenberg's definition to the discussion of decolonizing teaching and learning, the "structural advantage" can be connected to the colonial structural legacies that tend to remain in universities. The "standpoint" can be associated with the Western-centric positions and perspectives often centered in curricula. The "cultural practices" might be the impact which the knowledge produced across university classrooms and programs has on wider society. One of the ways in which the decolonizing agenda can have an institutional wide impact is through policy. But without action, policies become a passive approach to addressing issues.

3. "CRT in education rejects the dominant narrative about the inherent inferiority of people of color and the normative superiority of white people" (Dixson and Anderson 2018: 122): This can be connected to the "need to look beyond 'the deficit model' to explain the attainment gap" (Cotton et al. 2016: 477). The superiority associated with whiteness may manifest itself in a variety of ways including through Western-centric reading materials, unconscious bias, a lack of space for critical discussions of a wider range of positions, viewpoints, and a favoring of assessments rooted in Western traditions. The process of decolonizing involves questioning the privileging of Western contexts, approaches, and ideas.

4. "CRT in education rejects ahistoricism and examines the historical linkages between contemporary educational inequity and historical patterns of racial oppression" (Dixson and Anderson 2018: 122): Decolonizing efforts involve examining how colonial history has manifested itself in various forms within the university. These manifestations may lead to the unintentional exclusion of some students while benefiting others. Consequently, levels of engagement, retention, progression, and overall degree outcomes may be affected. One of the ways the latter is arguably demonstrated is through the existence of the BAME awarding gap.

5. "CRT in education engages in intersectional analyses that recognize the ways that race is mediated by and interacts with other identity markers (i.e., gender, class, sexuality, linguistic background, and citizenship status)" (Dixson and Anderson 2018): Intersectionality was introduced by Crenshaw (1989) in "Demarginalizing the Intersection of Race and Sex: A Black Feminist Critique of Antidiscrimination Doctrine, Feminist Theory and Antiracist Politics." "[T]he concept of intersectionality was originally identified and developed as a *mechanism*, a way to think about how these distinctions are socially constructed such that they depend on one another for meaning, which almost paradoxically can create vulnerabilities, erasures and gaps, particularly for members of groups defined by multiple axes of disadvantage" (Cole 2017: ix). A person's outward racial appearance can quickly become connected to racial stereotypes. Pigeonholing may also occur via stereotypes relating to class, gender, and/or sexuality to name some examples. Such categorizations simultaneously place individuals within a prejudiced hierarchy of socially accepted norms. Case (2017: 9) puts forward a model of intersectional pedagogy which "teaches intersectionality across a wide variety of oppressions," "aims to uncover invisible intersections," "includes privilege," "analyzes power," "involves educator personal reflection on intersecting identities," "encourages student reflection," "promotes social action," "values the voices of the marginalised and oppressed," and "infuses intersectional studies across the curriculum."

6. "CRT in education agitates and advocates for meaningful outcomes that redress racial inequity. CRT does not merely document disparities" (Dixson and Anderson 2018: 122): In Dumbrill's and Green's (2008: 494) analysis of academic space, they provide a "characterization of the social order that privileges White, male, 19–60 year-old, able-bodied, heterosexual, middle–upper class professional/managerial social locations." Decolonizing teaching and learning points out inequalities in order to move toward developmental action. As Dixson (2014: x) states, "the combination of theorizing and 'doing' is an important one for truly solving social problems." Ndebele, speaking of the South African context, reminds us "that fire can be a companion to invention; and that for fire to play its companion role, requires of those who use it a lot more thought, a lot more rigour in the thinking, a lot more thoughtful detail in the doing." Fanon (2005: 15) argues, "Decolonization [. . .] cannot be accomplished

by the wave of a magic wand, a natural cataclysm, or a gentlemen's agreement. Decolonization, we know, is an historical process."

Chapter Summary

As Stovall (2005: 198) describes, "[a]lthough introductory in terms of utility, CRT should be understood as a call to work." Similarly, Dennis (2018: 199) comments, "A decolonising education is an activist one [. . .] not a discipline but a practice of weaving the threads of resistance, opposition and insurgency to prefiguratively build a different world." The project of decolonizing in universities is not intended to fuel racial tensions. Although the decolonizing agenda is connected to the history of colonialism, it is not a form of retribution for past traumas. Discussions regarding the work of decolonizing should not be divisively located as BAME versus white. Such understandings act to racialize an issue which goes beyond race. For example, awarding gaps not only exist between BAME and white students, some institutions may have a greater challenge resolving gaps between students among the same racial grouping but from different socioeconomic classes. Universities are now starting to look more closely at disaggregated data too. Some institutions may focus on challenges relating to political divisions or conflicts between religious groups.

The decolonizing agenda looks to question hegemonic narratives and their influence on the teaching and learning experience, particularly upon students and staff from historically oppressed groups. Discussions concerning decolonizing teaching and learning will be difficult at times. However, the intention is for these conversations to be developmental. "Moving beyond critique is crucial because simply critiquing European dominance is by its nature another exercise in Eurocentrism" (Dumbrill and Green 2008: 499). The endeavor to decolonize teaching and learning should benefit all students entering university and all staff working within the institution. It is through the process of deeply reflecting upon who we are, how we see others, and how we are seen that a dialogue can be formed to better understand, share, and explore differing positions and viewpoints.

2

What Is Good Development?
With Contributions from Nelly Kibirige and Bernadine Idowu-Onibokun

This chapter begins with a brief outline of how continuing professional development (CPD) is often understood and perceived in higher education (HE). It then explores the connections and variances between CPD and what can be described as "good development" before putting forth a set of principles for the latter. Attention then turns to how engagement with decolonizing work is developmental and how collaborating with students can help facilitate challenging discussions. The chapter then considers the importance of seeking and creating new spaces for decolonizing conversations and work to take place. The chapter ends with contributions from Bernadine Idowu-Onibokun and Nelly Kibirige.

What Is Good Development?

Continuing professional development is a familiar phrase within HE as academics are expected to be active in CPD as part of good practice. A quick online search of the term immediately offers up a number of articles, organizations, and definitions relating to CPD. In an article by Johnston (2019) for a well-known site for academic jobs listings, CPD "refers to the process of tracking and documenting the skills, knowledge and experience that you gain both formally and informally as you work, beyond any initial training." This understanding of CPD points to the expectation that professionals are continuously engaged in the assessing and recording of their skillset and knowledge levels. On the CPD Certification Service (2019) webpage, it is noted that CPD "enables learning to become conscious and proactive [. . . and that engagement in CPD] ensures that both academic and practical qualifications do not become out-dated or obsolete." The latter description highlights how active engagement in CPD can help an individual to remain a competitive player within their career field. There is also an association here between CPD activity and temporality, with the suggestion that particular knowledge and skills can become redundant, thus requiring constant maintenance and review.

Within universities, CPD is often linked to formal training and activities that lead to some form of accreditation, qualification, or recognition. Professional development in HE, particularly when referring to academics, is often linked to the topics of "teaching development" and "teaching quality" (Parsons et al.: 2012). To help improve these areas, the completion of taught postgraduate programs such as the initial professional development Postgraduate Certificate in Higher Education (PGCert in HE) program may be written into a contract of employment for academic staff who have little or no teaching experience. The completion of such programs has shifted from being listed as "desirable" to "essential" on many academic teaching job specifications, illustrating how institutional demand affects levels of engagement with particular CPD activity.

Noncredit-bearing CPD opportunities can come in various forms, including conferences, training in new tools or software for teaching, workshops on innovative assessment, and new ways of communicating feedback. These are just a few examples of CPD activity that academics, technicians, professional services colleagues, and students may be engaged with outside of their compulsory duties. Unlike scheduled lectures and seminars, opportunities to take part in CPD may arise at any time, through an e-mail call for papers, an invitation to attend a guest lecture, or through word of mouth praising a particular course. It is then a process of reorganizing the work calendar and seeking relevant managerial or supervisory support, if necessary, to participate in that activity. What both earlier descriptions of continuing professional development have in common is the notion that CPD is the responsibility of the individual and ideally should be voluntarily sought after as part of good practice. Engaging regularly with opportunities to enhance one's knowledge and skillset and applying these in practice helps to ensure high standards of teaching and learning support. As a result, CPD activity holds a unique space in teaching and learning as it is often seen as evidence of an individual's commitment and passion for their role. For Fellows of the Higher Education Academy, CPD engagement also helps to maintain good standing (HEA 2013: 3).

When the outcome of a CPD activity is a qualification of some sort, the "professional" aspect of the development is emphasized. However, all CPD is personal in the sense of it being developmental for one's own professional careers, enhancing our knowledge of a subject, or becoming better equipped with skills to carry out current or future roles more productively. The discussion of the "personal" cannot therefore be ignored when discussing professional development. For Blackmore and Blackwell (2003: 25), "Continuing professional development requires a systematic career-long approach to performance review and development." When discussing a personal development plan or appraisal at work, evidence of high levels of engagement with CPD is often cited as demonstrating good practice. Does this mean that all CPD may be viewed as "good"? Is there a difference between CPD and "good development"? If so, what is this difference? And how might "good development" be understood?

Rogers (1988: 15) asks "whether, for education to be education, the goals must be 'good' [. . .] The problem is an old one: how to define 'good' in this context." Rogers points to the different ways in which people may see "good" in this context such as a "change in society," "increased freedom," "generate wealth (either for oneself or for society at large)," "rectification of social inequalities or the increase of cultural richness" (1988). These understandings of "good" are similar to reasons that may be associated with the act of doing good. If "doing good" involves having a positive impact on the lives of others, then the outcome of undertaking "good development" should have the potential to positively impact others too. However, the outcome of CPD activities can usually always be linked (directly or indirectly) to enhancing the experience of others within one's working environment. Commenting on the "ripple effect," Andresen (1995: 46) notes, "people who make a long-term commitment to their own professional development may have an impact on people around them." However, it is here proposed that "good development" situates the development of others, rather than the individual, at the center of the activity.

But as noted by Blackwell and Blackmore (2003: xiv), "the term 'development' is not without problems. [. . .] It also has patronizing overtones. In its customary interpretation, it is the staff who are developed through the institutions provision." But what if the institutional provision is lacking? What if it is the institution that needs developing by staff? Based on the discussions so far in this chapter, some characteristics of what good development might involve and lead to are listed:

1. The focus is less on the development of the individual and more on how that individual will be able to develop others.
2. The beneficial impact on wider society should be considered as part of the development's design and delivery.

3. There should be potential for developmental impact across an institution at all levels.
4. It should help to enhance relationships within the institution.
5. It should lead to increased levels of reflexivity among individuals toward one another.

The process of decolonizing teaching and learning fits in with this list in the following ways: efforts to decolonize teaching and learning are rooted in the desire to enhance the experience of students more so than one's own knowledge and/or skillset. As such, there is no accreditation, formal recognition, or credit-bearing certificate which is awarded to individuals who are engaged in the process. Although there are no set guidelines for approaching the designing of or delivery of decolonizing practices, the TRAAC model (outlined in Chapter 3) considers the ways in which questions raised in connection to conversations around decolonizing can impact relationships, learning environments, and wider society. As McGregor (2012: 4) notes, decolonizing pedagogies "help[s] learners come to recognize and know the structures of colonization and their implications; while engaging in activities that disrupt those structures on an individual and collective level [. . . to] facilitate engagement with possibilities for making change in the world." The impact which a decolonized university (in terms of both institutional structure and teaching and learning) may have on society is significant.

Developing and Decolonizing

Engaging in conversations that consider the questions raised by the decolonizing process can be understood as good practice and good development. The potential development of others (in this case, primarily students) is at the center of this process. "A decolonised curriculum is evidenced by a shift in subjectivity from the arrogant 'I' (of Western individualism) to the humble 'I'—to the 'I' that is embedded, embodied, extended and enacted" (Le Grange 2016: 9). Decolonized teaching and learning may potentially increase levels of engagement among students, which may in turn lead to students experiencing enhanced levels of belonging. The positive impact that the decolonizing process may have can be beneficial for the entire student body, as students become more reflective and responsive to different perspectives and positions. The subject of decolonizing teaching and learning has the potential to revitalize the way universities currently operate at both managerial and operational levels.

The momentum that currently exists has led to an increase in awareness about the topic among students and staff. Doharty, Madriaga, and Joseph-Salisbury (2020: 1–9) argue,

> despite the paradox of working under (what purports to be) a "decolonial" agenda, widespread calls to decolonize our universities have further embedded rather than dismantled whiteness, thus continuing to characterise the careers, wellbeing, and daily lives of faculty of colour [. . . as . . .] Institutions advance rather than dismantle racism by adopting the work of a few racially minoritised groups, but exploitatively draining the useful parts of their scholarship to meet institutional metrics and marketise fashionable buzz-words that appeal to social media hashtags.

In a collaborative online piece, Sisters of Resistance, Left of Brown, and Jenny Rodriguez (2018)

> question whether the rapid uptake of decolonising as the new buzzword of critique has become a new form of academic production that adds value to one's reputation as a critical scholar while also opening a pathway to profit through making the histories, bodies, and experiences of Black people and people of colour consumable and marketable, transforming them into a viable subject for the entrepreneurial academic agenda.

The renewed interest in the subject of decolonizing risks it being perceived as a passing trend. Such a perception gives those who question the value and benefit of decolonizing a reason to not commit energies into engaging and reflecting upon the ideas raised by it. Ahmed (2012: 60) states, "words have institutional lives." The latter points to how terms can take on meanings that may change, evolve, grow, and/or cease to be used within a university. Ahmed refers to "linguistic fashion: words come in and out of use by being used or not being used" (2012). The connection between trending words and their impact on the value of a topic of discussion is evident when turning briefly to the discussion of the term "woke." Staples (2018) offers up the following general explanation: "woke" "is an adjective, a verb and an outlook. The political term refers to a perceived awareness of social justice issues, particularly those affecting minority groups. The expression 'stay woke' originated in African-American culture." Offering a more detailed definition, Ashlee et al. (2017: 90) "define wokeness as critical consciousness to intersecting systems of oppression. Specifically, to be a woke person is to hold an unretractable embodied consciousness and political identity acknowledging the oppression that exists in individual and collective experiences."

In recent years, the term "woke" has been used in reference to a number of issues; this has occurred to such an extent that the description of someone as "too woke" has also come into being. Counterarguments to decolonizing include claims that such an agenda is too woke. Ramaswamy's (2019) comment on wokeness is referred to by way of responding to such a critique,

> The more woke is used as a slur, joke or shorthand to mock the hypersensitivity of the left, the more we need it. We need it to keep debating subjects in shutdown. We need it to remind ourselves that debates shut down in the first place is because they don't start on an equal footing: one person's intellectual exploration is another's marginalised life.

The process of decolonizing teaching and learning has the potential to change how the design of curriculum, delivery, activities, and assessments is reviewed, approached, and discussed. By embedding the subject into various avenues of discussion it can become part of everyday practice, rather than a process viewed as unfamiliar, detached, or controversial. But an embedding of the subject into university life and discourse should not lead to a dilution, simplification, or generalizing of decolonizing work, "defusing the decolonising incursion with more palatable alternatives" (Thomas: 2018). To help grapple with challenges involved in the decolonizing process, universities need to provide appropriate space and support for staff and students. McGregor (2012: 10) emphasizes this further: "for teachers to decolonize themselves, their identities and the ways they view education; supports (such as workshops or mentoring) [are needed] to ensure teachers are confident and prepared in using decolonizing pedagogies."

Working with Students to Form a Developmental Dialogue

The conversations and work carried out to decolonize teaching and learning should involve stakeholders across the institution, particularly students. This view is supported by Stevenson et al. (2019: 10): "Strategies should be put in place—with care and involving students—to decolonize the curriculum. That is to consider, and then address, how the values, norms, thinking, beliefs and practices that frame the curriculum perpetuate white, westernised hegemony and position anything non European and not white as inferior." It is not enough for students to have access to knowledges; they should also be empowered to challenge and create knowledges. Fung and Carnell (2017: 7) emphasize that students as partners and cocreators should be "empowered to challenge the status quo and bring about creative, evidence-based changes in their institution's practices." For Kupatadze (2018: 8), "neither faculty nor students should think of the partnership process as faculty's desire to improve their teaching, but instead, as a way of helping students develop a better understanding of the pedagogical choices made when creating an assignment, a course, or a curriculum." Unfortunately, as Jason Arday points out in Chapter 4 of this book, "research [...] has illuminated that BAME students are often given no agency or autonomy in collaboratively negotiating the canons of knowledge provided." The pressure on universities to decolonize has been driven by student protests and campaigns on an international scale. To not include students in this work would be to silence and take over student voices.

University teachers should look at their curriculums through their students' eyes. Prosser and Trigwell (1999: 59) note, "university teachers need to [. . .] think about the variation in students' experience and how it may affect the way students perceive and experience what they are designing and structuring." Going further, actively involving students in curriculum design and pedagogy wherever possible means not having to imagine what student perceptions and experiences may be. Through interviews with staff and students who had collaborated in "student-staff partnership projects" (329), Niculescu, Nagpal, and Rees (2020) found that "One interviewee referred to the need for staff to make themselves vulnerable and to create space for different forms of knowledge" (338). Staff and students both require support through this process, particularly those who are new to working as part of a student-staff partnership.

Bovill et al. (2016: 197–8)

> identified four roles students often assume in co-creating learning and teaching: (1) *consultant*, sharing and discussing valuable perspectives on learning and teaching; (2) *co-researcher*, collaborating meaningfully on teaching and learning research or subject-based research with staff; (3) *pedagogical co-designer*, sharing responsibility for designing learning, teaching and assessment; and (4) *representative*, student voices contributing to decisions in a range of university settings. These roles are not mutually exclusive; indeed, significant overlap may occur.

Another way of viewing student collaboration is in terms of a spectrum. On the one end, there may not be any opportunities for students to be involved in working together with staff, some may carve space for semi-engagement, and others may provide examples of productive collaboration, and on the other end, there is an emphasis on sustained teamwork through working with students as partners.

Academics cannot simply rely on their expert knowledge, teacher training, or experience of teaching to make informed judgments on the content of their curriculum, or the ways in which the material is taught, engaged with, and assessed. The relevance and appropriateness of a course or program arrive through consultation with students. Making sure that students are given sufficient space before, during, and after a program to voice their views concerning what they need to learn, what works well, and areas for further development can help to form a program that has been cocreated. As part of quality review processes, surveys are now factored in as a standard part of a module or program. Student feedback on core aspects of a program tends to focus on generic questions regarding teaching quality, timeliness of feedback, and relevance of assessment. Opportunities for hearing and responding to student thoughts on the issues of decolonizing should also be created. The dialogue calling for decolonizing draws attention to more personal experiences such as the connections made with the content, the students' sense of belonging, and the dynamics of relationships in the classroom. While efforts to decolonize have been fuelled by student voices, it cannot be assumed that all students are familiar with the subject of decolonizing teaching and learning. It also cannot be assumed that all students or staff are in favor of the decolonizing agenda. Conversations around the subject can begin by exploring individual perceptions and understandings of decolonizing. In doing so, a shared understanding of the values associated with the term can be negotiated and used to direct teaching and learning toward a collective goal.

In 2011 the government published the Prevent strategy (2011), which had three main aims: "respond to the ideological challenge of terrorism and the threat from those who promote it [. . .] prevent people from being drawn into terrorism and ensure that they are given appropriate advice and support [. . . and] work with sectors and institutions where there are risks of radicalisation." HE providers are required to comply with Prevent duty (Office for Students, Counter-terrorism—the Prevent duty), but the program has garnered criticism as it has been viewed as a threat to free speech (Stoughton quoted in Thompson 2019) and its review described as "strange" (Abbott quoted in Grierson 2019). In a document produced by the Muslim Council of Britain (MCB) (Versi 2015: 1), the MCB "echoes the concerns held by a wide number of stakeholders that the "Prevent" policy, has flawed analytical underpinnings and leads to the Muslim community being viewed through the prism of security."

Conversations about decolonizing need to be authentic to ensure that students and staff can engage in a developmental dialogue. This requires courage to have challenging conversations with respect and understanding. Without this authenticity discussions risk falling into the realm of the superficial, all well-meaning but with limited or no subsequent change to practice. Authentic initial conversations help to lead into bigger discussions around the work and vision. Tuhiwai Smith suggests questioning

> where that idea [of decolonizing] came from external to the university, who supports it, how that support is mobilised, how it is reflected in decisions, what the concrete projects and home lines are, what is the vision of change, how do people actually see a decolonising vision in every day practice in terms of who is in front of students, what kind of students, what kind of research, what kind of readership and administration structure. I would have all those questions that I think have to be thought about before a unilateral declaration of decolonisation. (Sociological Review Podcast 2020)

A shift in teaching and learning which questions tradition and moves toward something unfamiliar through the decolonizing process will undoubtedly face challenges, not only via resistance from individuals but due to organizational memory. As a result, it is not only the actions implemented to achieve the decolonizing agenda which should be granted attention but the communications which go alongside these. The importance of appropriately articulating the aims of decolonizing to different audiences within an institution will help encourage support and engagement with the agenda. Just as staff will have to engage with reflection and reflexivity in the process of decolonizing, so too will students. An environment needs to be formed so that the dislocation of one's position and thoughts can be explored respectfully. Universities need to ensure that appropriate support for students and staff is made available to help guide individuals mindfully and emotionally through this process.

At Rhodes University, "the Teaching and Learning Centre [. . .] began a series of *Curriculum Conversations* for the university community [. . . where] academics share ways in which they have conceptualised and responded to the need for curriculum transformation and decolonisation in their disciplines" (Quinn and Vorster 2017: 134). These stories were then assembled into a teaching resource. The example of continued dialogue around decolonizing at Rhodes can be implemented at universities in any country; they could also be extended to create a regular space for staff and students to come together and discuss different aspects of decolonizing teaching and learning. The creation of this new and developmental space could also be used to voice any concerns, hesitancies, questions, or disseminate good practice.

Fostering new spaces for the decolonizing agenda allows for creating conditions for success. As previously noted, the process of decolonizing teaching and learning is for the benefit of all staff and students. However, O'Mahony (2019) points out, "projects of inclusion are at the same time, projects of exclusion," "who is in? who is out?" Teachers need to be responsive to this when acting as developmental facilitators during student discussions of decolonizing. There should be opportunity and respect for all voices to be heard; no voices should be alienated or excluded from the discussion. It may also be that for some contexts and situations that traditional forms of discussion are found to be lacking when it comes to critically engaging with decolonizing. When such is the case, the task is to find or create new formats or spaces for interaction and developmental dialogue to take place. Methods of engagement can be experimented with and reflections upon what was shared may not necessarily be verbal in terms of output. The authentic spaces needed for an exchange of ideas around decolonizing may involve the development of new environments with new structures.

Confining discussions to the physical walls of the classroom will restrict the impact which decolonizing can have. The creation of both formal and informal spaces for the regular discussion of race and educational inequalities can help to embed challenging discussions into everyday practice. These spaces should be accompanied by transparent pathways of action so that issues and concerns can be taken further as appropriate. Without this, the spaces for discussion, while helping to develop a culture of authentic critical conversations, will be limited in their capacity for wider impact and practical change. What is needed are opportunities for reflection and dialogue which then productively informs the enhancement of teaching and learning practices.

One area of concern regarding conversations of decolonizing teaching and learning, whether staff are in favor, tentative, or against the decolonizing agenda is that of initiating conversations with students and/or colleagues. Navigating the discussion as well as the questions and challenges that may arise can be daunting, particularly if such conversations have not been carried out before. Points raised will likely be different for each group of participants, with every conversation offering up new responses and questions for further interrogation. Rather than fearing the unknown direction of these conversations, allow the questioning to form the structure of the discussion. Grounding the conversation in questions may be problematized by students who have come to expect that their teachers will provide them with answers. This may also be disjointing for staff who are used to being comforted by discussing a subject that they hold expert knowledge of. But it is this very process of being intellectually disoriented that will allow for an authentic exploration of the decolonizing agenda.

A developmental dialogue with students requires openness. This may come from the teacher explaining to students the purpose or hoped for intentions behind their efforts to discuss the topic of decolonizing in the classroom. The subject of decolonizing is therefore not dropped or pushed into conversation. Rather, it becomes located in context. The topic of decolonizing involves touching on a number of potentially sensitive issues, thus working with Student Ambassadors and colleagues in Students Union to understand how best to introduce the conversation can help to communicate messages in a clear and student-focused way. But there may be times where one or more individuals (whether students or staff) refuse to take part in conversations around decolonizing altogether. If there is a significant refusal to engage, how can a developmental dialogue take place? A starting point may be to understand the reasons for not wanting to engage.

Respectfully questioning why a person feels uncomfortable discussing the topic of decolonizing can lead to the formulation of ideas for how to respond to their concerns. This may come through the form of reassurance that the conversation is not intended to lead to judgments being made against individual persons but a critical exploration of ideas. It can also help to emphasize that conversations on decolonizing are being raised due to the continued privileging of Western perspectives and contexts across areas of teaching and learning. By accepting this as the foundation for discussion, the development of the conversation going forward is fuelled by the objective of addressing these larger issues rather than being focused on individual viewpoints. The conversation might also be made more developmental if guidelines are agreed upon among those participating in the discussion so that individuals are reassured of how the conversation will be facilitated and structured. The aim of this is not to soften discussions. Rather, as conversations about decolonizing are often challenging, it is important to consider ways in which an environment can be formed for high levels of engagement and action from staff and students across an institution.

Once conversations around decolonizing begin, space and opportunities to continue these discussions need to be made available and signposted to staff and students, leading to the implementation of relevant interventions at all levels across the university. As Trowell (2019: 21) comments, "Decolonising the curriculum provides an inclusive intellectual space for uncomfortable conversations and histories to be shared and opens up a wider cultural heritage which we can learn from collaboratively." Working with students as partners in the enhancement of teaching and learning "assume as fundamental the existence of dialogic structures and processes that embed student opinion and feedback and mandate accountability for subsequent responsive action" (Currens 2011: 186). With this comes the importance of listening and responding appropriately to student voices. Staff and students engaged in decolonizing conversations should be conscious to "respond" rather than "react" to points which may counter their own positions and perspectives. Being responsive will help to develop and extend discussions, while being reactive may lead to a closing off of conversations.

It is also important to reflect on which student voices have been heard. The discussion of student voices has been rather homogenous so far, which risks approaching students as one uniform group. While efforts should be made to work with students on designing, developing, and implementing interventions, the way in which student responses are sought should be evaluated for its inclusivity. Ryan Carty's contribution in Chapter 6 gives an account of when well-intended efforts to engage with students and respond to their needs fall short due to limited representation of student voices. Ryan describes how the

> decision for prices on Sports Awards tickets was made on 130 votes on Twitter and SurveyMonkey. We have over 2000 students that take part in sport and it is widely known at the university that Black and Asian students don't engage well with centralised/corporate forms of communication on social media from the university, so why was this used as our main way of making this decision?

This example underscores the need to thoughtfully review approaches behind engaging with and listening to student voices. The approach taken, resources used, amount of time allocated, questions asked, and the space created for discussion can all play a part in influencing who responds.

Quick routes to gauging student feedback may offer immediate results, but these become problematized if responses and resulting actions are made based only on the desires of a specific group. Relating this to the topic of decolonizing teaching and learning, while it may be difficult to gain the opinions of all students on the subject, it is nevertheless essential to try and understand the wide-ranging views which students may have on the topic in order to formulate appropriate strategies, policies, and interventions based on student needs, which will likely differ across institutions and programs. Reviewing which students have previously responded to calls for collaborative working can help to pinpoint if particular student groups are being listened to more over others. Without this, staff risk unintentionally targeting specific groups, meaning the responses and voices engaged with are not representative of the student body.

Contributions

The contributions in this chapter highlight student experiences through student voices. The first contribution is by Bernadine Idowu, who uses the activity and assessment segment of the TRAAC model to instigate discussion among a student focus group. The second contribution is by Nelly Kibirige, who responds to questions raised within TRAAC from a personal perspective, reflecting on experiences as a student, mother, and Students' Union president. Both contributions point to tensions around levels of inclusivity and the work that is still required to enhance the student experience for all groups. The subsequent chapter summary explores points raised in the contributions, connecting them to the wider conversations taking place in this book regarding decolonizing teaching and learning.

Focus Group Responses to Activity and Assessment Strategy among BAME Students in Various Disciplines

Bernadine Idowu-Onibokun

This contribution focuses on the lived experiences of three students from the following subject areas: biomedical science (faculty of life science and medicine), philosophy (faculty of arts and humanities), and mathematics (faculty of natural mathematical science). It is important to hear about the experiences of students situated in different disciplines. Too often we hear that Black minority and ethnic students are left behind, their comments are not addressed, they are ignored compared to their white counterparts, and they do not feel a sense of belonging.

This focus group explored questions based on those raised within the activity and assessment segment of the TRAAC model.

- How should lecturers show respect to all voices? Can you provide a good example and a bad example in your discipline?
- What should lecturers do to consider student groups in the assessment strategy? Can you cite an example of an effective and ineffective assessment

strategy in your discipline, alternatively suggest something you would like to see?
- In your discipline how inclusive are the teaching activities? Please give examples of inclusivity and non-inclusivity

How Should Lecturers Show Respect to All Voices? Can You Provide a Good Example and/or a Bad Example in Your Discipline?

Biomedical student: "I think it is important that lecturers should be aware that many students of ethnic minority did not feel heard or even felt comfortable portraying their 'voice.' Personally, I did not feel able to approach lecturers unlike my white counterparts who found it easier. I think it is important for students to be treated with equity. Students in the lecture hall may have had similar A-level grades, if not they would have grades which qualifies them to be in the room. Many students like myself had/currently have so much more to deal with, like finances, than just lectures. And even when voiced, at least by myself, very little was done to support me. In my experience, despite the well-documented disadvantages of black students compared to their white peers, universities do not offer much support to black students that target their specific needs (Griffiths 2015). During my undergrad, I experienced the loss of a friend and had to work during my degree. I expressed my struggles to a lecturer but felt as though it was just a waste of time. No help or real direction was given, I truly felt like a number in the university. [. . .] During my post-graduate degree at a different university, I had further financial difficulties, I had to work lots of hours. My lecturers, however, were understanding, they helped ease the burden by providing possible solutions and connecting me to the teams that would help me."

Philosophy student: "The best example I found was during a biblical Hebrew language seminar in which my lecturer and I descended into a conversation concerning gender constructs and gender bias in Ancient Israelite society. The reason I found the conversation so poignant and respectful was that it was conducted in a way which was new and surprising to me. The lecturer tried to maintain cultural relativism so there [were] no moral judgments made; equally there [were] no references to stereotypes or attempts to explain or 'sanitise' the information to further his agenda. Instead, he provided a wealth of information [which] we dissected together and drew our conclusions from. This is extremely important because I find that many times during academic discourse, personal experiences and general notions of morality find themselves as the foundations of arguments and analysis, and this steers the argument left ultimately. Furthermore, there is a tendency to maintain European ideological conventions and 'other' everything outside, of the normalcy of our domestic context. This manifests itself in disrespectful and often racist, sexist, or classist remarks which reinforces and sometimes justifies the inequality experienced by those disadvantaged by society. Consequently, this is the place in which lecturers tend to inadvertently and purposefully disrespect the voices of those who do not conform to the consensus of a particular educational institution, or the overall opinions of the wider socio-political context. It is the tendency of lectures, textbooks, and the general HE system to lump people, thoughts, ideologies, and cultural content under generic 'catch-all' groups. These include vague concepts like 'orientalism' (a term challenged and explored by Edward Said in *Orientalism*), and reducing the diversity of movements like feminism, or socialism to 'angry women policing men,' which undermines the work done by those such as Edward Said and Kimberlé Crenshaw to present nuance and depth to those 'othered' by traditional education and society."

Mathematics student: "I think that in order to respect all voices, lecturers must first understand the students and their backgrounds in order to do that effectively! It goes without saying that having a more reflective body of lecturers can aid in lecturers showing respect to all voices. There are often preconceived assumptions from a lot of lecturers that results in them making statements or acting [in a way] that may come across as offensive. For instance, I once went to a lecturer during their office hours to [ask them to] explain a concept to me in more detail, and whilst they did, I was welcomed with apathy at first, and was continuously asked, 'Why do you not know that?' Not to say that it was the lecturer's intention to be patronising, but an understanding of how students operate should perhaps be explored in a lot more detail to avoid instances like this."

The biomedical student made reference to Griffith (2015) when discussing how the educational (under)achievement of Black students has been well documented and researched. The research presents different reasons for this disadvantage. Therefore, it is important that Black students are not treated like a monolith of people but that they (educational institutions) take into consideration the unique experiences of economically and socially disadvantaged Black students (Griffith 2015). Therefore, it is imperative that the powers that be at various universities make available resources to support all students, but primarily students from BME backgrounds as they are considered to be the underachievers. The BME-attainment-gap has been spoken about in various universities, more needs to be done. An initiative by the government to bring about the Office for Students

(2020) is welcomed to ensure "every student has a fulfilling experience of higher education that enriches their lives and careers."

The mathematical student highlighted the lack of BME academics. Idowu (2018) in her *Guardian* article cites Dr. Winston Morgan where he comments on his presentation, "Why we need Black Professors," "Having Black Professors (Academics) designing and informing the curriculum will reduce the Eurocentric content of the curriculum."

What Should Lecturers Do to Consider Student Groups in the Assessment Strategy? Can You Cite an Example of an Effective and Ineffective Assessment Strategy in Your Discipline, Alternatively Suggest Something You Would Like to See?

Biomedical student: "I believe lecturers should dialogue with students more. Have meetings with student reps to get feedback on assessments and actually implement change. During my undergrad years these meetings were conducted but voices were represented by mostly the white student body and had no real follow [through] or impact/change."

Philosophy student: "I think that lecturers should move away from traditional methods of assessment, and include more inclusive practices like group projects, visual and audio mind-maps or student think tanks to prevent discrimination against those with learning disabilities as well as levelling the field for those who, like me, may not have performed as well in written pieces because they had not been given the most appropriate tools in secondary school. Assessments that include marks awarded for classroom participation and group discourse allow [for] both inclusivit[y] amongst pupils but also the ability for students to offer their own diverse opinions and thoughts on subjects and expand on their ideas. I would like to see a better relationship between lecturer and student in the future, which is based on a foundation of mutual exchange where lecturers take on board the different ideas of their students and mentor them. Furthermore, student think tanks for assessment criteria would allow students the ability to both see how and why they are being awarded particular marks, but also it allows them the space to criticize and challenge the marks awarded by lecturers. There was very little policing of marks within my department, especially as the nature of my degree was quite subjective. And so I think that there needs to be checks and balances in place to prevent personal bias, and to allow fair assessment for those who may not share the same vocabulary as their marker, and/or lecturer but makes coherent and concise arguments."

Mathematics student: "I think the assessment strategy in my discipline works to a large extent! There are only set topics covered and the exams styled strategy effectively allows me to engage with the theorems. I do [. . .] however think that for more practical subjects, e.g. Marketing, it would be interesting to visit firms and companies and see the theories that we learn in practice. Finally, as conducted at [. . .] LSE [. . .], stagger difficult modules to bring everyone on the same page. A lot of students come from backgrounds where they [have] cover[ed] topics already and hence understand the content a lot quicker than other students. Hence, for some modules, there should be an intermediate class or more skill sessions [. . .] to ensure that everyone is on the same page by the end of the year."

Both the biomedical and philosophy student talked about getting input from student reps and that they should be listened to and not ignored. Oldham and Dhillion (2012) found in focus groups conducted with BME students from the University of Wolverhampton that listening to students volunteering information must be taken on board. Questioning students on assessments, they found that students preferred essays, also presentations, and case studies.

In Your Discipline How Inclusive Are the Teaching Activities? Please Give Examples of Inclusivity and Non-Inclusivity

Biomedical student: "In terms of curriculum nothing stood out. For example, we had a module which included Blood Science, [but] Sickle Cell—a major disease affecting BME populations—was not discussed or taught in detail. The scientific publications we were asked to read, all the authors were white. There was no diversity in the content let alone the lecturers."

Philosophy student: "Within my discipline, I have found that inclusivity depends on two major factors—class participation and the choice of the module you take. This is due to how my degree was curated to maximise a student's ability to choose what they wanted to learn and to orient themselves around that particular interest. This way [of] learning allowed me the freedom to take modules that did not grade in the traditional essay manner, but also they tended to meander around a subject. I was offered the chance to explore different opinions and thoughts on particular subjects like existentialism, evil, and religion in general. However, this did not change the fact that as a student coming from an underfunded state school with a lesser economically robust background, I found university challenging and inclusivity only extended to a point. Especially as the gaps in my learning, due to a lack of preparation from my secondary school, meant that I lagged somewhat behind my peers despite my ability to engage in class. I found that while I was confident to express opinions and thoughts, it was noticeable that I was not receiving the same amount of private tuition and effort that many of my peers were. Inclusivity in the classroom is often promoted and sought after, yet I find there is a lack of inclusivity concerning the curriculum taught and the access given to those who are not privileged within the university school system. It is well known that diverse voices feel comfortable to express themselves[;] however, if the structure of the institution does not allow them access to the same places in which white, middle and upper-class men frequent, then the institution lacks inclusivity and I think under that criteria, many universities—including my own, fail."

Mathematical student: "Due to the rigidity of my discipline, it is somewhat difficult to include inclusive teaching practices as the solutions are either correct or incorrect, and the methods to approach the solution cannot be alternative to the set theory laid out. Nevertheless, something that I found extremely insightful when studying Economics was that the lecturer included Economic theories from a wide range of backgrounds to support/disprove arguments. Hence, there were theories from both genders, black economists and from different age[s] and backgrounds. I thought the range of views offered from their backgrounds gave me a well-rounded understanding of a lot of topics. So if this practice could be included in other disciplines, it could aid in making a lot of the courses and practices more inclusive."

Both the biomedical and philosophy students elegantly voiced their opinions on a distinct lack in inclusivity within the curriculum. Interestingly, however, the mathematical student stated that "their degree was inclusive . . . this practice should be included in other disciplines." Peters (2015) writes an informative article describing "Why Is My Curriculum White?" Eight answers are given with the last one written as follows, "Because if it isn't white, it isn't right (apparently)." I leave the readers to comment! Many authors have addressed the issue of inclusivity, and my belief is with students' constantly voicing their opinions, universities will have no choice but to implement change, sooner rather than later.

Conclusion

When approached to contribute to this book, I did not think twice as it was an opportunity for my BME undergraduates and postgraduate students, whom I mentor from various disciplines, to get heard. My mentees are not shy to share their experiences with me as they know I understand. They view me as a role model and a force who is a doer (as my coach always tells me) and wishes to be the change they need to see. They are happy to help, hence contributing to this focus group.

Many points have been addressed in this short article; I selected mentees from various disciplines, STEM, arts and humanities, and natural mathematical science, expecting their stories to be similar in places and different in others. Overall, I found their experiences were very similar:

- Lecturers fail to listen and understand what coming from a disadvantaged background looks like.
- Assessments were not inclusive.
- Lack of inclusivity in their curriculum, although an effort was made by the modules taught in the Mathematical degree program.
- None were taught by BME lecturers.

Having graduated from King's College London (KCL) with a Biochemistry Single Honours degree many years ago, I am yet to see many BME lecturers in science at KCL. I made a conscious decision to address this through a chance meeting with the president/principal of KCL, Professor Ed Byrne. He was very welcoming and suggested we meet. He not only listened to my concerns but acted on them. I was given a temporary part-time position in Diversity and Inclusion and made such an impact championing many projects related to the Race Equality Charter Mark, one of which was to develop a conference—namely, "BME Early Career Researcher (ECR)—How to Stay in Academia in 2017" (Idowu 2017). The conference was designed to empower BME ECRs by seeing and hearing the stories of BME academics from various disciplines, and be aware of the resources available, including mentoring and networking. The year 2020 marked its fourth year and it was conducted at Imperial College London in September. The feedback from previous conferences has been phenomenal; many BME ECR and academics have been inspired, secured academic positions, promotions, and are doing well, along with being visible role models.

In my new role, I contributed to the development of two degree programs, Biomedical Science and Pharmacology within the New School of Biomedical Sciences at the University of West London. I have made every effort to make it an inclusive degree. Lectures will explore diseases of every population, including those affecting BME populations. Reading lists will include books and scientific papers published by diverse authors. The lecturers will also be diverse, including BME and female staff of different ages. I am one of the course leaders; I am a Female Black British Born Award–Winning Scientist (Idowu et al. 2007), with a

Nigerian heritage. Black women are considered as a rarity in academia (Wilson 2017; Opara 2017). I sincerely hope that this contribution will lead to even more changes in various universities. There continues to be a high population of BME students in various universities and year on year the numbers are increasing (The National Archives 2020). Students wish to leave university with good degrees, which will lead to good employment opportunities.

De-Colonizing Teaching and Learning with the TRAAC Model

Nelly Kibirige

The following contribution is structured by headings that relate to each of the segments and corresponding questions in the TRAAC model. The model is engaged with from a personal perspective, from the position of a student, mother, and Students' Union president at London South Bank University 2018–20.

1 Teaching Approach

1.1 What Power Dynamics Are Generated from Your Approach?

In my very first week at university, a seminar teacher asked us all to introduce ourselves and state where we were from. He proceeded to ask us all to explain the difference between being born British, being English, and being a British citizen! He further asked us whether it was possible to acquire English status as you would acquire British citizenship. We were freshers from all over the world, eager to please, participate, and get to know each other, but what I saw was an individual trying to put people in their place. If you had "acquired" British citizenship, you would never be English, and it was very special to be English, a privilege which apparently a small number in the class possessed. There was clarification that individuals of color born in Britain were British but were not English. That sent my mind on a journey outside of the classroom! We were not in a citizenship class and from that moment forward, groups of people slowly started to form based on who they identified with. It was then very clear where the power sat. The trouble with power dynamics is that it severely impacts on the way people interact with each other and sets the tone for who has the upper hand, giving individuals the ability to control and influence other people's behaviors including gagging others from speaking up in meetings for example.

Learners should be grouped only by the one thing that brings them together, learning!

1.2 How Is the Learning Environment Participatory?

We quite often find that a handful of the same students participate time and time again. One has to question what it is that deters other students from interacting. In my role as SU president, during a consultation on participation, I had an honest but revealing conversation with a student who had a real and present anxiety about how their accent was perceived by others. They had been bullied and ridiculed for how they spoke, and they had since decided to say nothing! *Finding creative ways to engage the least engaged should be part and parcel of teaching and learning.*

1.3 What Variety Do You have in Your Teaching Approaches?

The trouble with pedagogy in the twenty-first century is that we are still using traditional methods of teaching on modern learners. Since learning is not a one-size-fits-all activity, I have always found it ironic to have been taught that there were several learning styles, but then not have been taught in the style that was mine! Throughout my life, I have gone through three-fourth of the VARK learning styles and believe I am still changing, showing that even once we've identified the type of learner we are, it is not set in stone, and circumstances, challenges, and the changing environment, all play into how we learn moving forward. *The style of teaching should be adjusted to meet current needs of the learners.*

2 Relationship

2.1 What Shared Connections Do You have with Your Students?

Learners have a natural tendency to respect and hold their teachers in high regard and that's great. But no fear, isolation, or complete divide should exist. Students need to feel a connection with their educators no matter how small. A lecturer once asked, "Put your hand up if you live/work in South London." Given the location of our university, that was almost half the population. Although there wasn't much else in common, already the guards were down because of the common connection we shared. *Find what connects you with your students and emphasize that, no matter how small!*

2.2 Have You Reflected on Unconscious Bias Toward Your Student Groups?

It is refreshing to see that institutions are offering unconscious bias training for staff. NUS have some useful resources that are accessible to members. I tasked my institution with developing and offering enhanced racial equality training which received unanimous support at EDI committee. Institutions should recognize where they need to make unconscious bias training mandatory and if not sufficient, full training on racial equality should be offered instead.

2.3 How May the Way Students Perceive You Affect the Learning Environment?

Think of a parent: your children love and look up to you, you are their first teacher, and they want to be like you! Take this and apply it to an academic. When I embarked on my HND in 2012, I had great admiration for my lecturers. I saw them as being exactly what I aspired to be! The majority had several qualifications plus a PhD. This was comforting to me and my peers. Moreover, having a highly qualified teacher with incredible emotional intelligence and oversight was refreshing. None came across as condescending. *The way your students perceive you will majorly impact their learning.*

3 Content

3.1 What Will the Benefits Be for a Multicultural Society?

Quite frankly, we are regurgitating knowledge and information from centuries passed. We pass it on and repeat with not much change in delivery plus the window for new academic citations is tight and tighter for academics of color. We need content that not only teaches individuals facts/figures but also has some takeaways for the multicultural society we are today! *Research your audience and customize their learning to them.*

3.2 What Perspectives/Contexts have been Considered?

Educators must consider relative perspectives for their learners. Two weeks ago, my four-year-old came home saying, "Mum, black people copy everything that white people do." To say I was gobsmacked is an understatement. Not only has my baby never referred to BAME people as Black (always used brown from his own perspective) but he's also never been critical of them/us! It turns out that on Martin Luther King Day, his 90 percent Caucasian school held an assembly, and it would appear that the narrative was misleading to my four-year-old. And he now refers to individuals as Black and copycats. *In this particular scenario, I feel that nonrepresentative institutions should bring in a BAME speaker to give talks on key issues affecting BAME individuals for the avoidance of doubt.*

3.3 How have You Considered Your Student Groups in Content Selection?

Your student groups are your go-to, be all and possibly end all. It is important to tailor your content to them and not just perform a tick box exercise. *Where possible consult and involve students in content selection. Trust them; they know.*

4 Activity and Assessment

4.1 How Do You Show Respect to All Voices?

As previously mentioned, know your audience, trust they know what's best for them, and respect their wishes. Nothing is more condescending than being told what's best for YOU!

4.2 How have You Considered Your Student Groups in Your Assessment Strategy?

We've recently updated our assessment criteria. It was a trial and error exercise in the beginning, but constant consultation with student leaders meant the institution finally got it right. *Make use of your student voice reports; these come directly from course representatives and from the "horse's mouth," so to speak. Use this information to form your assessment strategy.*

4.3 How Inclusive Are Your Learning Activities?

As a DDS student, I learned all too quickly the challenges faced by certain students and especially if you are DDS and BAME! There are far too many intersectionalities to name them all. It's the difference between having your care needs showcased on a projector as opposed to being called in confidence to discuss the extra time you need in in-class computer tests. Trust me, it makes a huge difference to your grades and self-esteem. *Ensure learning activities are inclusive for all protected characteristics and that safe and secure measures are taken to implement these with privacy as key!*

Chapter Summary

Both contributions point to examples of good practice by teachers who have made efforts to enhance levels of inclusivity. However, both Bernadine's and Nelly's contributions also highlight a number of areas affecting levels of student belonging and engagement that are in need of development. These areas include content, assessment, and staff communication. One student in the focus group suggests that a greater choice of assessment is a way of enhancing levels of inclusivity. This is mirrored by calls to diversify curriculum content and the staff body, points that are raised in both contributions. The way colleagues communicate and engage with students is also discussed by both Bernadine's student focus group and in Nelly's personal reflection. The language used, types of questions asked, and the way discussions are facilitated by teachers are shown to all impact on the student learning experience. These concerns raise questions regarding the teaching and learning environment that has been created as well as the general institutional climate.

One of the ways in which a more connected environment can be formed is through creating more opportunities for a developmental dialogue to take place. When the Philosophy student in Bernadine's focus group recalls a productive discussion with their lecturer in a biblical Hebrew language seminar, the student values the teacher's focus on exploring ideas without forcing a judgment or agenda on to the conversation. Both contributions center student voices and offer suggestions for enhancing inclusivity. Nelly also encourages staff to make efforts to find shared connections with students to form a rapport in class, and for all staff to undertake unconscious bias training.

The use of the TRAAC model to prompt conversation among the student focus group has led to a myriad of open, personal, and thought-provoking discussions.

Both Bernadine's focus group and Nelly's reflection also underline the usability of TRAAC, which can be accessed by staff and students as a tool for reflection and entry point into deeper discussions. Furthermore, individuals engaging with the model's questions have responded to the prompts in both specific and more general ways. This has illustrated how particular areas of discussion can extend into other related topics, which altogether help form a clearer picture of the challenges and spaces for further development in HE teaching and learning.

3

The TRAAC Model

This chapter summarizes the aim of the TRAAC model to provide a reflective and reflexive entry point to help encourage challenging conversations around decolonizing teaching and learning. By unpacking each segment of the model and exploring in detail the corresponding questions of each section, suggestions are given for how the model may be used. These are suggestions not instructions as the model is aimed to open up rather than restrict discussions. The consideration of each themed segment of the TRAAC model is grounded in critical scholarly discussions relating to Teaching, Relationship, Activity and Assessment, and Content.

Introduction to TRAAC

Academics are thought of as critical thinkers who have the ability to teach students to develop their critical thinking skills, yet there remains significant room for criticality when it comes to reviewing university teaching and learning. Shilliam (2018: 60) suggests, "the decolonizing project [has the] potential to deepen academic rigour and pursue intellectual challenge." Describing the nature of a decolonized curriculum, Leibowitz (2017: 93–4) says it "could be concrete in that it could imply a system led by design, but it is also abstract, it implies various more formal and more informal aspects of the experience of a student's university learning and the aspects that influence learning, such as social behaviour or residence life." When asked about the subject of decolonizing teaching and learning, it has been a challenge for some academics across disciplines to engage with the questions raised from this often sensitive and challenging topic of conversation as there is "no substantive 'decolonised' or 'decolonial' theory, to guide the transformation of the curriculum" (2017).

50 Decolonizing University Teaching and Learning

Although not a theoretical framework, this chapter outlines the TRAAC (Teaching Approach, Relationship, Activities and Assessment, Content) model. The model is grounded in questions raised within decolonizing scholarship (see, for examples, Dennis 2018: 202, Morreira and Luckett 2018, Sabaratnam 2017) and influenced by critical race theory. By encouraging the user to explore core aspects of teaching and learning including the design process, implementation of activities, and the interaction between staff and students in the classroom, the TRAAC model explores different areas in which inequalities may appear. The questions in each segment require the user to reflect on their own position and perspectives, as well as those which they have incorporated into their teaching. By doing so, the model helps to pinpoint the extent to which an individual's belief system influences their curriculum design and pedagogical approach. The consideration of unconscious bias leads to the exploration of how dominant social views can affect our own decision making and the role we play in perpetuating

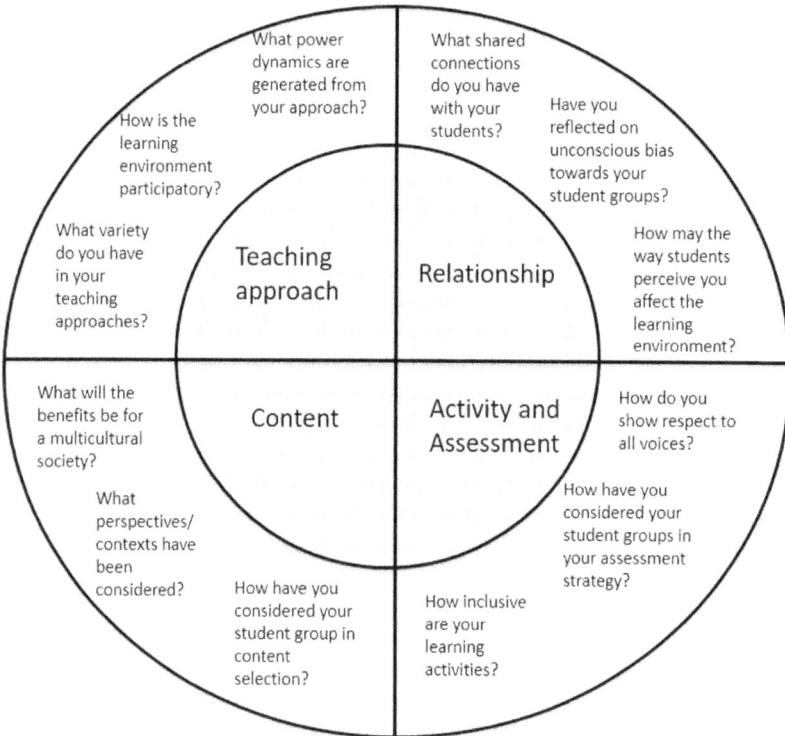

Figure 1 The TRAAC Model (Teaching Approach, Relationship, Activity and Assessment, and Content): An Entry Point For Challenging Conversations about Decolonizing.

or challenging these hegemonic perspectives within our educational settings. Though the questions in the TRAAC model may seem rather general at first glance, each one is unpacked in detail later in the chapter. The model may be used individually or as part of a group discussion (Figure 1).

Teaching Approach

> The questions in the "Teaching Approach" segment of the TRAAC model are:
>
> 1. What power dynamics are generated from your approach?
> 2. How is the learning environment participatory?
> 3. What variety do you have in your teaching approaches?

The consideration of teaching approaches is often grounded in the discussion of pedagogy. The exploration of pedagogy becomes limited if reduced to only being concerned with "how" something is taught. Discussion of teaching approaches should go beyond this simplification. Lusted (1986: 3) states, "What pedagogy addresses is the process of production and exchange in this cycle, the transformation of consciousness that takes place in the interaction of three agencies—the teacher, the learner and the knowledge they together produce." The collaborative aspect of teaching and learning is here emphasized in Lusted's consideration of pedagogy. This is important as it draws attention to the value which students have in the production of knowledge within a classroom. Students are a vital element in this process of production. The description of teachers and learners as "changing and changeable agencies" (ibid.) points to the altering power dynamics that can occur during the teaching and learning process, inside and outside of the classroom. Both staff and students need to be engaged in dialogue, learning from one another with the output being the creation of knowledge.

For Zembylas (2017: 495), "decolonising pedagogy aims at interrupting Eurocentric knowledge at the level of the classroom with the hope that these interventions help undermine historical distributions of power structures." The power dynamics at play within a classroom setting can act to either help or hinder the learning environment. Icaza and Vázquez (2018: 119) comment, "decolonisation of the university should include a transformation of the relationships established in the classroom and across the university.

The classroom is a space in which power hierarchies and forms of exclusion often get reproduced." Power dynamics in the classroom change through the roles which staff and students play. The extent to which students have the freedom to choose how they engage with the teacher, discussions, and peers affects the type of role they have, and the power which comes along with that particular role. As a starting point for exploring the distribution of power dynamics, it is helpful to consider who holds the power in your classroom and how it is managed. The answer to this depends on how power is understood.

At university, a teacher's power is less associated with their authority to manage the behavior of students and more related to the influence they have over what is taught and how. It is here understood that power in a university classroom is linked to how students are being *led* to learn. Such power may be expressed explicitly or implicitly, consciously and unconsciously. When an individual(s) deliver a class (here a "class" may refer to lectures, workshops, seminars, and tutorials whether in person or online), an array of teaching approaches may be used. Some individuals may favor a certain style or approach to teaching. A teacher-centered approach ensures the creation and communication of knowledge are predominantly held and retained by the lecturer. Meanwhile, through the student-centered approach, the teacher becomes more of a facilitator than instructor. "Students react positively when allowed to make decisions about their own learning" (Harden and Laidlaw 2012: 80). The power dynamics are typically less hierarchical in a student-centered classroom, offering greater opportunities for students to be involved in the production of knowledge. Trigwell and Michael Prosser (2004: 421) comment, "in subjects where teachers adopted more student-focused approaches to teaching, their students adopted a deeper approach to learning."

However, the choice to be more teacher or student focused should be context specific, responding to the needs of the class. As students within a class will each have preferred ways of learning, it is unlikely that one particular approach will be beneficial to all. As a result, staff should consider their support strategy for students on their program. This includes the support offered to aid with transitioning from further education to higher education (HE) study. Support should include appropriate embedded support, provisions for additional optional support, and extra signposting to resources and guidance which students may find useful. When support is made explicit and accessible through various avenues by staff, students' mental health and general well-being are highlighted as priorities.

Being teacher focused should not suppress the student voice and being student centered should not involve pressured student interaction. Adapting approaches may assist in developing an environment that is more considerate of those it has been created for. "Establishing an open discussion climate is a prerequisite for conducting effective discussions" (Dean and Joldoshalieva 2007: 178). The power dynamics generated during a class may also be affected by the extent to which opportunities are created and how much time is given to interrogate knowledge and explore a range of perspectives and positions. When time is given, consideration should also fall on "what" questions are posed and "how" they are asked. For example, as Regan (2010: 11) points out, "*how* people learn about historical injustices is as important as learning truths about *what* happened." The "demystification" strategy (Dean and Joldoshalieva 2007: 179) may be employed here. "The strategy differs from discussion in that existing arguments are analysed, whereas in discussion, arguments are generated" (2007).

The approach to the organization of seating arrangements can also affect the way in which staff behave and engage in class. Further, the choice of teaching approach can affect the extent to which the teacher moves around the room or makes use of the space around them. Todd and Robert (2018: 65) commenting on the school system note, "The way in which space is utilized [. . .] is reflective of a Western paradigm. [. . .] hierarchy is built into the classroom by the way in which teachers and students take up space within the classroom." The same can be said of many university classrooms and it is the way in which this taking up of space occurs that can alter the power dynamics at play. Due to the allocation of teaching rooms often being outside the control of teachers, the layout of a room may not always lend itself to being malleable to the purpose or objectives of the class. Even when the physical layout of a room cannot be altered (e.g., in the case of lecture theaters where chairs cannot be rearranged), the teacher can respond by adapting their engagement with the environment around them. They may walk around the room and/or make other efforts to speak *with* rather than *to* students, breaking down the distance and traditional power dynamics of lecturer and student.

Experimenting with the use of online platforms, forums, and asynchronous modes of engagement can also help uncover different power dynamics between staff and students, creating opportunities for shared reflections on teaching and learning experiences. However, the incorporation of technological tools should take into consideration cost for students (in terms of equipment and/or software needed), accessibility, whether any support or training is needed, and if other options can be made available for students unable to engage in this way. Engaging in peer teaching observations can help to uncover what power dynamics are generated from our teaching. Going to observe others teach and developing through peer feedback can help to fill the gaps in our knowledge as it can be difficult to understand how our actions and approaches are being interpreted and understood by others.

Relationship

> The questions in the "Relationship" quarter of the TRAAC model are:
> 1. What shared connections do you have with your students?
> 2. Have you reflected on unconscious bias toward your student groups?
> 3. How may the way students perceive you affect the learning environment?

Describing the university classroom as "Another site of decolonization," Mbembe (2015) goes on to state, "We cannot keep teaching the way we have always taught. [. . .] In an age that more than ever valorizes different forms of intelligence, the student-teacher relationship has to change." Forming an educational relationship between staff and students begins like any other relationship, with getting to know one another. In this way, the "Relationship" segment of the TRAAC model explicitly connects with the "Teaching Approach" segment as the creation of spaces for dialogue can be used as an opportunity to form a working relationship between staff and students. A participatory and open atmosphere can encourage students to engage with classroom discussion. Once greater levels of trust in the environment are developed, students and staff may feel comfortable sharing more personal anecdotes and stories from their own lives in connection to the topics and issues being discussed in class.

Storytelling can provide a creative way of enabling people to engage in a deeply critical manner by encouraging them to share and tell stories to one another. The power of storytelling as a decolonizing approach and tool for inclusivity has been discussed by scholars in different fields of research (Bisht 2017; Dumbrill and Green 2008). The act of storytelling is personal yet communal at the same time with values and lessons being shared. The behavior of a group during shared storytelling is one that is united as people are sat around together on equal footing. "Stories in Indigenous epistemologies are disruptive, sustaining, knowledge producing, and theory-in-action. Stories are decolonization theory in its most natural form" (Sium and Ritskes 2013: ii). While students should feel empowered to speak knowing their stories will be respected, it should not be an expectation that students share their personal experiences. Reflecting on different avenues of entry into deeper discussions across areas of study is important as they can significantly impact on students' teaching and learning experiences.

The first question within the "Relationship" segment of the TRAAC model refers to the shared connections a teacher may have with their students. "Shared connections" have positive connotations, an encouraging starting point for developing rapport between people. Between staff and students in a classroom, these shared connections might be things you can see or can't see. For example, a teacher may be of roughly the same age, or share the same racial appearance, as some of the students in their class. On getting to know their class, staff may find they share the same religion, cultural traditions, or social background as some of their students. However, without knowing how each student self identifies, shared connections cannot be presumed. Shared connections may be used to create a learning environment that enhances the level of belonging among students as the distance between the traditional hierarchy of teacher and student is decreased. But shared connections can lead to assumptions being made, which may be positive or negative. Generalizing assumptions about particular groups can prevent an acknowledgment of the individual. Shared connections with students do not give staff the entitlement to behave differently toward these students than those they do not feel they have connections with. Shared connections should not be used as a way of legitimizing the crossing of professional boundaries. The question on shared connections also implicitly asks individuals to consider those they feel they do not have shared connections with, and how connections can be formed with these students so as to develop a classroom environment that is inclusive for all.

The second question in the "Relationship" segment of TRAAC asks individuals to reflect on unconscious bias. Whether individuals are familiar with unconscious bias or not, there is value in reflecting on what it is and how it influences our decisions and interactions. Reflective practice plays a prominent role in programs such as the PGCertHE but they don't always look at areas of unconscious bias or decolonizing. For Domínguez (2019: 47), "for all of its 'innovations,' and eagerness to account for a diversifying world, teacher education remains a deeply colonial endeavour. Worldwide, it is a process undertaken by predominantly white institutions, preparing predominantly white novice educators, and, though steeped in discourses of diversity and multi culturalism, still presuming the centricity of Eurocentric thought and ideology." Whether someone has reflected on their unconscious bias requires more than a yes or no answer. Where an individual considers there to be a seeming lack of unconscious bias toward students, consider whether this exists because students are being viewed as one homogenous group with the same identity.

It can be helpful for staff to note down how they would describe their different student groups and examine what their descriptions reveal about the ways in which students are being positioned or located in comparison to themselves. Developmental activities focused on the topic of unconscious bias and relevant resources should be offered to all staff involved in teaching and learning support, embedded into various forms of training and reviewed regularly. Acknowledging that unconscious bias exists within all individuals is the first step to removing hesitancies toward addressing bias in teaching and learning. Staff should also make efforts to be active in responding to the existence of these biases. One way in which this can be done is by considering how unconscious bias might manifest in different aspects of teaching and learning, from course design through to delivery, and assessment.

A person's unconscious bias can affect how they approach and engage with students. Unconscious bias held by staff may lead to greater attention being given to students whom they have shared connections with. This therefore risks a disconnection with students they feel a lack of association with. When thinking about the unconscious bias one might have toward a particular group, it is worthwhile considering which student groups are not reflected upon and why. Doing so may reveal other biases which might have an impact on the teaching and learning experience of other student groups. If a team, department, or institution has a high number of part-time, contract, and/or hourly paid staff, these colleagues may not have sufficient time to get to know their students well and reflect on biases that may manifest themselves in actions and communications. Strategies and training need to be in place (as they should for full-time staff) to help prevent colleagues' behavior and decision making from being informed by stereotyping and unconscious bias. Reflecting upon and responding to unconscious bias can be a revealing developmental activity for students as well as staff. While staff are regularly told to consider the makeup of their classrooms, time should also be spent exploring how students are perceiving staff.

The third question in the "Relationship" segment of TRAAC considers how the way students perceive staff may affect the learning environment.

Fomunyam (2017: 6801) conducted a case study in South Africa using open-ended questionnaires focused on decolonizing the engineering curriculum. The findings revealed that "those who pointed out that teaching and learning enhanced the decolonisation project argued that the quality of academics used and the diversity took the decolonisation project a step further" (2017). Although Fomunyam's study focuses on the South African context, the issues raised are relevant to universities in other countries too. The number of BAME staff appointed as professors or working in other senior roles has been significantly and continuously lower than white staff across UK universities (Adams 2018; Coughlan 2018; University and College Union 2016).

The lack of diversity among senior staff means that BAME students are not seeing enough BAME role models during their university life. In a study of how race impacts the university experiences of BAME students at Goldsmiths College and Goldsmiths Students' Union, Akel (2019: 17) notes, "it became clear through the data collection process that many students favoured building student-academic relationships with their tutors when they shared an ethnic identity." The latter points to how levels of student engagement would arguably increase if there were greater opportunities to connect with staff who may be perceived as potential role models. The lack of diversity among staff "risks reinforcing a cycle in which BAME students not only perform less well but are less likely to see themselves reflected in academia" (Rehman 2019).

Students should also be encouraged to reflect on the issue of shared connections in the classroom as this can help to inform colleagues of how student perceptions of staff may affect levels of engagement. The diversity of the student body should be reflected across aspects of the university including the teaching team. Lack of diversity among staff might limit the sense of belonging some students may have within their program. Short-term interventions such as invited guest speakers can help to address a lack of diverse role models, but a refreshed recruitment strategy would form part of a longer-term strategy. The extent to which the diversity among staff affects student belonging can only be discovered through engaging with students as collaborators. End of course surveys ask students to comment on the support they received from tutors and their experience of being taught by the team generally. While the benefit and value of these surveys continue to be debated, the heavy reliance upon them currently means they should also make efforts to address issues concerning diversity and how this may have had an impact on the student experience.

Activity and Assessment

> The questions in this segment of the TRAAC model are:
>
> 1. How do you show respect to all voices?
> 2. How have you considered your student groups in your assessment strategy?
> 3. How inclusive are your learning activities?

In Meda's (2019: 8) case study of South African student views of decolonizing one student says, "It is also about laying bare the failures of the heterosexual, patriarchal, neoliberal capitalist values which have become so characteristic of the country's universities." The student's statement touches upon decolonizing concerns globally. Showing respect when decolonizing curricula involves more than including a range of readings that focus on marginalized groups or contexts across a curriculum. As Chadderton (2011: 74) stresses, "Marginalised groups such as women; non-white people; lesbian; gays; bisexuals and transsexuals (LGBT); young people and people with disabilities have been, and continue to be pathologised, dominated and even exploited through both qualitative and quantitative research. [. . .] the fact remains that research plays a role in the marginalisation process." Simply including varied course content across a program does not therefore address the issue of the marginalization of voices.

The way in which knowledge is understood, interpreted, and critically evaluated is different between individuals. Content may be taught in a particular way, but this does not mean it will be understood the same way. The developmental environment created by staff should be one that is open to challenging opinions. The questioning of a particular perspective, including that of the teacher's, is not a challenge of authority, but a learning opportunity for both staff and students. When it comes to assessment (both formative and summative), staff should reflect on the students within their cohort when designing the assessment strategy. While a particular mode of assessment may favor some students, it will simultaneously be more of a challenge to others. Giving students a choice of assessment types where possible may help. But doing so requires a review of which type(s) would be appropriate.

Whichever assessment type is chosen a support strategy needs to be in place throughout the timespan of a program. This strategy should include embedded support, optional support, and additional support. Timings of such support and who delivers it should also be factored into consideration. Embedded support is that which is scheduled as a core part of the teaching timetable. Embedded support may include a customized workshop on approaching the assessment or a scheduled opportunity for students to raise questions or concerns. Optional support may be offered in the form of a mock assessment in which students may receive feedback. Additional feedback may be extra guidance made available online or assessment exemplars. Furthermore, the phrasing and formatting of the assessment guidance (no matter what mode the assessment takes) need to be accessible for all students.

A learning activity may be understood as any activity of which the purpose is to extend knowledge about a particular subject. Types of learning activities include focused discussion groups, peer-assisted learning activities, and the use of informal formative assessments. The type of learning activity selected should depend on the aim of the activity and the students you are working with. For example, to introduce a new complex theoretical concept to a group of first-year undergraduate students through a paired learning activity without dedicated teacher support beforehand may cause more confusion than clarity. As students have different preferences in terms of how they receive, engage, and respond to information, there will likely be some students who find certain learning activities to be easier to participate in than others. Classroom discussions and group work may draw out the communication and leadership skills of more vocal students while alienating shyer and less confident speakers. Assigning rotating roles for group members can assist with preventing group discussions from being dominated by one or two members but can also lead to some feeling pressurized into participating in a way they find uncomfortable. Experimentation with learning activities should be encouraged, accompanied by the understanding that they can be changed as necessary.

Content

The questions in the "Content" quarter of the TRAAC model are:
1. What will the benefits be for a multicultural society?
2. What perspectives/contexts have been considered?
3. How have you considered your student groups in content selection?

The critical discussion of HE teaching and learning should make efforts to consider the post university impact which students on the program will go on to have in wider society. The connection between university and the public is discussed by Gebrial (2018: 19), "public discourse might seem far from the academy's sphere of influence, but 'common sense' ideas of worthy knowledge do not come out of the blue, or removed from the context of power—and the university is a key shaping force in this discursive flux." The ways in which knowledge(s) is created and explored within the classroom have an impact on how students may approach, interrogate, and go on to understand different social issues. La Belle and Ward (1994: 176-7) comment how "Proponents of multiculturalism in higher education have moved from teaching about differences to promoting change based on difference and from simply acknowledging growing campus diversity to actively empowering students and others to build on this diversity." Unpacking what is understood by "multicultural" can open up discussions as to how a particular program of study may impact aspects of wider society. Consider, for example, the areas of society which the program of study relates to most obviously and the aspects of society that it connects to in more subtle ways. Pinpointing these links can help to inform the curriculum and pedagogical design of a program as well as the assessment and feedback strategy.

Smith (2012: 63) writes, "The globalization of knowledge and Western culture constantly reaffirms the West's view of itself as the centre of legitimate knowledge, the arbiter of what counts as knowledge and the source of 'civilized' knowledge." To decolonize a curriculum involves more than diversifying a curriculum in terms of globality. Choices also need to be made in regard to which situations and environments within these locales are considered as part of the exploration of a particular issue. Furthermore, the lens through which these contexts are seen plays a significant role in how a topic is understood. This lens could be that of a particular perspective held by a certain person(s), a certain framework or approach. The publisher or location of where research is published can also influence this lens due to a hierarchy that has developed which stigmatizes non-Western publishers. Students are taught to assess the legitimacy of sources before citing them. Lesser-known journals and materials published outside of the West are often called into question for their validity as an academic source.

Consequently, a hierarchy of publishers and materials is perpetuated. This can be further problematized by journal indexing. "Indexation of a journal is considered a reflection of its quality" (Balhara 2012: 193) with authors searching for indexed journals as a preferred site for publication (Dhammi and Haq 2016: 115). Commenting on the problematic process of gaining this status, Hirmir notes, "To become an indexed journal, one has to already have a number of publications with articles [. . .] bibliographies that reference articles, which in turn are published in indexed journals [. . . producing a] self-affirming process of knowledge production which we want to break free from" (Istratii and Monika Hirmer 2020: thirty-three minutes).

The response to this is not to devalue known journals or publishers but highlight the equal value of scholarly contributions by lesser-known academics and non-Western publishers. The use of technology can increase access and develop opportunities and spaces for engaging and sharing of resources. Experimenting with different mediums is not to ignore the usefulness of traditional resources but to open up the doors to knowledge on a wider scale. Supporting students in their critical exploration of sources and interrogating assumptions regarding the validity of lesser-known publishers will lead to greater awareness and appreciation of a variety of sources of all modes from across the globe.

In the 2011 National Union of Students survey,

> 42% of Black [African, Arab, Asian and Caribbean descent] students [. . .] answered "No" to the question, "Do you feel the curriculum on your course reflects issues of diversity, equality and discrimination?" Student comments focused on the concept of a "mainstream" way of thinking which excluded students from diverse backgrounds, and a lack of courses focusing on BME-specific content. (Miller 2016: 74)

Almost a decade later, the same issues still exist. In Goldsmiths's recent study of BAME student experiences, 49 percent of respondents did not feel their "course content was representative of the lived experiences, achievements and works of Black and minority ethnic people" (Akel 2019: 18). Qualitative evidence on the experience of BAME students at SOAS University similarly reveals feelings of exclusion and criticizes the limitations of content and perspectives covered (Decolonizing SOAS Working Group 2018: 5). Highlighting the continuation of issues on BAME student belonging in documents like these helps to encourage the need to recognize and address these issues at all levels of a university. The difficulties outlined are not confined to these institutions but point to wider concerns of BAME students' experiences within HE across the sector.

When choosing what materials to include within a program, the decision of what materials to exclude is simultaneously considered. What is not taught can also speak volumes about the program; this is known as the null curriculum. For Provenzo Jr (2009: 3), "the null curriculum teaches what is valued and what is not valued by society. As a result, traditional values and power structures are reinforced, and minority opinions and values are often marginalized and given little value or credence." In regard to materials that are incorporated, what topics, themes, and issues are covered but underrepresented? Rather than trying to achieve balance between topics, attention could focus on questioning the reasons as to why certain materials are included/excluded over others. It is not only what is made explicit in a curriculum that should be examined but also that which is hidden.

Portelli (1993: 343) differentiates between the "formal curriculum [...] which is officially recognized," "the actual curriculum, that which is actually carried out," and "The hidden curriculum [which] is usually contrasted with the formal curriculum and may form part of the actual curriculum." "At a micro-level, the hidden curriculum is expressed in terms of the distinction between 'what is meant to happen,' that is, the curriculum stated officially by the educational system or institution, and what teachers and learners actually do and experience 'on the ground,' a kind of de facto curriculum" (Sambell and McDowell 1998: 392). Cotton et al. (2013: 192) note, "In higher education, [the hidden curriculum] may be made up of the societal, institutional or lecturers' values that are transmitted unconsciously to students."

Chapter Summary

Chapter 1 of this book touched on issues concerning history, race, and politics and how they connect to the subject of decolonizing. Although the terms "history," "race," and "politics" are not used in the TRAAC model, this is not an avoidance of terms, or a shying away from difficult conversations. Rather, the purpose of the model is to provide a starting point for supporting challenging conversations. The questions require the user to reflect on their position, perspectives, identity, and those of their students. The purpose is to provide an accessible model that can be used by anyone involved in teaching and learning support for reflection and forward planning. The questions raised in TRAAC will not be new to teaching practitioners as they are ones considered regularly as part of formal review processes. However, it is hoped that employed holistically (with the understanding that the questions in each segment cover a wider scope of consideration as unpacked), the TRAAC model can help to act as an entry point for deeper critical reflection in regard to decolonizing teaching and learning.

4

Bringing Together Materials for a Decolonized Curriculum

With Contributions from Jason Arday and Joanne Dunham

This chapter focuses primarily on the "Content" and "Activities and Assessment" segments of the TRAAC model. It begins by outlining the different ways curriculum can be understood and how this affects teaching approaches and students' learning experience. Extending on discussions in Chapter 2 of working with students in the decolonizing process, this chapter further underlines how valuing student voices when developing a decolonized curriculum means student needs, contexts, and lived experiences are acknowledged in the process. The chapter also highlights the influential role which library can play in the decolonizing agenda and the value of working closely with library colleagues to bring together materials that work toward a decolonized curriculum. The chapter ends with contributions from Jason Arday and Joanne Dunham.

What Makes a Curriculum?

"[H]igher education is characterized by specific modes of selection and organization of the knowledge taught, which makes the analysis of curriculum construction particularly relevant regarding teaching staff and institutions" (Barrier et al. 2019: 38–9). This chapter considers the ways in which materials can be brought together and explored to help produce a decolonized curriculum. By way of starting this discussion, it is important to clarify what is meant here by "materials." The following discussion refers to materials as resources that form both the primary and secondary learning resources used by staff and students inside and outside of the classroom. These materials may include written, online, recorded, or other mediums of learning resources and guidance materials that may be shared before, during, or after class. The selection of these materials directly connects with the assessments that are set for students.

It is also central to explore the various associations and meanings of the term curriculum. In Annala et al.'s (2016: 171–2) "systematic literature review [...] of the state of studies on curriculum in HE [in sixty-two articles]," four different ways of approaching curriculum in curriculum studies were found:

1. An emphasis on the syllabus to be taught
2. The product of a curriculum in terms of a graduate who has the knowledge and skillset to contribute to a continually changing workplace and society
3. The curriculum as an interactive process between staff and students
4. Curriculum as praxis, emphasising action and reflection. (2016)

Similarly, in Fraser and Bosanquet's (2006: 272) study of twenty-five semi-structured interviews with academic teachers from an Australian university exploring conceptions of curriculum, the following categories were described:

- The structure and content of a unit (subject);
- The structure and content of a programme of study;
- The students' experience of learning;
- A dynamic and interactive process of teaching and learning.

The first description given by both studies is that which emphasizes the content of the curriculum. In light of discussions on decolonizing teaching and learning, this does not only involve decisions as to what to include as core material; it also asks the teacher to question what knowledge is being held up as more valuable and of having greater importance than others. Trigwell and Prosser (2004: 411) note, "An important part of what may be needed to change actual teaching and perceptions of teaching is knowledge of what the teachers themselves see as their own approaches to teaching, and how these approaches are experienced by students." Staff need to reflect on the message which they wish to communicate to students about diversity, belonging, and equality through their choice of materials.

Both studies also point out the theme of student experience as being one way of understanding curriculum. While students share a classroom, they do not all experience the same teaching and learning environment. Thus, approaches to designing curriculum should also support students to negotiate their own place in the curriculum. De Lissovoy (2010: 286) calls for a "a deep destabilization of our notion of curriculum, since it becomes less the name for an organized content or educational experience, and more the designation for the process of construction itself of an unprecedented knowledge." De Lissovoy puts forth a "Pedagogy of lovingness. [. . .] This orientation can be distinguished from the simple attitude of 'caring,' which is influential in progressive education, in centering an awareness of cultural difference while developing an enlarged solidarity that reaches beyond the local and the nation to participate in the construction of a global community" (2010: 289).

Whichever way an individual conceives curriculum, it should be accompanied by the realization that their approach affects the type of role they take on as a teacher. This is because the way we understand curriculum influences how we teach, which affects classroom dynamics and student perceptions of staff. The extent to which a teacher has control over the shaping of their curriculum also plays a part in this. When teachers feel they lack agency within an institution, this prevents the teacher from being able to create and communicate a curriculum which they believe will best fit the needs of their students. Outside factors may also impact on the degree of influence which staff have on curriculum design as professional body and vocational career requirements can significantly limit assessment creativity. When such is the case, program teams can reflect on how reforming the interactive learning process can help to make up for the lack of control elsewhere.

When planning a curriculum, higher education (HE) teacher training courses and programs often discuss topics such as learning outcomes, content selection, learning activities, and assessment. The discussion of these topics is frequently discussed in light of Biggs's constructive alignment (no date: 1), where "all components in the teaching system—the curriculum and its intended outcomes, the teaching methods used, the assessment tasks—are aligned to each other. All are tuned to learning activities addressed in the desired learning outcomes." However, as Bovill and Woolmer (2019: 414) point out, "this framework assumes that the teacher retains responsibility for identifying learning outcomes and the ways in which assessment, teaching and evaluation will align, and it does not address issues of power and privilege in the production of knowledge. This system-based approach can appear so tightly bound that it unintentionally limits flexibility and possibilities for student-staff co-creation."

Biggs's model emphasizes the "what"—what needs to be covered, what needs to be learned, and what needs to be assessed in order for alignment between topics to be connected and fluid. The transparency of the relationship between learning outcomes, content, and assessment is vital to ensure students understand what is expected of them from the program. This clarity also helps students to relate their learning throughout their modules back to the wider aims of the program, further strengthening their understanding. However, the focus on the "what" may lead to what Dunham and Tran (2019) refer to as the "forgotten stage of designing curricula." They describe this stage as one that "Explores the deeper levels of learning which students will hopefully achieve. [Involves] [r]eflection by the academic upon the choices they make in terms of curricula and pedagogy. [Requires] [e]ngagement between academics and library staff to form more thoughtful decolonized curricula and inclusive collections." The idea of the forgotten stage encourages consideration of how the program in question is located in terms of wider community, and the impact and benefits that the learning may have on society.

The deeper levels of learning which students will hopefully achieve connect the learning which takes place during the program to the application of knowledge which might occur after completion. Addressing this forgotten stage involves critical reflection as good practice when planning and designing a curriculum. Being critically reflective and reflexive when making choices regarding the design of a curriculum enables one to produce and explain the thoughtful strategy behind the selection of materials, activities, and assessments. This involves thinking about the extent to which a teacher's own position and perspectives express itself in curriculum choices, and how much space is available for other positions, contexts, and perspectives to be explored.

The forgotten stage calls for collaboration between academics and library colleagues to share knowledge and create new resources in light of decolonizing needs. And "decolonising the curriculum must go beyond updating reading lists" (Nwonka 2019). "Decoloniality infers an active undoing, deconstructing, or delinking from coloniality, and in the library or archive this is a different concept to the process of diversifying collections, or ensuring that multiple narratives are represented. Decoloniality can focus for example on a process of re-contextualisation" (Crilly 2019: 9). As discussed in previous chapters, decolonizing is not a call for an eradication or replacement of materials but a call for a more mindful approach to the exploration of materials and issues so that the relationship between students, staff, their academic programs, environment, and wider society can be better connected.

It can be difficult to design a customized curriculum based on the students in the classroom ahead of time. For some teachers, they may not have any information about their student cohort ahead of meeting them at the first class. To plan a program based on the most accurate and up-to-date student data is therefore often an unrealistic task. However, what staff often do know or can reasonably discover are the general past trends and typical characteristics of their particular student cohort. Such information may include approximate ratios of BAME to white students, home and international students, the number of students who have outside commitments such as work and caring responsibilities, the percentage of students who are the first in their family to enter university, and the typical routes of entry for their students. While the accuracies of such information will change each year, knowledge of past trends and the typical makeup of a student cohort can nevertheless be helpful in indicating the potential likely challenges that students may face during the course of their study.

For example, students who are the first in their family to go to university may feel they lack an immediate role model to discuss the particular struggles that come with HE studies. For those who are balancing their studies with outside work or family commitments, their engagement with the program may be limited. For commuter students, the detachment which comes with being located away from campus may also affect their engagement with peers and the university more widely. These student characteristics can at times overlap. Research has found that "commuter students are more likely to: work part-time; have family or carer responsibilities; be the first generation in their family to attend HE; be from a lower socio-economic group; have a low income; be mature; and have a BAME [. . .] background" (Maguire and Morris 2018: 12 citing Donnelly and Gamsu 2018; Thomas and Jones 2017; Woodfield 2014). Such knowledge can be employed by staff to design a program that takes into consideration the needs of their students, implementing appropriate interventions as necessary to offer deep levels of support. However, teaching staff need to be conscious of how knowledge of these indicators may unconsciously influence the expectations they may have of particular students. Furthermore, for commuter students and students who are trying to find balance between a number of personal and professional commitments, it is even more challenging to find sufficient time to contribute to student-staff partnership projects that focus on codeveloping curriculum. Asynchronous modes of engagement can help respond to this as it enables students to engage in their own time.

Approaching students with compassion can be developmental for both students and staff. Discussing the pedagogy of compassion, Gibbs (2017: 3) notes compassion is "usually conceived as a personal response to the vulnerable and those that suffer. It is a strong emotion and one that is more likely to lead to action than sympathy or empathy, although all three prove a compelling mix for a humane society." In Vandeyar and Swart's (2016: 141) case study arguing for a "pedagogy of compassion as a possible approach to addressing and transforming education in post-apartheid South Africa [. . . One of the findings was that the] implementation of a 'pedagogy of compassion' enabled the teacher to dismantle polarised thinking and to shatter the polite silence of post-apartheid South African society." The power to change mindsets and encourage openness toward new ways of thinking connects compassionate pedagogy with the work of decolonizing. Waddington (2018: 2) underlines how if "Compassionate pedagogy [. . .] is to flourish, [it] must challenge [. . .] dominant paradigms' [. . .] Compassion inevitably expresses itself in the fight for justice." Again, such features of compassionate pedagogy mirror the core values of the decolonizing agenda.

Valuing Student Voices When Developing a Decolonized Curriculum

When classroom conversations are framed as interactions that have the potential to impact on society, discussions are transformed from ones that not only question academic debate but consider how they may play an active part in their own way in shaping and reshaping wider social discussions. The student voice in the latter setting is a more powerful one than that of a typical classroom. The relevance of program content to student lives, backgrounds, and experiences can enable greater connections to be made between what is learned and a student's lived experience. Assemi and Sheikhzade (2013: 82) comment, "In experiential null curriculum, students neglect or pay little attention to some contents because these materials do not relate to their life or it is incongruous with their needs." Feeling a greater level of connection to materials might support a student's ability to engage in class discussion. This may then help students to apply learning to lived experience and simultaneously help them to critically reflect upon experiences in light of knowledge learned.

The makeup of a classroom, whether physical or online, consists of staff and students. A classroom would not function without the two coming together. In Meda's (2019: 8) case study of student understandings of decolonizing, students emphasize the need for a contextually relevant curriculum. To design a program without making efforts to understand in detail, the needs of students lead to the design of a program that is biased. This bias may be unconscious, coming through the choices made in relation to content, activities, approaches, and assessments. Varied choices may be integrated in an effort to be inclusive, but the extent to which these inclusions lead to improved outcomes of grades and an increased sense of student belonging depends on the level of criticality behind the rationale, how they are implemented, explored, and reviewed by staff and students throughout the program.

One of the ways in which the subject of decolonizing can be explored early on with students is through the engagement of selected pre-reading or in-class reading materials. Maloney (2012: 281) discusses the positive impact which a Diversity Book Display Initiative can have on campus, "The mindful leveraging of collections not only provides opportunities for student learning regarding diversity and inclusion, but also can be a platform to build collaborative campus relationships and elevate library visibility." At Goldsmith University (2019), library colleagues are asking students to recommend texts as part of the institution's "Liberate our Curriculum" and "Liberate our degrees" initiatives. What these examples show is the influential role the library can play in helping to progressing the decolonizing agenda. Not only are colleagues across institutional libraries developing projects for decolonizing but as libraries are both student and staff facing, they help to connect voices and develop a wider conversation on decolonizing teaching and learning.

As Joanne Dunham notes in the Chapter 4 contribution,

> Library collection development in its purest form should be diverse, inclusive and speak to all perspectives. However, the Eurocentricity of published content, how it is classified and arranged in libraries continues to speak to the era of colonization. As the institution attempts to decolonize, embrace diversity and inclusivity in its research and teaching, the expertise of Librarians in knowing and understanding what content is discoverable, how to find it and appraise it should be exploited.

Students could be given a text that considers the issue of decolonizing within their particular subject discipline. These could then be used to open up discussion among the group, encouraging students to put forth their own positions and perspectives on the text. The following questions may be subsequently posed to students: What are their first impressions of the materials? What are their expectations from the program? What are their desired outcomes? These questions can help to build a rapport between staff and students through the teachers' efforts to better understand the connections between the personal and professional among students.

For some subject areas it may be difficult to make significant changes to the content of a curriculum, thereby seemingly hindering the process of decolonizing altogether. For Brodie (2016) "This means that those within the discipline must consider other aspects: curriculum processes, such as critical thinking and problem solving; pedagogy—how the subject is taught and, as a number of people have argued, addressing the issue of identity." Brodie's article focuses on mathematics, but as a few of the contributions in this book highlight, flexibility of the content of a law curriculum can also be restrictive. When selecting materials for a program it can be helpful to consider how student cohorts are mini reflections of wider society. Doing so brings to the forefront discussions concerning the sustainability of the program and the impact which would be hoped for in connection to content and community.

One of the professional values of the United Kingdom Professional Standards Framework (UKPSF) "Acknowledge[s] the wider context in which higher education operates recognising the implications for professional practice" (AdvanceHE 2019: 3). The statements of the UKPSF are general in description so that they can be applied across categories of fellowship. One example of the "wider context" referred to might be the topic of graduate employment and the pressure among academic staff to integrate and develop what is sometimes referred to as the "employability skills" of students during the course of a program. Other examples of this wider context are issues regarding access to HE and the awarding gap between BAME students and white students.

The HE sector is directly affected by economic, political, and social changes but can also affect society too. Therefore, the conversations, research, and other outputs from universities can play an important role in influencing change both within an institution and more widely. Gorski (2008: 515) argues "that attaining [. . .] an intercultural education requires not only subtle shifts in practice and personal relationships, but also important shifts of consciousness that prepare us to see and react to the socio-political contexts that so heavily influence education theory and practice." Encouraging students to consider how their classroom may be perceived as a microcosm of wider society or a society in itself may encourage deeper levels of critical discussion. For Osman and Hornsby (2017: 4) "the classroom is not only a microcosm of what society is but what it can be if we take social justice seriously." As Eizadirad (2019: 205) notes, "The objective of a decolonized education model would be to internally motivate students to care about themselves and their communities through relationship building, empowerment, reflexivity, and a sense of shared responsibility while acknowledging inequality of opportunity as a systemic barrier to achieving success." Students are thus empowered not only in their own lives but as persons who have the potential to make an impact on networks they are a part of and those beyond.

Consideration of the makeup of specific student cohorts when selecting materials helps to ensure that content covers a range of perspectives and contexts. Olaleye (2019), giving a keynote at the Addressing Barriers to Student Success conference, noted, "decolonization requires sustained collaboration [. . .] that knowledge is not owned by anyone [. . . and that it is important to] ensure knowledge production reflects a multifaceted society." This should be a collaborative effort. Module leaders and colleagues involved in front line teaching are likely to have better insight into what students do and do not enjoy. Speaking with past program leaders can also offer an insight into how preferences have changed toward learning and teaching, including choices relating to activities and assessments. Going beyond the standard end of program surveys to carry out focus groups and/or informal discussions with students can push further the review of topics relating to content selection to more accurately understand issues of student engagement and enjoyment. Showing respect to all voices means that "Educational spaces have to be opened up to the multiplicity of student voices" (Vandeyar 2019: 7). Creating opportunities for students to become active contributors to the design of a curriculum can help to decrease the gap between staff and students more generally.

While surveys pinpoint what areas of a module or program students have responded well and less well to, authentic conversations with students can offer ideas relating to how successful areas can be scaled up in a way that would benefit a larger number of the student cohort. Commenting on case studies which involved facilitated discussions between students and lecturers, Rumpus et al. (2011: 252) underline how "the work demonstrated that the reflections students made, and their opinions and suggestions, were more powerful when given directly in narrative form in the students' own words. [. . .] These methods carried greater credibility with staff than previously used methods of information gathering such as the fairly standard module/course questionnaires." Involving students helps to produce a curriculum with meaningful opportunities for a wider range of students to connect and participate with the program.

Contributions

The following contributions by Jason Arday and Joanne Dunham extend the conversations around diversifying curricula and materials. Jason considers how whiteness, and the continued privileging of Eurocentric knowledge, hinders the development of a truly inclusive curriculum for students. Joanne highlights the influential and diverse role which library colleagues can play in helping to develop conversations around decolonizing collections. Both contributors emphasize the need to listen and respond to all voices and engage with different positions and perspectives to create curricula that are appropriate to our current multicultural society. The contributions are followed by a discussion of the issues, ideas, and themes raised by the authors and how these connect to wider discussions of decolonizing touched upon in this book.

Trying to Break the Monopoly: Diversifying Our Curricula within the Academy

Jason Arday

Introduction

Anti-racist education holds the potential to truly reflect the cultural hybridity of our diverse, multicultural society through the canons of knowledge that educators celebrate, proffer, and embody (Peters, 2015). The centrality of whiteness as an instrument of power and privilege ensures that particular types of knowledge continue to remain omitted from our curricula. The monopoly and proliferation of dominant white European canons do comprise much of our existing curriculum, and consequently this does impact on aspects of engagement and belonging particularly for Black, Asian, and Minority Ethnic (BAME) learners. Within HE, campaigns such as the Decolonising the Curriculum Movement and Why Is My Curriculum White have sought to challenge and dismantle the existing orthodoxy by advocating a curriculum that reflects the multiple histories of Black and Indigenous populations globally but particularly within the UK.

Anti-racist education in Britain provides a cornerstone for reconceptualizing how knowledge is proliferated and who should be the custodians of particular types of knowledge particularly within the classroom environment where historically the gatekeepers to knowledge have often resembled the white middle class (Leonardo, 2016). Within the UK and the Academy more generally the liberal assumptions of multiculturalism have been integral in uncovering and dismantling the hidden power structures that were responsible for inequality and racism in institutions. Educational institutions, in particular, continue to be complicit in reproducing white privilege. The dearth of Black and ethnic minority gatekeepers to knowledge in the Academy has been a contributing factor in sustaining systemic racism and stereotypes against ethnic and minority groups. While traction regarding this issue continues to gather momentum nationally within the UK and globally, the curriculum and pedagogies that pervade within our institutions continue to remain a site for the systemic reproduction of racism.

This chapter succinctly explores how pedagogues might attempt to decenter and decolonize the dominant Eurocentric canon. Within this treatise, the exploration presented focuses on the importance for diversifying our curriculum and providing a curriculum that is reflective of our ever-increasing multicultural society. In attempting to endorse a curriculum which encourages inclusion and facilitates belonging, aspects examined consider the impact of a narrow and restrictive curriculum on ethnic minority students and how the omission of diverse histories and multicultural knowledge canons facilitate marginalization and discriminatory cultures within the Academy for students and academics alike.

Occupying a space which attempts to dismantle and deconstruct normative orthodoxies remains difficult due to a reluctance generally by custodians of the Academy and gatekeepers to knowledge to disrupt the canon in favor of something more egalitarian and representative of our diverse multicultural society. Within the UK there has been a continuing critical mass of students and academics that have sustained calls to decolonize the curriculum and diversify the canon at universities "by ending the domination of Western epistemological traditions, histories and figures" (Molefe 2016: 32). In particular, anti-racist scholar-activists have called for the end of dominant ideologies that position "white, male, Western, capitalist, heterosexual, European worldviews in higher education as the dominant knowledge canon and discourse, in favour of more inclusive lexicon that embodies global 'perspectives, experiences and epistemologies' as the central tenets of the curriculum" (Shay 2016).

Nwadeyi (2016) argues that colonialism, segregation, and other divisive vehicles for entrenching white supremacy have impacted how educational spaces construct knowledge and the historical contexts that comprise the curricula that we advance and consume. The framing of Black histories and the systematic omission of their contribution to global society facilitate an historic amnesia that creates a very narrow and constrained view of society and more notably the actors that comprise these knowledge canons. The effects of this continued marginalization on academics and students of color facilitate a learning space which is not reflective of increasing diverse student populations (Tate and Bagguley 2017). This is perhaps symptomatic of the entrenched institutional racism which still influences much of the discriminatory terrain in the Academy and society more generally (Shilliam 2015).

Challenging the Dominant Eurocentric Curriculum in Higher Education

Curriculum within HE has been a significant factor in attempting to discern issues concerning engagement, belonging, and marginalization. Consequently, recent research (Andrews 2016; Arday 2019; Bhopal 2014; Rollock 2016) has illuminated that BAME students are often given no agency or autonomy in collaboratively negotiating the canons of knowledge provided. In many cases, ethnic minority students are engaging with a curriculum that does not reflect their socialization, worldview, history, or lived experience. There are several arguments (Andrews 2016; Delgado Bernal and Villapand 2016; Leonardo 2016) to suggest that any body of knowledge solely produced by only white scholars is not truly reflective of a multiculturally diverse society and negates the contribution of Black scholars to contributions or canons of knowledge. There have been commentaries (Miller 2016; Leonardo 2002) proffered which suggest that applying a broader canvas to contributions of knowledge would actually limit the potential aspirations of BAME students, leaving them without access to "perceived" necessary historical, philosophical, and intellectual grounding. Such claims fall down upon the basic premise that the Academy is inherently white, and often through this supremacist guise of normativity, knowledge is often cultivated and constructed through an exclusive and narrow lens that has historically omitted the contribution of people of color as constructors of knowledge (Andrews 2019; Arday 2019).

Pedagogically, there is an obligation within our HE institutions to ensure that the knowledge provided is historically representative of an ever-changing global community. In attempting to unpack the power and privilege that pervades this discourse, it is important to assert that the continual advancement of a nuanced and constrained curriculum also disadvantages white students with regards to broadening and challenging their own worldview particularly against dominant discourses and stereotypes concerning people of color (Leonardo 2016). Within the UK, we have begun to observe a resistance toward the knowledge only being advanced through these canons with movements such as Why Is My Curriculum White? and Why Isn't My Professor Black? Fundamentally, both campaigns share a commitment toward decolonizing the Academy and diversifying a dominant Eurocentric, white curriculum that does not acknowledge nor reflect the contribution of people of color and the diasporic, historical lived experiences of ethnic minority students and migrant populations (Delgado Bernal and Villalpando 2016; Dei, Karumanchery and Karumanchery-Luik 2004).

Recent studies (Arday 2019; Ahmed 2012; Hamilton 2016; Shay 2016) have continued to query not only the lack of transformation in the HE sector but also the mechanisms which continue to sustain such an exclusionary curriculum. Such cultural and structural mechanisms include poor diversification among academic staff and omitting students of color from curriculum design processes (Delgado Bernal, and Villalpando 2016). Thus, many efforts to change the zeitgeist involve an inevitable disruption of whiteness; however, the centrality of this phenomena occupies and monopolizes much of the pedagogical practices that transpire within the Academy (Cotton et al. 2016; Leonardo 2016). The centrality of the whiteness to be disrupted maintains a historical legacy that is deeply rooted having been imposed through colonial mechanisms as a "symbol of purity" undermined by a notion that this knowledge canon is the only legitimate and verifiable knowledge claim to knowledge (Sardar 2008). This whiteness is still engaged in daily open and/or subtle racism and marginalization of Black people. The landscape and current structure of HE require dismantling in order to be fully representative and more inclusive. There is a collective responsibility required in dismantling racism within HE if the sector is to serve its function to promote social mobility and improve individual lives through the vehicle of education. An overhaul of the current system may seem insurmountable upon initial consideration, but university institutions must work harder to address the deeply entrenched inequalities that blight and compromise equality and equity within the sector.

There have been aspects of the Eurocentric curriculum that have attempted to present a multicultural discourse; however, an important distinction to assert has been the reluctance of the Academy to address the colonial past and its impact on present society. Senior leaders tasked with this responsibility often do not strategically prioritize this agenda despite being tasked with a remit to facilitate the best learning experience for all types of learners. BAME students by proxy of paying tuition fees subscribe to the idea of an inclusive curriculum that challenges, uncovers, and dismantles the hidden power structures that are responsible for inequality and institutional racism (Pilkington 2013). This forges an essential part of what still remains a largely exclusionary curriculum. Fundamentally, the problem stems from a lack of diversification among Academy staff that is truly reflective of ever-increasing diverse student populations.

Beyond just having greater representation, diversifying academic staff cohorts also facilitates different forms of pedagogy that dismantle and disrupt the historical landscape of education. Within this landscape, educational institutions in particular have played a fundamental role in reproducing white privilege and sadly HE has been complicit in reinforcing racist and stereotypical ascriptions against ethnic and minority groups through varying tools of whiteness such as the racist microaggression (Leonardo 2016). Attempting to dismantle the physical, cultural, and intellectual environment of the Academy is problematic because as Peters (2015) states, it is legacy built on white domination. Penetrating the curricula to produce something that is wholly representative is something that must be considered by parliamentarians, policy makers, and senior leaders within universities. Such action is urgent as the BAME attainment gap (current attainment gap between white and Black students qualifying with a 1st or 2:1 degree is currently at 24 percent) widens and a significant reason for this deficit has been the omission of culturally diverse curriculum in favor of curricula which largely only represents, acknowledges, and celebrates white endeavor (AdvanceHE 2018).

Conclusion and Recommendations

The landscape and current structure of HE require dismantling in order to be fully representative and more inclusive. There is a collective responsibility required in dismantling racism within HE if the sector is to serve its function to promote social mobility and improve individual lives through the vehicle of education. An overhaul of the current system may seem insurmountable upon initial consideration, but university institutions must work harder to address the deeply entrenched inequalities that blight and compromise equality and equity within the sector.

While universities continue to remain a reflection and microcosm of society, they should be committed to structurally and culturally facilitating the needs of a multicultural and diverse learning community. This becomes even more prevalent with increasing tuition fee costs for students in an increasingly competitive landscape. Therefore, the learning space must be reflective of a curriculum that embodies and reflects all students' lived experiences, particularly from a cultural and historical viewpoint. For universities to truly embrace the ideals associated with diversity, there must be recognition among institutional leaders, parliamentarians, policy makers, and the sector more generally to address the deeply entrenched systemic problems that reinforce inequality within the Academy (AdvanceHE 2018).

There are three factors that impact this discourse: structural, organizational, and cultural:

Structural: The autonomous nature of HE means that institutions must invest more funding (specifically student tuition fees) on diversifying internal structures to ensure students as consumers are provided with an inclusive experience that is reflective of multicultural hybridity particularly within the university space.

Organizational: Universities must consider the importance of an "inclusive curriculum" that not only speaks to students lived experiences and cultural history but decenters dominant Eurocentric discourses as the only canon of knowledge to be considered. Institutions should engage more collaboratively with students to design curricula, for example, students should have a significant role in shaping the type of curricula provided and have equal agency to that of academic staff, in attempting to be truly inclusive.

Cultural: Universities and the sector more generally must accept that the Academy is unequal and, in many cases, reinforces inequality. Resistance by universities in diagnosing and acknowledging the problems that permeate the BAME attainment gap reinforces a culture of inequality. This has been a significant barrier toward effecting positive change. To ensure penetrative and sector-wide change, BAME students and staff must be a part of the curriculum design process and consulted during revalidation and modification processes to university degree programs.

Decolonizing the Curricula: The Academic Library Supporting the Decolonized Curricula in Learning and Teaching

Joanne Dunham

Academic libraries have long supported the learning and teaching endeavor of the university through their collections, information literacy training, and liaison with academic staff delivering teaching. Librarians are well versed in adapting their skills and their collections to the new areas of pedagogy and research. In recent years this has meant turning toward the challenges of decolonizing their collections and supporting academic staff in the redesign of their curricula as they look toward creating inclusive teaching models to reflect the diverse student populations taking their module.

What Is the Role of the Library in Decolonizing the Curricula?

As Archivist L'ael Hughes-Watkins states, work undertaken by archivists and librarians can and has led to social change (Hughes-Watkins 2019: 41). In Academic libraries this is exemplified by increasing activity in this arena as a result of the "decolonising the curriculum" debate following the Rhodes Must Fall movement and Is Our Curriculum White? campaigns. Libraries around the world have begun to look at how their collections and staff can play a role in helping to progress the decolonizing work of an institution and support staff and student bodies by acting as a conduit for access to diverse and inclusive learning and teaching resources. This work looks at academic liaison activities including analyzing, advising, and finding content for reading list creation with teaching staff; using information literacy skills to find nontraditional resources; reviewing embedded information literacy skills within modules to ensure that all voices are represented; working with the student body to identify, add to, and create collections that represent student voices; reviewing traditional classification schemes to arrange collections; and reviewing the use of language in how services are provided and communicated (Charles 2019).

There are examples in the UK of how academic libraries have been working in their institutions on this agenda from Liberate our Library at Goldsmiths (Liberate our Library; Clarke 2019); Decolonising the Curriculum (Bournemouth University); and How to Decolonize the Library at the London School of Economics (Damen 2019), among others.

Marilyn Clarke at Goldsmith University Library is working collaboratively with their Students' Union to "liberate our degrees" and has put this issue front and center as part of their library strategy to Liberate our Library (Clarke 2019).

At Leicester there has been various activities in this area as part of the Education Excellence Programme the Library has been involved in leading on. This has included making operational the work of the Inclusive Curriculum Stream by establishing a working group within the library; working with the student body to create a "Represent" collection of material and associated reading list; working with curriculum learning developers to review resources and collections including coverage, advising on how to find alternative sources; reviewing information literacy sessions and examples used in training sessions; and talking with publishers about the content that they provide and the diversity of their resources.

Taking library collections as an example, there is a clear distinction between decolonization and diversity. Diversity relates to who is in the collections, which voices are heard; decolonization is more related to the description of the collection, how it is classified, what terms are being used (Khan 2019). There is a danger that diverse readings can be interpreted as tokenistic and something paid lip service to rather than an integrated and vital part of the curriculum, module, and course (Nwonka 2019). The importance of libraries lies in three areas: place, content, and people (Dame 2019).

Using TRAAC in a Library Context

The TRAAC model has offered a useful way to reflect on library services and resources both in a way that supports the learning and teaching endeavor and toward how its collections represent the diversity of the institution. This helps resource discovery to look beyond traditional content. Furthermore, conversations with academics, students, and content providers are framed in a more participatory context and information skills training demonstrates cultural competence (Foster 2018 ALA). As a result, collection development, information literacy, and library services can be developed and provided in a more holistic, integrated, and inclusive way.

Teaching Approach

The library can be viewed as an extension of the classroom with its extended opening hours, group working areas, and flexible learning spaces. The library, even in an environment where much has been made digital and can be accessed anywhere, is a place that students view as a safe place to study while on campus. The library has become a complement to the classroom, and library staff need to view it in the same way as a tutor would view their teaching room. With a blend of learning spaces including individual traditional study spaces, group study areas, and more relaxed study spaces designed with a user-centric approach, students can continue to learn and study in a space that suits their need. Librarians can support teaching and learning by matching library space to pedagogic needs in spaces that reflect different learning styles.

Academic libraries have evolved with the changing nature of the communities they serve. Group working areas with associated technology allow for discussion and ready access to resources. In contrast, individual study places in a range of formal and informal styles speak to the diverse range of students. As a central building at the heart of campus with long opening hours across seven days a week, the library has adapted to support more than the academic needs of the students. Activities such as permitting and providing food and drink during library hours, creating areas of quiet and silent study, addressing student health and well-being by providing leisure collections, access to academic skills support, access to welfare, counseling and accessibility services provide a holistic approach. This has been well received and supported by students. Library staff have welcomed the opportunity to work with the Students Union to create and develop activities as part of the wider university activity that ensure student well-being and support.

Relationship

Libraries have always had a mandate to serve all its user community, and as this community becomes more diverse a wide range of voices need to be connected with. There are a variety of ways this has been achieved from the more formal liaison activities with Student Staff Committees, Academic Committees, and meetings with Officers of the Students Union to student fora, focus groups, linking with student societies, campaigns, and interest groups alongside the use of Student Champions.

The Read@Leicester campaign was initiated in 2016/17 stemming from studies on the reading practices of young people entering HE. Reading for pleasure as opposed to just for academic purposes provides one way of exploring wider perspectives. In 2018/19 one of the books chosen by students was the *Good Immigrant*, edited by Nikesh Shukla (2016). This opened up a wide-ranging debate and led to lectures and workshops based on its content.

In 2019/20, the library created a leisure collection alongside initiating a campaign called "Represent," in which the library is working with the student body and Student Champions to recommend books, both fiction and nonfiction, to represent their diverse voices. One of the challenges in setting up this collection has been engaging students and staff to participate. Momentum developed during the first semester as greater awareness of the campaign grew. The strength of being able to provide this opportunity has been borne out by the positive feedback from students who have welcomed the ability to suggest books, which they can borrow, or just read in a dedicated reading space within the library. When providing a recommendation, many students speak about giving visibility to underrepresented authors and their own voices.

The diversity of the library workforce risks hindering the connections between libraries and their communities as the profession is predominantly white and female. In 2015 over 86,000 (96.7 percent) professionals working in the library and information profession across public, academic, and commercial libraries were identified as white (Hall 2015). The lack of staff diversity and shared lived experiences could affect how our diverse student community engages with library staff when interacting and seeking support. Attracting a more diverse staff profile could potentially influence levels of students seeking support and engaging with support services on offer, particularly academic skills support to improve student outcomes.

There has been work at a national level in the UK from both the Chartered Institute of Library and Information Professionals (CILIP) and the Archives and Records Association (ARA) in 2015, Society of College, National and University Libraries (SCONUL) in 2018/19 and a BAME library staff survey published in 2019 (Ishaq and Hussain 2019). There is a CILIP special interest group and BAME staff forum and further work announced by both organizations. Locally at Leicester, we have worked with our Equality Diversity and Inclusion (EDI) unit to hold workshops, online learning, and discussion groups to increase awareness of our diverse community, unconscious bias, white privilege, and other equality issues. Library staff have also led a group discussion to reflect on the role of the library in serving its population and ways of creating the best environment for learning. The Library at Leicester has also been working with recruitment to attract a more diverse range of applicants to library jobs. This has included reviewing the images portrayed on the library website, revising job descriptions, advertising in places specifically aimed at the BAME community, holding recruitment days to short list, involving students in recruitment panels, and tracking recruitment data to look at our equality.

Activity and Assessment

The academic library has long been involved with providing library instruction with the aim of embedding information literacy skills into the curriculum. Many academic librarians with a subject specialist role have undertaken formal teaching qualifications. However, many taught sessions are one-off instructional training workshops on how to find, access, appraise, and use the many resources the library provides. Library staff in these roles usually have little or no prior interaction with a class before the session and only have limited time in the lesson to create a connection with students. Cultural awareness and cultural competence of librarians is a key requirement for these teaching activities. This can be achieved through involving librarians in teaching sessions in the curriculum, peer review, and liaising with teaching staff about the students they are teaching, as well as developing their competencies through training and development.

The American Library Association Diversity group has developed a framework for cultural competence by which Librarians can measure their cultural competence. Standard 5 addresses library information skills training requiring librarians to assess how their "instructional methods, practices, and resources are widely accessible and reflective of the broad diversity of learning styles, language abilities, developmental skills, and cultural perspectives represented in the learning community" (ALA). Elizabeth Foster (2018), in her article on cultural competence in library instruction, advocates a reflective practice approach to one-off instructional training. As with teaching, one-off instructional training should be flexible, creative, and open to experimentation to be truly inclusive.

At Leicester, our academic liaison librarians have initiated a decolonizing curriculum working group which meets monthly. This group has largely discussed diversifying library collections and the range of resources it signposts; working with departments on the inclusive curriculum and holding training workshops for library staff across the region. Members also are part of Leicester's Educational Excellence program for Inclusivity that is comprised of colleagues from library, professional services, academic staff, and students. The coming together of different stakeholders raises the cultural awareness of the group. This allows the group to discuss, research, collate information, and reflect on their training, liaison activities, and collection development.

Content

The American archivist, Hughes-Watkins (2019), reflecting on her work in creating archives, states, "I wanted to be part of a process that made the invisible visible" when speaking about hidden voices in hidden archives. A core purpose of academic libraries should be to make content visible, provide the tools to enable its discovery, and influence the creation and provision of content from the community it serves. Arguably this starts with the academic body in relation to what and how they are researching, what and how they are teaching. From a library perspective, long-established academic liaison activities, subject knowledge, expertise, and information skills put them in a prime place to affect library collection development. This has to be a partnership between library staff, academic colleagues, and students.

Library collection development in its purest form should be diverse, inclusive, and speak to all perspectives. However, the Eurocentricity of published content, how it is classified and arranged in libraries, continues to speak to the era of colonization. As the institution attempts to decolonize, embrace diversity, and inclusivity in its research and teaching, the expertise of Librarians in knowing and understanding what content is discoverable, how to find it and appraise it should be exploited.

The rigidity of cataloguing and classification standards for a library's physical collection such as Dewey Decimal and Library of Congress created in the nineteenth century use terminology that could, and does, alienate diversity. Abstracting and indexing discovery tools are predominantly capturing material published in the Western world and very few include any form of nontraditional content, or content published outside of Europe or North America. Critical appraisal skills tend to marginalize nontraditional content by discounting the quality of the resource due to how and where it is discovered. If content is not easily discovered, then increasingly it becomes marginalized. The rigidity of physical collections is not there in the digitally connected library enabling linking and access to a diverse range of content. The American Library Association cultural competence framework standard 4 highlights the need for library staff to think beyond the traditional methods for considering, purchasing, reviewing, creating, describing, reflecting, and including the needs of their diverse communities (ALA).

At Leicester, we have started reflecting on this and implementing changes through the creation of reading lists, applying critical thinking to "nontraditional" library content, improving discovery and signposting, reviewing terminology, involving the community to create diverse collections, and influencing publishers and providers in the content they are making available. We are reviewing the way diverse voices are included across indexing and resources with a view to reflect this during instruction and discovery skills training. Furthermore, we are identifying and signposting to a range of nontraditional resources such as self-published content, newsletters, YouTube, social media (Twitter, Instagram, etc.), local and regional news, and blogs.

Chapter Summary

The contributions in this chapter point to challenges facing universities in light of efforts to decolonize and the ways in which institutions can play an active role in progressing this agenda. Jason's contribution begins by problematizing the lack of diversity of knowledges being produced and communicated through university curricula due to the maintenance and ongoing privileging of Eurocentric canons. The same issue is discussed by Joanne, who raises the profile of how library colleagues can play varying roles in breaking down this tendency to rely on Western knowledge. These roles include finding varied content, nontraditional resources, greater inclusion of student voices, reviewing traditional classifications, and becoming more mindful of the language used in communication.

What is touched upon in both contributions is the shift from diversifying to decolonizing curricula. For both contributors, the success of this shift relies on stakeholders across the university becoming involved and working collaboratively on decolonizing. Jason draws attention to the reluctance "generally by custodians of the Academy and gatekeepers to knowledge to disrupt the canon," address the colonial past, and its ongoing impact. Jason's recommendations for structural, organizational, and cultural change underscore the significant shifts in attitude, approach, and action needed to fully acknowledge and respond to issues which the decolonizing agenda aims to address. The shared issues and ideas that both Jason and Joanne touch upon draw out the connectedness of conversations taking place across different areas of a university. Though the contributors hold different roles and responsibilities, their contributions highlight the shared areas of concern and challenges faced for all stakeholders trying to engage in the task of decolonizing.

Both Jason and Joanne also comment on the need for universities to adapt and change in the current climate in order to appropriately address student needs around inclusivity and decolonizing teaching and learning. Jason's contribution emphasizes the essential support required from senior leaders to prioritize the decolonizing agenda across an institution through addressing staff diversity, policy changes, and curriculum reviews. For such changes to take place, senior leaders need to familiarize themselves with the complexity of the decolonizing agenda and implement mindful interventions as appropriate to their context. Joanne praises the ability of university library staff to adapt their focuses based on student needs and engage in a variety of activities and campaigns that concentrate on decolonizing. Both contributions have been prompted by the TRAAC model. Joanne's contribution is structured using the segment headings of the TRAAC model. This helps the reader see ways in which changes can be made across library roles and responsibilities. The contributions thus help to extend the usability of the model by evidencing its accessibility by academic and professional services colleagues. The segments of the model not only are relevant to teachers working on revising a course or program but cover areas of consideration that are pertinent to other university stakeholders too.

As this chapter has shown, bringing together materials for a decolonized curriculum is not simply a task of internationalizing a reading list, incorporating global case studies, or including the perspectives of marginalized voices. Moving away from passive inclusivity toward active efforts to decolonize curricula involves questioning how individual materials, positions, perspectives, and contexts play a part in forming a wider picture of a program. The extent to which materials are supportive of the decolonizing agenda should be interrogated as the favoring of Western-centric structures may still be at play. The reasoning and motivation behind the design of the curriculum should be communicated to staff and students succinctly, supported by a clear assessment strategy. Questioning how learning is led creates opportunities to reflect on how power dynamics in the classroom can affect the learning experience of students. Thoughtful consideration and responsiveness to student voices are vital to creating a curriculum that students can relate to and find connections between their academic and personal life. The approach an institution takes toward enhancing equality, diversity, and inclusion should be customized to the needs of that particular organization.

5

Moving Away from Passive Inclusivity

This chapter focuses on the Contents and Activities and Assessment segments of the TRAAC model. It discusses how the decolonizing agenda aims to move away from passive inclusivity and surface-level changes when reviewing curriculum design and delivery. It then explores the extent to which the relationship between researcher, participant(s), and methodology can form a decolonized space for research to be carried out. The chapter then reviews teaching practices that can affect levels of student belonging and strategies that can be employed to enhance levels of belonging. Discussion of the use of English as the primary language of instruction in the majority of UK higher education (HE) classrooms is also touched on by way of looking at the relationship between language and student experience in light of the decolonizing agenda. The chapter then considers the role which technology can play in the process of decolonizing before discussing ways in which the culture of assessment can influence student perceptions of a program and the discipline more widely.

Moving Away from Passive Inclusivity

All aspects of program design and delivery should be reviewed to ensure that efforts to develop a decolonized curriculum on paper are also achievable in practice. Otherwise, the curriculum design becomes flawed by its own passive inclusivity. This phrase has been used before in a context outside of teaching and learning. Grossmann and Creamer (2017) in their examination of the Transition Town Tooting (TTT) initiative, which aimed to help communities with low carbon living as per the "The Transition model [which was] designed to increase local resilience to global scale threats" (163), described TTT's approach to recruiting members, as "passive inclusivity" (174). "Rather than actively seeking to recruit new group participants [. . .] operating under the assumption that, by adopting an 'open door' policy, participation in TTT's core group is accessible to all community members" (2017: 174–7). By not taking any action toward enhancing levels of inclusivity, passive inclusivity occurs.

Moving away from passive inclusivity means moving away from superficial inclusivity. The phrase "passive inclusivity" is put forth in this chapter by way of describing those learning and teaching opportunities that are aimed at supporting the needs of a wide range of students, but which are lacking in their implementation. This can sometimes lead to students feeling excluded from their learning experience. When signs of passive inclusivity are noticed yet not changed, the approach to addressing issues regarding inclusivity becomes a tick box exercise. Some examples are:

- An internationalized reading list but where traditional canonical texts and Western contexts remain the primary point of research
- The use of technology-enhanced learning tools and online approaches without sufficient user support and where knowledge and skills of staff and students are assumed
- The introduction of nontraditional forms of assessment but which are not based on student needs

Surface-level changes do not lead to effective changes toward enhancing the student learning experience. Such efforts may read well on paper but the impact and outcomes on student retention, attainment, and feedback need to be reviewed to know whether such efforts are making improvements in reality. Duff (2003: 703) comments,

> In its passive mode, inclusion is simply a matter of not trying to prevent access; in its active mode, it involves offering encouragement and assistance to those who would gain access [. . .] [I]n many, especially private, contexts, passive inclusivity might be all that should be expected of us [. . .] In other contexts, though, inclusivity demands positive action.

A significant amount of scholarship has focused on how diversifying and internationalizing a curriculum can help to achieve greater levels of inclusivity. Highlighting greater levels of visible globality across a module or program helps to familiarize students with a variety of contexts and studies. This is indeed important and behind these choices should be reflections and reasoning as to why they were chosen, contemplation of how they might be effectively explored in class, and what opportunities will be given for students to thoughtfully question and critically discuss the knowledge(s) put forth to them. Mahtani

(2019: 25) comments, "by internationalising the curriculum, we will pave the way to achieve a decolonised curriculum to ensure that students should no longer have to ask the question: Why is my curriculum white?" Just as a lack of diversity in the curriculum would be detrimental, a diversified curriculum created for diversity's sake highlights rather than values difference.

When trying to incorporate a range of perspectives and contexts, efforts to revise a module or program reading list offer a relatively quick way of making such changes. A revised reading list offers visible proof of change as it can be used to show the difference between the past and present focus of a program. However, if additional readings have simply been added on to the supplementary reading list and the focus on core content remains the same as in previous years, then any actual change to teaching and learning becomes immediately limited. Moy (2000: 128) similarly notes, "The danger of marginalizing occurs when minority cultures are viewed as mere appendages to the regular curriculum."

The connection between curriculum content and student belonging should not be underestimated. In a jointly written article, one graduate student reflects upon their learning experience: "The scholarly works assigned in classes did not represent my community or resonate with me. This led me to the erroneous belief that I did not belong in the academy" (Ashlee et al. 2017: 94). Writing from an international student's perspective, Gohlan (2019: 24) recalls student concerns about the lack of diversity across materials being met with responses such as "Are you saying we need to give students extra reading? They don't do the readings anyway!" Gohlan describes how "Articles by people of colour and/or women are present only when the topics centre around discussions of race and gender. Intersectional critique was absent" (2019). Working with colleagues in the library can lead to pushing past the reliance on traditional texts and open up new avenues of incorporating a wider range of learning resources. The reading list then becomes revised not only in terms of what content is covered, what voices are being listened to, and what contexts are being explored, but is altered in terms of what formats and mediums are included.

The inclusion of literature that is not normally considered as part of a discipline's traditional canon cannot simply be assumed as helping to increase levels of inclusivity and therefore form a decolonized curriculum. For example, while the focus of some materials might highlight the issues of a marginalized group of peoples, the approach, methodology, and/or theoretical framework may still be upholding forms or structures that favor the dominant group. Blackburn and Smith (2010: 626) discuss the challenge of "working against homophobia within a largely heteronormative framework." Heteronormativity is described as "a way of being in the world that relies on the belief that heterosexuality is normal, which implicitly positions homo-sexuality and bisexuality as abnormal and thus inferior" (2010: 625). When bringing together and evaluating materials for a decolonized curriculum, consideration should not only fall on the content that is explored but how issues are approached and examined within the literature too. For Moy (2000: 130), "The task of religious educators is to design a multicultural curriculum in which not only the Bible, but also theology, can be taught from a variety of racial-ethnic perspectives. Otherwise, church education, by presenting only a European American viewpoint, will continue in its failure to confront the heresy of American racism."

Selecting literature to include in a curriculum should involve questioning the space in which research is carried out. Zavala (2013: 60) recommends looking into how "modes of participation ensure that the interests of historically marginalized peoples are represented, especially when they are carried out within colonizing spaces, such as universities and public school bureaucracies." An examination of the position of the researcher and those being researched uncovers the particular power dynamics that may underlie research processes and findings. Johnson (2020: 91–2) stresses the "need to develop critical methodologies that examine structures, including the structuring of academic institutions that fix (non-white) racialised bodies as deviations that stand out against a white background [. . .] and use dialogical thinking to frame interactions [. . .] as an opportunity to share different knowledges about our lives and experiences of racialisation." The motivations behind research and the space in which the work is undertaken is another area that requires attention. The creator of the space, the development of it, and the way the space is managed might also feed into the extent to which a decolonized space is created.

An illustration of the latter is explored by Simpson's (2001: 138) consideration of how Traditional Ecological Knowledge (TEK) "is used or not used in Canada in terms of Aboriginal rights, and the role of Aboriginal paradigms, Aboriginal knowledge and Aboriginal processes." Simpson discusses how many Aboriginal people view participatory action research as a way for Euro-Canadian researchers to study and access Aboriginal knowledge (2001: 140). Consequently, "To a large extent Aboriginal people are unhappy with the idea that TEK can be written down and integrated into the frameworks of western science and contemporary development paradigms [. . .] separating the knowledge from all of the context (the relationships, the world views, values, ethics, cultures, processes, spirituality) that gives it meaning" (2001: 139). It is therefore not only the focus of the research being explored that needs to be questioned. The approaches, methods, contexts, and strategies employed also need to be problematized. Dumbrill and Green (2008: 493) comment, "With European thought established as the norm in today's society, modern academics with no intention of colonizing Aboriginal peoples still do so. Bringing Indigenous knowledge into a Eurocentric academy forces such knowledge to fit into an overarching European framework." Simpson's work points to how some aspects of a research project may be inclusive while others are not. This leads to questioning whether research can ever be decolonized across all areas and what this might look like.

Enhancing Belonging through Our Materials

Feelings of belonging inside a HE classroom and wider university life in general play an important role in the student experience. But what does belonging in a teaching and learning context actually mean? Strayhorn (2012: 3) offers the following definition for belonging at college: "students' perceived social support on campus, a feeling or sensation of connectedness, the experience of mattering or feeling cared about, accepted, respected, valued by, and important to the group (e.g., campus community) or others on campus (e.g. faculty, peers). It's a cognitive evaluation that typically leads to an affective response or behaviour." Feelings of belonging should help students to feel empowered to raise questions while surrounded by supportive peers and colleagues. If this is what belonging can be said to be, how can it be measured? Levels of engagement may be one answer, but attendance records and data concerning the amount of time a student may be spending on a program's virtual learning environment platform can be interpreted differently. Student retention and attainment may be another way of looking into levels of belonging, but while such information may help to show which students are continuing and progressing well, it does not offer an explanation as to why this is not the case for all students.

It has previously been argued that when materials are made relevant to students, engagement levels increase as students become more connected to their curriculum. As a result, feelings of belonging are enhanced. But materials cannot be expected to speak for themselves, their exploration needs to be facilitated by the teacher who helps to open up different avenues for further discussion. In a study which explored the impacts of integrating "Aboriginal cultural knowledge/perspectives [. . .] into the Social Studies curriculum in a Canadian inner city school" (Kanu 2005: 1), there were significant improvements in grades and self-confidence within the "enriched classes" (2005: 6) in comparison to regular classes. "There was a pass rate of more than 80% among the Aboriginal students who were regular in the enriched classroom, [. . .] compared to 44% pass rate among regular attendees in the regular class" (2005: 11). It was not only the integration of new materials that led to these improvements but the ways in which these were taught. The care and ability of the teachers to communicate knowledge were highly valuable and were commented on by students (Kanu 2005).

The language in which materials are communicated is another area for consideration as language choices can influence levels of student belonging. The power which language holds is emphasized by wa Thiong'o (2009: 20): "Language is a communication system and carrier of culture by virtue of being simultaneously the means and carrier of memory." In South Africa, campaigns such as #AfrikaansMustFall have influenced universities to employ English as the favored language of instruction as "Afrikaans language policy has historically been used to exclude black learners" (BBC 2019). Changes to language policy have occurred at the University of Pretoria and Stellenbosch University (Karrim and Seleka 2019). The economic and political power of the United Kingdom and United States has enhanced the increased use of English on a global scale.

Discussing the context of Australia and the dominant language of standard Australian English, Truscott and Malcolm (2010: 6) argue that "language mechanisms includ[ing] language testing, education curricula and the media [. . .] serve to—undermine the legitimacy of and discriminate against certain non-dominant groups [. . . encouraging] speaker communities to accept—automatically, unconsciously and therefore without resistance—the hegemonic ideologies of the dominant socio-political group." Caine (2008: 9) suggests English Language Teachers (ELT) should "investigat[e] the nature of the diaspora of English and the reasons underlying its subsequent dominance worldwide, and then re-examin[e] traditional assumptions, held by teachers and students alike."

The primary employment of English within a UK HE classroom for students whose first language is not English can create a number of challenges during the student learning experience. Paul Breen in his Chapter 8 contribution points out that "within some [English for Academic Purposes] contexts, there is a sense that the onus is upon students to adapt to western ways of thinking, writing and presenting." The use of English at university can be both inclusive and exclusive at the same time. Low confidence levels in speaking English may lead to limited classroom engagement and peer dialogue. Savvas Michael in Chapter 8 criticizes the language used in legal assessments stating that they fail to reflect 2020 multicultural London and the UK. They draw on situations that are simply not relatable to students, particularly of working classes but even less so to students of BAME backgrounds. In fact, the use of nonlegal quintessentially "British" words or phrases in these problem questions can severely impact a BAME student's performance, even if their knowledge of the law is good.

Savvas's comment points to how the choice of language should be more mindful of the multicultural classroom and society we live in.

Gomes (2018: 201) underlines the need to "investigate and accept shared responsibility for ameliorating colonialism, including linguistic imperialism." Although Gomes focuses on US postsecondary institutions, first-year writing programs, and international students, the ideas raised may be relevant to wider discussions on written assessments and employing English as the primary language of communication within HE UK classrooms. These include "Treat prior cultural and rhetorical knowledge as an asset for learning and a resource for writing; Recognize students' experience and expertise with culture and language; [. . .] Treat students' educational and rhetorical needs as culturally situated" (2018: 221). Classrooms offer opportunities to interrogate the relationship between language and knowledge. It is also important to acknowledge the limitations of language and question the extent to which a decolonized curriculum can be achieved through problematizing the language of instruction. By doing so, students and staff become engaged in a critical dialogue that is a learning experience for all involved.

Decolonizing Technology

As digital tools and online learning environments continue to be developed, the HE sector is becoming ever more digitalized. In March 2020, as a result of the coronavirus pandemic, universities across the UK began shutting the doors to their campuses as teaching and learning moved online. This meant students and staff had no choice but to find ways of adapting to *"emergency remote teaching"* (Hodges et al. 2020). The virus caused a significant worldwide disruption of the familiar as new modes of engagement, learning environments, assessments, and approaches to teaching and learning became the new normal. The lack of preparedness that many institutions experienced meant "Universities that fail to successfully transition to online education in the wake of the novel coronavirus pandemic could be at risk of permanent closure, but other institutions could gain financially from the disruption, an expert has claimed" (Bothwell 2020).

The pandemic quickly forced the sector to review what was feasible to carry out online and what was not. It continues to be debated how much of our pre-Covid-19 teaching and working practices should be returned to.

For Morris and Stommel (2018) "A Critical Digital Pedagogy demands that open and networked educational environments not be merely repositories of content; rather, they must create dialogues in which both students and teachers participate as full agents." Hybrid pedagogy for Stommel (2018) "does not just describe an easy mixing of on-ground and online learning, but is about bringing the sorts of learning that happen in a physical place and the sorts of learning that happen in a virtual place into a more engaged and dynamic conversation." The employment of technology and its impact on levels of access and participation is complex, and the extent to which students can easily gain access to online materials also needs to be considered. For example, issues relating to internet speed can impact on a student's ability to stream lecture recordings, while some countries may have censorship policies in place which mean students may be restricted from accessing particular websites, services, and platforms. Efforts to carry out research online via search engines are subtly influenced by popularity algorithms which themselves have not been tested for assumptions which may hinder inclusivity and decolonization. These search results may unconsciously influence our perception of materials we come across online. As Richardson Jr (2011: 1) points out, "the most authoritative pages may not be retrieved at the top, rather only the most popular pages. Not surprisingly, an English language website is most likely the top page or even fills the first pages of the retrieval set. I suppose you could call that a kind of cultural imperialism."

Ogden et al. (2015: 1–2) argue that the web "remains grounded in particular conceptualisations of information exchange, ownership and progress that are tied to a Western scientific rationality." They go on to note that "A de-colonial approach to the Web re-centres the focus from a false binary of open versus closed, towards an approach that considers the cultural situatedness of protocols for information sharing, and the online and offline relationships that determine access" (ibid: 2). For Clark and Gorski (2001: 39)

> multicultural education as a field, must be more active in critically analyzing the Internet as an educational medium and in examining ways educational technology, especially the Internet, serves to further identify social, cultural, educational 'haves' and 'have-nots.'" As a result, they go on to argue that "multicultural education [. . .] must direct its efforts toward closing the worker–leader divide, in all its manifestations, that Eurocentric education established and perpetuates (2001: 41).

The inclusion of varied activities and assessments in a program can sometimes be more positive on paper than in practice. Well-thought-out intentions and detailed plans may for a number of reasons become unsuccessful when implemented in practice. For example, an effort to make more effective use of seminar time may lead to the introduction of a flipped classroom approach or experimentation with blended learning in the hopes of increasing levels of student participation. However, depending on the complexity of the subject matter which students are expected to digest independently before class, such approaches may result in greater confusion and anxiety. Furthermore, the financial cost of certain technologies can be high and staff training on how to support particular tools is often left to individuals which impacts on workload and staff morale. Student engagement and feedback toward technology (in its various forms) can be also mixed when not enough support is given.

There is nevertheless great potential in the role which technology can play in the process of decolonizing. Pohawpatchoko et al. (2017) discuss how the Native American Museum and Technology Workshop created opportunities for collaboration between the museum and Native American high school students through technology. The work was grounded in cultural constructionism (Pohawpatchoko 2015). This involved "merging, mixing, and coalescing separate ideas into a unified whole. [. . . Fostering] the agency of individuals to enable participation and reverse unequal access to theory and digital resources. In this sense, cultural constructionism can be seen as opening an Indigenous cultural narrative" (Pohawpatchoko et al. 2017: 54).

For the relationship between technology and education to be successful, there needs to be clear evidence of how the needs of students are acknowledged and incorporated into the design and delivery process. Valdez and Thurab-Nkhosi (2019: 194–5) comment that online and blended learning "requires educators to explore the identities of their students, rethink the content and the ways in which this content is presented [. . .] open[ing] spaces for teaching and learning [positioning] online and blended learning as a potential disruptor." As was seen from the previous example, levels of genuine collaboration are enhanced when approaches consider the culture, aspirations, and voices of the students.

Decolonizing the Culture of Assessment

Morreira and Luckett (2018) pose a set of questions to help decolonize classrooms with one being "How far do your teaching and assessment methods allow students to feel included without assuming assimilation?" This question underscores the importance of assessing students in a way which allows for equal participation and engagement, as well as touching on the value of considering varied student identities, experiences, and contexts when designing assessment. Cohering materials for a decolonized curriculum suggests that the activities and assessments within a program should also be decolonized. This raises the following questions: What would be described as a decolonized activity and assessment? How can an activity and assessment be decolonized? One way of approaching these questions is through examining the design of activities and assessment strategies as these play a vital role in communicating to students the intentions of program.

If students have previously been primarily assessed through group tasks and project work, they may find the transition to HE studies more challenging due to the traditional tendency to assess through individual essays and exams. French writer and philosopher, Michel de Montaigne, born in 1533 has been described as "the man who invented the essay" (Gopnik 2017), a form which continues to play a prominent role in the culture of university assessment today. Academic essays are accompanied by expectations pertaining to structure, form, and tone. Within each subject area there will also be an expectation that students have engaged with essential reading which typically consists of texts that make up that disciplinary canon. The framework of an academic essay can therefore be restrictive as students are required to conform to expectations pertaining to style and content. As Peter Jones notes in his Chapter 8 contribution, "The essay's insistence on an 'appropriate' language register, including a particular style and tone, grammar and vocabulary, raises further questions about its 'diversity' credentials."

In an interview conversation with O'Sullivan (2019), Daswani notes,

> We are held back by an internal prestige system that forces us to write for a very specific audience and expects us to perform citational prostrations so as to confirm (and conform to) the authority of others' words. We get trapped in a circular pattern of seeking confirmation by citing the same people and often reproduce a system of privilege that exists.

Though Daswani's comment is made in reference to Anthropology, the message is applicable across areas. For Dei (2016: 48),

> The decentering of the written text would allow orality to be considered an equal and equally efficacious medium. [. . .] The voiced or the oral text is equal to the written text in terms of its capacity to articulate theory and praxis; as is the

educators capacity to track and evaluate the students ability to synthesize and integrate class materials, readings, and lived experiences through the oral of voiced analysis and the visual-cognitive of written analysis.

If a course assesses students only through timed exams, the assessment strategy is one which tells students that the program's intention is to teach through repeated testing, the focus is on understanding content, and that memory recall is valued as a vital skill within the discipline. While some students may respond well to the latter, others may find the assessment strategy to be one that forms a competitive learning environment which may cause students to disengage. Discussing the shortcomings of exams, Dawn Reilly's contribution in Chapter 8 makes reference to "a joint research project [by] the Institute for Policy Studies in Education, and London Metropolitan University (2011) [which] suggest[s] that assessment by examination disadvantages BAME students compared to their white peers." Exam-based assessment strategies also tend to rely on a teacher-centered approach to teaching and learning that would emphasize traditional hierarchy and power dynamics in a classroom. A qualitative study of the hidden curriculum with thirty-six undergraduate students in a medical school in the UK found that "One of the principal ways in which students learnt about the importance of hierarchy in medicine is through teaching that involved humiliation" (Lempp and Seale 2004: 771) and half "reported that competition rather than cooperation is the defining characteristic of medicine" (2004: 772). Though the findings of this study may not be applicable across all medical schools, it points to wider concerns of the impact which a competitive environment can have on students' teaching and learning experience.

In contrast to the format of timed exams, "One premise of project centred learning is that the student work produced is very diverse, which has the potential to challenge the view that the teacher is always the holder of expertise in relation to the work" (Orr et al. 2014: 36). The subtle messages which can be expressed through the design of activities and the assessment strategy can play a part in creating a participatory, connected or disconnected learning environment for students. For Sanford et al. (2012),

> Electronic portfolios also offer an alternative to traditional hierarchical assessment practices that often serve to fragment learning and alienate students from their own learning. Through the development of a rich array of learning artifacts, students take greater responsibility for their learning and recognize the relationships between different learning experiences in courses, outside experiences, and practicum experiences, making connections where none existed previously.

Chapter Summary

This chapter has emphasized the value of the decolonizing agenda to push discussions and practice regarding teaching and learning further by moving away from passive inclusivity. The latter has been outlined as being superficial inclusivity, limited efforts to extend, and develop curriculum and pedagogy through what may be perceived as tick box exercises. An example given was on the cohering of reading lists. It is not enough to add on diverse texts to a collection, a review of recommended resources should consider a variety of factors including content, contexts, voices, mediums, and the priority given to these. Discussions in the chapter also pointed to the importance of questioning the extent to which the relationships, dynamics, and approaches involved in carrying out research can create a decolonized space. Enhancing student belonging through learning resources requires teachers to create spaces and opportunities for critical discussion, spaces that value and are open to all voices. Technology continues to play a role in innovating teaching and learning. With universities worldwide struggling to be responsive to the needs of students and staff during the Covid-19 pandemic, technology has been key to the survival of the sector.

Toward the end of this chapter, attention turned to exploring the culture of assessment. What may work in one discipline may not translate as well to another. But experimentation with approaches should be encouraged. Strategies which may not seemingly be wholly transferable might nevertheless comprise of aspects that may be adapted for another area of work. What is consistent across disciplines is the need for clarity of assessment which can come through marking criteria and rubrics. It is usually the program team who are involved in creating these. Including students in the process of deciding how guidance is communicated, structured, and formatted can enhance student levels of understanding on assessment guidance. Bearing in mind that any lack of understanding regarding the criteria can affect a student's overall engagement with the assessment, clarity of these is fundamental. For Louie et al. (2017: 25) the process of involving students can lead to a breaking down of hierarchies, "By not insisting on being the sole arbiter of assessment, naming, and defining fundamental terms and methods within the course, teachers are modelling Indigenous democratic values of negotiation. Negotiations, within this context, flatten the hierarchical structure between the educator and student, while eliminating the adversarial components of assessment."

Teachers should encourage students' critical thinking, not a supposed "right way of thinking" based on personal or popular disciplinary viewpoints. Teachers should therefore reflect on the ways and extent to which they are leading student learning. The curriculum is partly shaped by the way content is taught which communicates to students what and who are considered authoritative, important, and valued. Cunningham (2013: 5) points to how "The question remains [of] how can lecturers reflect on their own diversity and teaching approaches and ensure they are practising inclusively." It is helpful to consider the extent to which activities and assessments have been chosen for reasons connected to disciplinary tradition, and whether or not there are relevant justifications for the continuation of these traditional forms. Decolonizing work does not have a definitive end point or fixed space, and what may be imagined as a completely decolonized assessment, activity, classroom, or curriculum may never be fully achieved or agreed upon.

6

Staff and Student Perceptions

With Contributions from Ryan Carty, Rahma Elmahdi, and Emilie Fairnington

This chapter begins by briefly explaining unconscious bias and its potential influence on teaching and learning. It stresses the importance of reflecting on our own biases, how these have arisen, and how they can be tackled so that they do not negatively impact on the student learning experience. Decolonizing practices requires reflection and reflexivity upon our own positions and perceptions and calls for these to be interrogated. Through examining one's relationship with hegemonic narratives, we can explore how these are negotiated, questioned, or perpetuated in our classrooms. The chapter also considers the importance of students engaging with unconscious bias training and reflexive activities too. Discussion then moves on to assess the power of seeing diversity within classrooms and universities generally, and how a lack of visible role models for BAME students can affect levels of belonging and aspiration. The chapter ends with personal reflections from Ryan Carty, Rahma Elmahdi, and Emilie Fairnington.

Relationships and Unconscious Bias

The way a person is perceived influences the way others interact with them and can, to a certain extent, affect how the individual behaves and perceives themselves. Perceptions, much like first impressions, can have a long-lasting effect on relationships. Within a university setting, unconscious bias can lead to the treatment of particular students differently. Similarly, the way students perceive their teacher may affect levels of trust, commitment, and interest in a particular session, course, or program. Focusing on the "Relationship" segment of the TRAAC model, this chapter considers the ways in which shared connections or a lack of connections between staff and students might influence the classroom atmosphere, and how perceptions and assumptions made by both parties can affect the learning environment.

According to Phillips et al. (2005: 4), "Because we are all products of a shared colonial history, we are all subjects of the enquiry." The relationship one has to this colonial history and how it continues to affect lived experiences differs in form and to varying degrees among individuals. One way our connection to history can manifest itself is through unconscious bias. "Implicit or unconscious bias happens by our brains making incredibly quick judgments and assessments of people and situations without us realising. Our biases are influenced by our background, cultural environment and personal experiences. We may not even be aware of these views and opinions, or be aware of their full impact and implications" (AdvanceHE 2019). The influence which unconscious bias has over our decision making is therefore a powerful one. By grappling with our unconscious biases and reflecting on the ways in which they can be addressed, decision making can become more mindful taking into consideration how external factors and experiences from the past may affect our initial responses.

By tackling the issue of unconscious bias, some universities have made efforts to develop and deliver unconscious bias training (UBT) for staff. In Atewologun et al.'s "evaluation of rigorous studies on the effectiveness of UBT, [findings] indicate a mixed picture" (2015: 5). They go on to note, "UBT can be effective for reducing implicit bias, but it is unlikely to eliminate it. [. . .] For organisational level change to happen, organisational structures, policies and procedures must be targeted directly, perhaps overhauled" (2015: 6–8). Although UBT may not lead to the removal of unconscious bias, it may help individuals become more aware of their biases and how these can impact decision making in all aspects of life. One of the recommendations for improving the retention of BME staff offered by Bhopal, Brown, and Jackson (2018: 138) is to make "training on unconscious bias compulsory and active bystander strategies as embedded elements of training." For teachers, knowing how unconscious bias might influence judgments and treatment of students within the classroom setting is of great value.

Unconscious Bias and Its Impact on Teaching and Learning

A reduction in levels of unconscious bias among university staff can lead to a more participatory learning environment and enhanced student experience. It has been discussed in previous chapters how personal experiences and culture can influence an individual's teaching style, approach, and decisions in relation to curriculum design. The exploration of unconscious bias looks into these subtle influences in more detail as they can affect how teachers engage, respond, and make judgments about students thereby increasing or decreasing the levels of inclusion for some students within the classroom. This process might involve, as Vandeyar (2019: 4) notes, "The ability of teachers to understand their own belief systems as well as the value systems of their learners may affect how successful they are in responding to diversity in the classroom."

When reflecting on individual belief systems in relation to teaching and learning, it is helpful to consider how and why one entered into their higher education (HE) profession. There exist many roles within an institution and the ways in which the same role can be engaged with varies across a team. The same job can be approached differently among colleagues, underlining how personal experiences, culture, and other factors such as unconscious bias feed into the personalization of the role one takes on. In addition, while numerous colleagues may have the same role, their personal description of the job can contrast greatly. Considering how one would describe their role at university helps to reveal how they see themselves as being located within their team, department, and wider institution. How one describes their responsibilities may uncover the extent to which an individual feels they have autonomy and freedom in their position.

Critically assessing one's own attitude toward HE, personal hopes for the future of the sector, and the role one can play in forming this ideal reminds us of the wider context in which the job is located, prompting consideration of the broader impact which our roles can play in society. The motivations behind why an individual enters into a career in HE will differ from the reasons which students have for studying in HE. Students' reasons for registering on to a degree program will also be different among their peers. Within a classroom, individual experiences and worldviews come together in a shared learning experience. It is within the power of the teacher to create space for these ranging perspectives to come through in discussion. Unconscious bias may lead a teacher to create opportunities for those students who they believe share similar views to their own to voice their perspectives. This can create a discussion which becomes easier to facilitate and manage but suppresses the voices of others. The seeming encouragement of a particular worldview acts to assert the identity of those who support it, simultaneously undervaluing the positions and identities of students who do not. Teachers should examine efforts made to create opportunities for worldviews and belief systems to be shared and how personal student stories can be interwoven into the learning experience.

The process of decolonizing teaching and learning is an uncomfortable one. Boler and Zembylas (2003: 117) put forth a "pedagogy of discomfort [. . . which] emphasizes the need for both the educator and students to move outside of their comfort zones. [. . .] A pedagogy of discomfort recognizes and problematizes the deeply embedded emotional dimensions that frame and shape daily habits, routines, and unconscious complicity with hegemony." They go on to note that "By closely examining emotional reactions and responses [what the authors call] emotional stances—one begins to identify unconscious privileges as well as invisible ways in which one complies with dominant ideology" (2003). Such an approach could be applied to efforts to decolonize teaching and learning. Classroom responses can be analyzed to uncover how dominant ideologies are shaping discussions and the extent to which students are aware of their influences. Problematizing responses and encouraging greater examination of personal perspectives create opportunities for different worldviews and positions to be voiced.

An ethnographic study by Zembylas "analyzes the ways in which emotions are constituted and mobilized by teachers to respond to growing diversity and multiculturalism in schools [. . . and] suggest[s] that constituting an ethic of discomfort offers opportunities to challenge structures of power, privilege, racism, and oppression" (2010: 703). Zembylas uses the term "ethic of discomfort" from Foucault (1994) and notes how through "Using discomforting feelings productively through dialogue and emotional negotiation, some teachers were able to transform experiences of frustration, anxiety, and ambivalence into one of possibility" (Zembylas 2010: 714). Although the study focused on three Greek-Cypriot multicultural primary schools and the way teachers engaged with immigrant and minority students, the approach discussed can be transferred to the HE sector in the UK. In spite of growing diversity in UK HE classrooms and inclusivity issues continuously listed as high priorities in university strategies and agendas, stereotyping and unconscious bias continue to play a part in preventing classrooms from being as participatory as they could be. Encouraging staff and students to engage with a pedagogy of discomfort and embedding such an approach across the institution may help to break down comfort zones which have been limiting the development of decolonized teaching and learning.

While the availability of UBT for staff is increasing, it is also important for students to be aware of their own biases and how this may affect their levels of engagement with teachers and peers. Depending on a student's instant reaction toward their teacher, assumptions are made early on by students as to whether they feel an immediate sense of connection or disconnect with their teacher.

These perceptions may be made based on the individual's age, racial appearance, the way they are dressed, their accent, to name some examples. Such perceptions may even affect the level of trust experienced by the student toward the teacher. Unconscious biases can also affect the way a student perceives their classmates, influencing immediate judgments as to who they would like to sit next to, be friends with, learn from, learn with. This can lead to a lack of fruitful peer learning and collaboration due to hesitancy to fully engage with one another inside or outside of the classroom.

UBT training for students is lacking, but occasions for students to engage in discussions on unconscious bias are necessary for HE classrooms to be authentic spaces for critical teaching and learning. One way of grappling with unconscious bias is through the selection and discussion of particular materials. For example, a text can be given to students which highlights the context, role, background, and other characteristics of the author. Students can be asked for their opinion on this text, which can then be compared to a text written by another author of a different context and background, but whose arguments are similar to those of the previous author. Such a task draws the students' attention less to the arguments of the text and more to who has written it. Students might find themselves favoring one author or offering opinions that have been subtly influenced by unconscious bias. Encouraging students to reflect and examine their own responses in light of biases helps to develop their critical thinking skills and enhance their own reflexivity. Efforts to gain increased awareness and strategies for responding to unconscious bias need to happen individually and as a group. Students can then become better equipped to be more mindful of their biases when interacting with peers and teachers. Such knowledge and skills will also benefit students in the wider multicultural society.

The Power of Seeing Diversity

The image of a diverse HE classroom is commonplace. But the image of a diverse staff force is much less so. Kernohan's article for WonkHE (2020) is a recent example of the growing interest in the need to address the lack of staff diversity at senior levels. Not only is this problematic for staff, particularly for colleagues from historically oppressed groups but the lack of visible diversity among staff can also demoralize students. Discussing the use of the term "diversity," Ahmed (2012: 53) notes, "[s]cholars have suggested that the managerial focus on diversity works to individuate differences and conceal the continuation of systematic inequalities within universities." Giving a keynote on race, ethnicity, identity, and co-identification in HE, Miller (2020) calls for the dismantling of structures and the creation of new ones to enhance levels of inclusivity among staff recruitment, arguing, "there is a lack of ethnic and cultural reference points" for BAME students which can lead to "potential estrangement due to perceived lack of 'authenticity.'"

When the diversity of the student body is not reflected in the makeup of staff, then questions about belonging and power begin to arise. The statistics of staff employment draw further attention to this. In 2017/18 "Among academic staff there were more males than females" (HESA 2019), and while "Universities are seeing record numbers of BAME students in attendance [. . .] this diversity has not translated to staff, particularly at senior level" (Khan 2017). If the majority of staff are white across all departments and particularly at senior level, then the suggestion is that white colleagues are more knowledgeable across disciplinary areas and are somehow better suited for senior roles. Consequently, the following is also suggested—that BAME staff are less knowledgeable and somehow less suitable to be appointed for senior positions. The composition of staff therefore communicates the message that BAME staff do not have as much autonomy, influence, or power within the institution in comparison to their white peers. For BAME students, this may lead to feelings of unbelonging and the view that while BAME students make up a large percentage of the student body, they will not be able to achieve as much as white students.

The power of seeing diversity in staff recruitment enables BAME students to see role models they can relate to, connect to, and aspire to become. When BAME staff representation is lacking, opportunities for students to witness BAME colleagues being high achievers are limited. Consequently, this may negatively impact on the confidence of BAME students who may doubt the achievability of their own goals. Clay's case study of nine students in a HE creative arts institution found "seeing staff from similar backgrounds was an important factor in confirming that students' choice of subject could lead to viable careers in the industry and/or university. [. . .] The visibility of BAME staff engendered a sense of agency, and signalled the means to be successful within the discipline" (2018: 103). The power of seeing diversity therefore lies in the impact it has on the thoughts, confidence, and "psychological effect" (Miller 2020) of the student.

The connection between what students see and the associations they make toward particular staff and students plays an influential role at university. The Equality Challenge Unit (2013: 6) note, "If people are always presented with an image of certain groups of people in certain roles then the association becomes automatic and influences our view of that group of people and that role. For example, 'vice-chancellor' should not be synonymous with 'male', in the same way that 'secretary' should not be synonymous with 'female.'" It is important that the successes of BAME staff do not go unnoticed or unacknowledged; these should be shared and celebrated. Action-oriented discussions should also focus on how to develop an anti-racist working environment and decolonized institution through shared accountability and responsibility; such work cannot be delegated. An inclusive and supportive culture also helps BAME colleagues to progress within the institution.

The Relationship segment of the TRAAC model looks at shared connections between staff and students. But acknowledging a lack of shared connections can also be used as an entry point for building rapport through showing respect and understanding. HE teachers are now designing and delivering programs that have to take into consideration student cohorts that are vastly different to a decade ago. The rise in the number of students living at home and balancing several outside commitments alongside their studies means the lived experience of current students is often in great contrast to the past experiences which many university teachers are familiar with. An honest acknowledgment of this unfamiliarity helps to express understanding and respect for students' lived experiences. Any offers to help will then be received by students as more genuine proposals of support. Teachers should reflect on any unconscious bias(es) they may have toward students and how these biases may be affecting the expectations they have of students.

Contributions

The following contributions from Ryan Carty, Rahma Elmahdi, and Emilie Fairnington offer personal reflections on their teaching and learning experiences. The contributions are followed by an exploration of the issues raised and a summary of the chapter.

Experiences in HE

Ryan Carty

This contribution is a personal reflection on my experiences within HE framed using the TRAAC model prompts. I had my ability to excel in education questioned many times during school, college, and at university by teachers and lecturers for various reasons, mainly for not fulfilling my potential—this is something many young Black people hear. On reflection, I am not surprised that I excelled in educational environments where teachers, lecturers, and support staff took the time to care and understand me. In this contribution, I reflect on personal experiences to highlight how authentic diversity and a participatory and respectful learning environment can significantly impact a student's learning experience.

Learning Environment and Unconscious Bias

I was not the perfect student, but the majority of teachers attributed my problems in sixth form to being solely my fault. Teachers made comments such as "you come in class with your hood up and don't do anything in class." My understanding of what teachers meant by this was: you dress like a hoodlum, like all the other Black boys around here and that explains why you're not engaged with your studies. The Head of Sixth Form once told me, "If you don't change your ways, you'll end up dead or in jail soon," a phrase often heard by young Black males in South London. As an emotionally developing sixteen-, seventeen-year-old with many personal problems to deal with, what was I meant to do with these comments? As teachers and educators, weren't these people supposed to be inspiring me to do the best I can in life?

Privately, I was struggling mentally and going through counseling for the third time in my life. As a result, these comments from teachers further contributed to my already incredibly negative mindset and opinion of myself. These experiences and others also amplified my lack of trust and unconscious bias against authority figures in education and led to me developing unconscious bias toward white people, particularly those from middle-class backgrounds and not from inner-city areas. However, now I make efforts to challenge my unconscious bias daily due to meeting many good white people all over the country in my life.

Growing up I wasn't the worst at football, so I left sixth form on mutual consent and trialed at three semiprofessional clubs, including Tonbridge Angels FC. At the interview, I was questioned about my reference from sixth form, which consisted of just four words: "Ryan has great potential." In spite of this short reference, I was accepted on to an educational football program based at Hadlow College. I studied BTEC Level 3 Sport Performance and Excellence and lived on-site for two years. In my first few months, I was immediately out of my comfort zone as I was one of two Black students/students from an inner-city area in a block of twenty-four students, which was a big shock to me. The other blocks weren't too dissimilar to this which overall housed around 130 students. As time progressed, I explored campus more with my small group of friends from London and other inner-city areas. From here, I grew in confidence and began to understand countryside culture. However, this brought a new challenge. Did I like the new me I was growing into? Would my childhood friends accept the new me? I even began to make subtle changes to my music taste and dress sense, who was I becoming?

During this time, a lecturer who grew up in South London joined the sport program. Some staff members thought that my friends and I feared rather than respected him due to his experience of being in the army, which was nonsense. The boys from South London respected him because he understood "the ends" and us as South London boys. No other member of staff attempted to create a relationship with us like he did at the college. I should also mention that I got distinctions and merits in the majority of assignments in his modules due to feeling more engaged and involved in the classes. In the second year, I was somewhat of a figurehead on campus. With this reputation, I managed to enhance integration of student groups on campus. For example, at college parties the DJ started playing music that my friends and I identified with as this attracted our group of friends, which made everyone on campus tag along with us. This had a positive effect on the revenue the bar got from parties and the amount of engagement the parties had from students. However, despite increased integration and acceptance of inner-city and Black culture, I noticed that the handling of disciplinary procedures differed between countryside students and students from inner-city areas. An example of this was when I was treated differently to a white student following an altercation they started with me. This resulted in me being unable to attend graduation, being kicked off campus and having my grades capped. This affected my university options when I eventually decided I wanted to study for a HE degree. Consequences for the white student were nowhere near as severe.

On reflection, if more lecturers had created a relationship with me, I would have told them I was affected by a range of things during my time at college such as my missing friends and family. The latter meant I felt as though I couldn't relate to many people at the college other than my football teammates and friends from "the ends." In addition, family problems, struggling with traveling to work on the weekends, the pressure from coaches to take football more seriously, and managing studies and training everyday meant I always felt exhausted. Overall, I was an overwhelmed nineteen-year-old struggling mentally and physically with life. In my second year at college, I also found out I had ADHD, dyslexia, and dyspraxia through a private test my mum paid for after being dismissed by doctors and teachers for years. This explained not all, but many of my struggles in life. With this information, I began to think that maybe with the right support, I could do well in education.

Inclusivity of Learning Activities and Respecting All Voices

Fast forward to August 2014, I passed college completing my assignments while working in Glasgow at the 2014 Commonwealth games. From here, I enrolled at the University of Bolton (UoB) through clearing where I studied for four years. I didn't really enjoy my time at Bolton, but I matured significantly there. At my trials in my first week, I noticed a divide in the first and second football team. The second team had predominantly Black players and the first team was predominantly white. However, both teams were equal in ability with some second team players being stronger than first team players. When I became chair and club captain, I began to change this. Through these roles and my jobs in the sport department, I began to positively impact the UoB sport student experience.

Despite all the work I was doing to enhance the student experience while studying, eventually graduating with a First (1:1) in Sport and Exercise Science, I couldn't help but notice that I received significantly less credit than various white students and staff members. I realized I had to watch how I communicate and with who due to the reputation it could get me. I also had to work twice as hard to get recognition. Reflecting on this, many students from a Black or Asian background were treated similarly to me, and I believe this resulted in a lack of engagement with staff from these students. I attempted to play a role in resolving this by running focus groups with every sports club to get real views and opinions from students. After many challenges and successes, I left UoB with a fully formalized Student Sports Council that allowed students to formally voice their views on all things sport related.

Exploring Connections and Perceptions

Many staff base their teaching and learning ideas on what it was like "when they were a student," which was often at a totally different university, typically with a different demographic, or years ago at the same university. From this, many staff just expect students to get involved in the environments they have created without actually understanding the demographic of students. My legacy at the University of Bolton was topped off the year after I left, when the sports clubs reached three cup finals and won three league titles, a feat that had never been achieved by UoB in British University and Colleges Sport (BUCS). Many students attributed this to the three and a half years of work I had put into improving the student experience. This raised the question: Why did it take so much effort to make this happen? Why were so many people against helping me? Why was I treated so different? Surely it wasn't because I was a young Black male from an inner-city environment?

I then moved to work at De Montfort University (DMU), where I really rediscovered my identity. Working in a department of thirteen staff members where I was the only Black person meant I had to really hold true to my values. I often felt like my opinion was valued less than others by some staff. Had I worked at a university which did not have such a diverse student body, this would have proved tougher and I may have succumbed to the mentality of changing to be accepted. However, DMU is unique because its Black and Asian students actually make up the majority of the student population with a high proportion of those students coming from South London. So, despite feeling like I had a lesser voice in the department I worked in, I owned my blackness because that meant I could communicate with the majority of the student population in a way that others could not. Therefore, by just being me, our engagement with a more diverse range of students increased significantly.

Considering a Range of Perspectives, Contexts, and Student Voices

It is important to make efforts to engage all student voices and to ensure that the voices being listened to are representative of the student body. At DMU, our departmental methods of reviewing student satisfaction always resulted in high student satisfaction rates. But if only particular student demographics were engaging with reviews, the results become problematized as we are not hearing students' voices from various backgrounds. As an example, we used Twitter and SurveyMonkey to decide on prices for Sports Awards 2020 tickets. One hundred and thirty students voted from around 2000 that engaged with sport. Staff knew from my observations and work done by the brilliant Decolonising DMU team that Black and Asian students don't engage well with centralized and corporate forms of DMU communication, so why was this used as our main way of making this decision? Further thoughts and questions came to mind that were fueled by my existing bias: Why didn't I feel safe enough to contest the way we made this decision more forcefully? Especially after seeing the significant lack of diversity within the 200+ students and staff that attended Sports Awards 2019. Was it because I was scared of being perceived as the angry Black person due to previous experiences of being labeled as aggressive? Was I scared I would be judged or disciplined for being an outspoken Black person? Was it because I was scared to offend those that are used to being privileged?

HE Sport is in a league of its own when it comes to diversity. I discussed the question under the "Relationship" segment of TRAAC: "*How may the way students perceive you affect the learning environment*" with over fifty different students and staff members (many of which reached out to me and were both alumni and current students/staff). These conversations showed me there was a clear feeling of unconscious bias in sport, particularly toward Black and Asian students. Despite raising these concerns, the department (some colleagues more than others) were of the belief that they were doing all they could to improve inclusivity in Sport at DMU. It's important to have continuous critical conversations about diversity and inclusivity so that the work does not become unintentionally deprioritized.

From white males at top sporting universities making racially offensive comments at the BUCS Conference and referring to them as "a joke" in front of me, to seeing pictures of around thirty to forty university sport department senior managers and all of them being white, to BUCS starting an inclusion board without any goals for improving engagement with Black, Asian, and Minority Ethnic students, told me that for the boy who grew up in South East London, I refuse to work anywhere that does not share the same thoughts I have on equality and diversity, especially in HE. However, creating an environment where everyone can feel at home and have a voice matters to me very much as I remember the teenage me that didn't want to study at university because of my life struggles and the strength and resilience it has taken to overcome them.

Conclusion

The TRAAC model helped me to structure my thoughts and identify where I could expand on ten years of experiences. Recalling some memories proved challenging; this coupled with my learning difficulties meant that the TRAAC model helped me to structure my work. One of many things I was taught by my specialist mentor was the importance of structure for me. In addition to her, I mainly attribute my success of achieving a First (1:1) to the support of my main notetaker and sport psychology lecturer because they genuinely cared about getting the best out of me—even more so because our backgrounds couldn't have been any more different. Having these people in my life meant I had to tackle my unconscious bias further because, of course, not all people/white people in authority positions are bad, so why should good people have their reputation tainted because of the actions of others? Further, why should I have to think this way? Honestly, it gets exhausting sometimes. Many staff members fail to understand the impact their words and actions can have on young people. Thankfully, going into my next venture I have a great team around me and can progress knowing my importance in young people's lives, so I will always try to be mindful of my words and actions while helping young people work toward being the best version of themselves.

Self-Reflection and Self-Reflexivity: Decolonizing Teaching Essentials

Rahma Elmahdi

In writing this contribution as an exploration of how we might decolonize teaching and learning (DTL) in HE, it became clear to me that I needed to address reflection and reflexivity when exploring questions raised in the TRAAC model. A necessary first step in adopting teaching practices that support decolonized learning is understanding our own experience in the colonial systems of the academy and how these shape our present-day teaching. This serves not only as an important reminder of the need for decolonized teaching as a tool for structural change but also as a reminder that one's reflexivity in practice is necessary for the creation of an optimal learning environment for students exploring knowledge in a decolonized classroom. Dennis (2018) argues that in order to help our students recognize different forms of understanding, knowing and explaining the world, we must first recognize *our own* form of explaining the world. Therefore, "before I can ponder what possible actions are required [to decolonize education] I must first identify [the] space from which I might speak" (2018: 196). If a teacher brings into the classroom unresolved Eurocentric structures of their previous experience without having interrogated what this might mean for themselves and their students, the challenge of creating the environment of a decolonized classroom which facilitates access to voices and visibility of knowledge forms that are normally unseen and unheard, becomes even more challenging.

Reflection is a skill I have only recently come to develop, having considered it a time-consuming, unconstructive exercise when it was first introduced to me in my later years as an undergraduate and only put to use as a young professional for portfolio purposes. I reflect on the many years spent learning about systems, institutions, and cultures that I rarely related to or saw myself in and yet was somehow expected to seamlessly assimilate to. Little of my color, speech, interests, or class was present in the lecture theaters or common rooms of my undergraduate years. I never once had a Black professor or lecturer give me a lecture or tutorial and those other well spoken, public school educated men and women of color who did give me classes seemed to instill in me even more of a disconnect than I had before; obviously, there is no issue with race here. My feelings of isolation and inferiority were surely due to my own lack of intelligence and/or dedication. The ever-present and growing disconnect with my identity as a Black woman raised on a north London housing estate, along with my five siblings by our single Sudanese mother was not one that had a place in the everyday activities of one of the country's most prestigious universities. With this increasing realization, and the further I became embedded in the academy, the more the feeling of imposter syndrome (not an uncommon one among the high achieving and competitive students at such institutions but heightened in a student like myself) consumed me.

The pressure to succeed in such environments calls for assimilation into the dominant culture. To be broken and subsequently remolded into the form of the prevailing hierarchical, Eurocentric ethos. This was made clear to me early in my academic career and I quickly found myself becoming complicit in my own othering, accepting the language and behavior I now have the knowledge to name as "microaggressions" from colleagues and seniors alike as the price to be paid for being allowed to progress within "the system." I was grateful to have a place at the table, no matter the cost to me personally. My complete assimilation was in fact so successfully achieved, that it wasn't well until after my last graduation, ten years after starting as an undergraduate at university, that I even began to critically question the name of my institution; Imperial College London or the motto, still proudly displayed in Latin within the university crest and translating to "scientific knowledge, the crowning glory and the safeguard of the empire." The exclusive nature of these literal colonial badges was celebrated as a point of pride.

The lack of faces such as mine was silently (but unquestionably) known to be a sign of the true prestige of our institution. Academic achievement was white, male, and wealthy. That is what I learned and internalized and the success I've experienced within academia is in itself nothing short of confirmation of the extent to which I was successfully assimilated (or I am at least perceived to be) into the colonial narrative of the modern British university. Reflection is a necessary first step for a teacher wishing to DTL in their own classroom. It requires that one first makes meaning of their experiences, rationalizing and linking them for the intention of personal and professional self-growth (Rodgers 2002). In attempting to explore your relationship with students as a teacher or facilitator in a decolonized classroom, you must reflect on your own experiences within the academy, how it has shaped you and link these to your thoughts, actions, and interactions with your students.

The TRAAC model asks three key questions in helping to facilitate reflective and self-reflexive teaching. First, under Teaching Approach and again within Relationship. When asking the questions, "Have you reflected on unconscious bias towards your student groups?," "What shared connections do you have with your student group?," and later "What power dynamics are generated from your approach?" It is necessary to both reflect and utilize self-reflexive methods. In my reflection, I am able to rationalize or "make meaning" of my own experiences within academic institutions to understand my thoughts and feelings of myself and how I am able to justify these through internalizing the practices and philosophy of a colonial worldview. By doing this fully and honestly, and developing a language for the process underway, I am then able to link this to my experiences in teaching, realizing that I had inevitably developed biases toward various student groups. These unconscious biases are present and manifest in several ways, but due to their unconscious nature being by definition difficult to identify in one's own thinking, are hard to recognize.

Opportunities for these reflections to take place are, as anyone who has taught at a university knows well, often difficult to find. Considering whether you have reflected on unconscious bias toward your student groups, however, is good practice, as are efforts to make time to identify these as early in your interaction with students as possible. Take the time before meeting your students, perhaps when you are preparing your introductory or ice-breaker session for example, to reflect on your unconscious bias. This is a good time in which to undertake this reflection as it is the point at which you have not yet met the individuals within the group but are developing an idea of the group characteristics and how you will engage with the group.

The time preparing before your introductory session is also a good opportunity to address the question "What shared connections do you have with your student group?" This period is particularly useful for reflecting on this question, alongside your unconscious bias, because it is a point at which you have not yet made interpersonal connections with individuals within the group that might later lead you to construct the "exceptions to the rule" narratives that are such an important factor in the persistence of our unconscious bias in our teaching. In practice, if you are addressing the Relationship aspect of this model effectively ahead of actually meeting a new student group, you can explore the unconscious biases that will come into play once you meet your students group, while simultaneously confronting the shared characteristics that you have with your students that will inevitably come into play to help you maintain those biases.

A teacher wishing to teach in a decolonized classroom must make a concerted effort to face the biases which they hold but may be loath to confront as they are likely to be at odds with their own self-image (Burke and Crozier Burke 2014). Self-reflection for decolonized teaching therefore is a deeply personal and sometimes uncomfortable process. This reflective process is, however, necessary as without doing so, one continues to place themselves in a position of unrealistic "objectivity" in relation to their students and therefore continues to actively create an exclusive teaching environment (Bell and Santamaria 2018). (Self-)reflexivity is how an actor and observer simultaneously "takes account of themselves or the effect of the personality or presence of themselves on what is being investigated" (Hobson 2004: 364). When applied to the question of the power dynamics generated by one's interaction while teaching, an active awareness of who you are and how your experiences, potential biases, thoughts and feelings inform your actions in the moment is required.

Two of the most influential theorists in the area of reflexive practice, Dewey (1933), who first explored reflection as an intellectual and emotional practice in education, and later Schön (1983), who further developed the concept of reflective practice, distinguish self-reflection from self-reflexivity by highlighting the characteristic of self-awareness in the moment as opposed to the "meaning making" of our experiences that is the main feature of reflection. It is in many ways more difficult to achieve self-reflexivity in day-to-day interactions than it is to put the previously discussed self-reflection techniques into practice. Self-reflexivity is, however, a key tool in assessment and management of power dynamics within the class. Power dynamics are often fluctuating and therefore require evaluation and reaction in the moment. In facilitating class discussions, for example, interactions between individual students and student groups can change quickly, and importantly, so can the situation of the facilitator for these interactions. An effective means of identifying the opportunities in which one might address the question of power dynamics in the classroom and where they are changing are points at which there is tension. This might manifest as discomfort in yourself, which you perceive in individual students or new tensions in student interactions.

This might not, however, be something that is easy to identify or work through. In working hard to prove my worthiness of a position as a teacher among a group of students educated within a hierarchical paradigm, for example, it was a great relief to me to find that I could occupy a space of authority. Redirecting the power that comes with the position of authority (particularly having had difficulty in attaining it to start with) is difficult and requires a mindful awareness of positionality. This reaction to redirect power from the authority-novice dynamic is essential for moving away from the replication of the established classroom hierarchies that maintain a colonial teaching norm. Challenging your students in those moments where they begin to perceive the knowledge you share as of value because it comes from you as an authority as opposed to critiquing that knowledge itself requires a presence in the moment and reaction to mitigate this through self-reflexivity.

Personal Reflections on Equality in Education and Sport

Emilie Fairnington

This contribution is a personal reflection of my experiences throughout life and how experiences surrounding HE has helped shape my ideology and passion for inclusion. Throughout the contribution, the TRAAC model has been used to help frame my reflection and highlight the importance of understanding the need for authentic diversity within HE but especially in HE sport. When using the TRAAC model in my reflection, I used it holistically as I feel all the different segments interlink with each other. Further, to ensure that authentic diversity happens, you need to think about the questions in each segment together. I would personally recommend that both staff and students, especially student groups such as sport clubs, use the model to help them to become more inclusive in what they deliver. For me, the model makes you think about what you are doing and whether you are being inclusive, so it is a great way to start your decolonizing journey, and hopefully, over time the questions presented in the model become second nature.

One of the key parts of my reflection is about where I came from and the environment that I grew up in. I was born in Scotland but grew up in a small northern town called Wooler, which is situated close to the Scottish borders. Similarly, to the majority of northern towns in England, there was not much diversity among the people who lived there; well in fact there was no diversity at all as there was only one lady who was not white! Unfortunately, due to so little diversity many people who live in areas similar to where I grew up are led to believe the perception that the Black and Asian community are all like what they see on the television in the various charity advertisements. This is down to the little education and representation that is provided within both the education system and society. If people's views and perceptions are not challenged and informed, how can diversity and inclusion within society grow?

I, however, have been incredibly fortunate to have had a number of opportunities to experience different cultures and faiths as I have traveled to different areas of the country and the world. This was where my interest and passion to learn about different cultures and people started. I remember in middle school we had one lesson all about the slave trade, and this was the first time I had really seen the segregation between two races. It destroyed me to know that my ancestors most likely would have been involved with such a disgusting movement and I couldn't understand why we were not learning more about this period of history or about Black history in general, such as the Black Civil Rights Movement. This sparked me to start developing and gaining my own knowledge about the world, and one resource that really stuck in my mind and had a positive, powerful influence on my ideology was Spoken Word. I first listened to Spoken Word when one of my high school teachers showed us a Suli Breaks Spoken Word video about education in our assembly. The way he communicated and the points he made really resonated with me, so I sought out more of this genre. Three individuals who I learned a lot from and still listen to are Suli Breaks, Prince Ea, and Nego True—I continue to share their work with people I meet. On reflection, I would say this is the part of my life where I began to understand the importance of diversity. Although I probably still had no idea what the term diversity really meant, I knew that the world was not equal for everyone.

As mentioned and indicated earlier, representation of a diverse demographic is incredibly important, but it wasn't until I started studying at university that I realized and understood fully the power of representation. I began studying Forensic Science in 2014 and graduated in 2017, but I never left the institution after graduation as I was lucky enough to secure a job in the sports department. I became one of four Graduate Sport Development Assistants, and after my year contract ended, I was grateful to be kept on continuing in the role. I then had the opportunity to gain a promotion into my current role as a Sport Project Coordinator in Participation. I also volunteer my time to coach the men's university basketball third team. Studying and working at this university has provided me with so many opportunities and experiences, but most importantly it has fueled my passion for inclusion, so I think that it is important to head back to the beginning of my university journey.

Moving to study at university was a positive culture change for me, and I think it was something I was striving for as my interests and morals were somewhat of an alien concept to many of my fellow classmates where I grew up—for example, my musical interests. I really enjoy listening (and dancing) to Afrobeats, Soca, Grime, and Hip Hop, but where I grew up people thought this was all just "noise" or "bad language."

With regard to my interests, one of the first things that I did when arriving on campus was sign up to the Women's Basketball Club because I absolutely love the sport and hadn't been able to play in the past few years due to being ill, so I jumped at the opportunity to get involved. I would go on to learn how important it is to get involved within a sport club at university, as it is not just a great way to make lifelong friends but it is also a way to develop your own skills in the sport, as a person, and career wise. As a sport, basketball is predominantly played by the Black community, and this was no different at the university I attended. When looking at us as a team, I was the person who was visually different due to the color of my skin. But as a person I didn't feel any different because I had the same interests, morals, and beliefs as my teammates. However, it became apparent to me that even though I didn't see a difference, other people, predominantly white people, did and I would constantly get comments about it.

Throughout my time as a student at university I learned a lot about the Black community from both my friends and my teammates as they educated me on their culture and shared stories of what they had experienced due to the color of their skin. I realized how privileged I was to have a voice that would somewhat be listened to, unfortunately due to my gender I am treated differently to my male counterparts, but I could be heard places where my friends and teammates couldn't. This was where my inclusion passion began. In my second and third year of university I got involved even more within the basketball club and the university by becoming captain of the women's basketball first team, Basketball ambassador for the university, secretary of the basketball club, and a few other different roles. It was within these roles that I started to use my voice and knowledge to educate others on inclusion and push for change. For example, my fellow committee members and I pulled the university up on their marketing material for Varsity, the biggest sporting event of the year. The material that had been produced was not diverse and didn't represent the university at all which has a unique student demographic of Black and Asian students being the majority at the institution.

Even more importantly, as a club we did not feel represented as the majority of our players did not see themselves in the material, and university sport departments wonder why Black and Asian students don't engage with them. If you don't identify with something, then why would you feel like that opportunity is aimed at engaging you? It was apparent that diversity was not at the forefront of their minds since they had asked the clubs which had little to no diversity to be involved and the only Black student that was involved was stuck at the back against a Black backdrop so could hardly be seen. Since we as a club raised this point, the Varsity material has demonstrated the institution's student demographic. Reflecting on this time, I can't help but notice that as a club we did not receive the same recognition as the predominantly white clubs, and we had to work twice as hard and make our own opportunities in order to succeed.

I think my experiences and the knowledge I gained while being a student really empowered me to continue to try and make a positive inclusive change within HE sport. As a member of staff working in this sector, I think it is incredibly important to ensure that all student voices are actually respected, represented, and listened to in the activity that is offered and that these voices reflect that of the student demographic. Although everyone's journey and experiences are different, there can be overlaps in the experiences people have had. For example, being Scottish is something that I am incredibly proud of, but throughout my life my identity of being Scottish has always been questioned by people due to me living in England. I used the way I felt to think about how I could run an event that would allow underrepresented students at the university to demonstrate their pride of their country while helping them look after their physical well-being.

I decided to run a Futsal World Cup due to the sport being incredibly popular around the world and students were able to enter the tournament as their chosen country. Between fixtures they had the opportunity to educate others about their culture and country's history. Being able to connect with the students had a positive impact, and most importantly the students all enjoyed themselves. They started to engage with the weekly recreational sport sessions at the university. One thing that I think is key in creating a positive society is understanding your own unconscious bias because everyone has them, but it is the way you act and respond to them that matters. If you take the time to educate yourself and understand others, then an inclusive environment can be created.

Chapter Summary

The contributions in this chapter have all been written from a personal reflective viewpoint. The experiences discussed connect the storyteller with the environment and people around them. By doing so, the contributions point to individual and collective responsibility to confront ongoing challenges relating to racism, student belonging, and problematic power structures. While Rahma's contribution focuses on particular TRAAC questions, Ryan's contribution is structured under headings relating to the TRAAC model, and Emilie employs the model holistically. All have engaged with the model in personal ways, underlining how there are no expectations in the way in which the model should or should not be used. Ryan, Rahma, and Emilie share the experience of being in positions of authority where they are looked up to by students. Their past and present roles differ but what is shared between them is their position for many students as role models. It is clear through the contributions that all are mindful of how they are perceived by students and colleagues. What is powerful is how the authors reflect honestly and openly about their academic and professional journeys, not shying away from the difficult situations and personal conflicts they have experienced.

Rahma raises the importance of engaging in reflective practice as a process that enhances one's personal and professional development. The questions drawn on from the TRAAC model instigate valuable reflections relating to Rahma's journey and the impact this has had on her identity along the way. Ryan's reflections point to Singh's (2020) underlining of the "large body of evidence confirming that BAME students face a variety of conscious and unconscious discriminatory practices in traditional classroom settings. For instance, BAME students' behaviour is more likely to be rated harshly compared to similar behaviours performed by white students, and staff tend to express more positive and neutral speech toward white students than toward BAME students." Ryan's feeling that he had to "work twice as hard" is mirrored by Eddo-Lodge in the article, "Why I'm no longer talking to white people about race" (2017). In the piece for *The Guardian*, Eddo-Lodge describes how "mum told me to work twice as hard as my white counterparts" and comments "We do not live in a meritocracy, and to pretend that simple hard work is enough to elevate everyone to success is an exercise in wilful ignorance" (2017). Such feelings are also unearthed in a report which looked at "BAME staff experiences of academic and research libraries," where it was found that "BAME staff feel under pressure to perform to a higher standard than their white counterparts and feel that they are being monitored. This was especially the view among those who believed their ethnicity particularly stood out" (Ishaq and Hussain 2019: 5).

Emilie's contribution also personally looks back on childhood experiences and reflects on how personal interests and passions have gone on to influence the ways in which Emilie works with students. By making an effort to seek out a plurality of knowledges, Emilie became mindful of privilege and how certain voices have been listened to more than others. While Emilie and Ryan pay attention to issues relating to equality within the discipline of sport, all the contributions talk about identity and belonging. What Rahma's, Ryan's, and Emilie's contributions highlight is the power in addressing inequalities by challenging their existence, persistence, and influence. Their contributions draw attention to how the sharing of personal narratives can open up wider conversations that resonate with a number of people. This can lead to encouraging others to question and challenge what are problematically accepted as dominant norms.

Singh and Masoca (2019: 4) comment, "A defining characteristic of the 'new' racism is that it is so subtle that it is very difficult to identify, and often takes place without the use of overt derogatory racist language associated with the traditional forms of racism." Such behavior not only impacts on the individual but risks developing a culture where microaggressions are tolerated and normalized. Jason Arday also touches on microaggressions in an earlier contribution. For Huber and Solorzano (2015: 298 cited in Lander and Santoro 2017: 1012) microaggressions are "a form of everyday racism used to keep those at the racial margins in their place." In a qualitative study by Lander and Santoro (2017: 1008), it was found that "Black and Minority Ethnic (BME) teacher educators in England and Australia working within the predominantly white space of the academy [. . .] felt marginalised, and encountered subtle everyday racism manifested as microaggressions that contributed to the academics' simultaneous construction as hypervisible and invisible, and as outsiders to the academy." Formal acknowledgment of the existence and influence which microaggressions can have on the well-being of staff through institutional policy can play a part in preventing a culture of normalized microaggressions from increasing. This can be accompanied by spaces to critically discuss microaggressions, staff training, and a formalized route for reporting microaggressions that may feed into local and wider processes involved in reporting discrimination.

This chapter has focused on staff and student perceptions. This has included a consideration of how the way colleagues perceive themselves influences their behavior in the classroom, which causes students to respond to them in particular ways. Staff perceptions of students based on unconscious bias can also lead to different treatment of students. UBT and other strategies to reduce these biases can help prevent instinctive assumptions and judgments from dominating decision making over mindful thought processes. Students should also be informed of how unconscious bias can influence their interactions with teachers and peers. The perceptions students have of individual teachers can affect levels of rapport, trust, and engagement. Student perceptions of staff diversity can also affect their sense of belonging, motivation, and aspirations. Greater diversity among staff to mirror that of the student body can play a part in decolonizing a university and enhancing the learning experience for a wider body of students.

7

Delivery and Power Dynamics

Approaches to delivery are affected by the learning environment, whether this be class size or the type of room (physical or virtual) to name some examples. This chapter focuses on the "Teaching Approach" and "Relationships" segments of the TRAAC model. Eizadirad (2019: 203) comments, "Decolonization as a process and pedagogy will be different and unique to each setting and spatial location in relation to the unique power relations embedded within each space." Different approaches have different effects on inclusivity and accessibility. The chapter begins by reviewing how power dynamics between students and staff in the classroom can be affected. This can lead to decreased or increased levels of engagement, hierarchy, and belonging. The chapter then goes on to explore the issue of trust in the classroom, how it can be given, received, shared, and fluctuated. It ends by considering how knowledge is produced, for whom and by whom. This discussion also looks at the ways in which language can be divisive and inclusive, and how narratives by one group about another can lead to perpetuating stereotypes and inequalities.

Exploring Power in the Classroom

Power dynamics within a classroom setting will always exist. However, the perception of these dynamics may be different among individuals. A teacher may believe that their classes create space for critical discussion and peer learning, while student feedback might suggest otherwise. Power dynamics in a classroom can be negotiated and changed depending on the behavior and actions of the individuals within it. Therefore, as Ball (2013: 30) describes, "Power is not a mode of subjugation, or a general system of domination and indeed power is as much about what can be said and thought as what can be done—it is discursive. Power is not merely prohibitive it is productive." In order to help ensure that the dynamics within a classroom are produced and negotiated productively, an exploration of the ways in which they exist and can be created is needed. "Every particular deployment of power implies certain possibilities of struggle and resistance—a resistance that never takes the form of a total rejection of 'power,' but which rather will be manifested as struggles aimed at the particular and distinctive configurations of power" (Schmidt and Wartenberg 1994: 288). Power within a classroom can be experienced in many ways. It can be developed, taken, shared, explicit, subtle, and hidden. Power can also be expressed in different ways.

As mentioned in previous chapters, the continuation of colonial power structures in universities can influence the teaching and learning experience. However, as Merriweather, Guy, and Maglitz note (2019: 132), "The impact of structural and systemic power is not always apparent to learners, who attribute the ensuing interactions to individual idiosyncrasies, personalities, and personal experiences. But structural and systemic power determines what is allowable speech and who is allowed to say it." Speaking of coloniality and decoloniality, Domínguez (2019: 52) puts forth the following:

> If coloniality is marked by patterns of inequitable power, hierarchies of knowledge, and a Eurocentric zero point. [. . .] Decoloniality is, in short, the destabilization of the zero point; accepting a world in which epistemic experience can, and should, be plural, and to reject expectations of cultural, academic, and social mimicry, while embracing a lived commitment to unravelling the ways coloniality has foreclosed upon these possibilities in our daily lives and institutions.

One of the initial steps to be taken toward decolonizing teaching and learning involves acknowledging where and how coloniality continues to exist. Keval (2019) tells teachers to recognize "how positions operate through networks of historical and contemporary power relations" and encourages them to ask themselves: "When I look around me, where do networks of power coalesce and what role does colour, race, language, gender, class, disability, etc play in this?" (2019). The latter discussion is extended upon in the previous chapter on the power in seeing diversity.

An important role of the teacher is to instill trust within the classroom so that a participatory atmosphere is formed. David Yeager, an assistant professor of psychology at the University of Texas, comments, "When students have lost trust, they may be deprived of the benefits of engaging with an institution, such as positive relationships and access to resources and opportunities for advancement" (UT News 2017). In order for students to feel that they belong in a classroom environment, they need to trust the teacher. For staff to feel like they belong within an institution, there also needs to be trust with colleagues. A number of studies have explored the student-teacher relationship in terms of trust in schools (Basch 2012; Lee 2007). In a 2019 study of "Race, Relational Trust, and Teacher Retention in Wisconsin Schools," key findings showed that "African American teachers feel lower levels of trust with other teachers [. . .] White teachers feel less trust with principals of color and are less likely to stay in schools with a principal of color, more students of color, and more teachers of color" (Jones 2019). Although the locale of this study is a specific one and not all teaching contexts will share comparable statistics and findings, what the study highlights and is relevant to the context of HE is how ongoing racial challenges within the education sector impact both the experiences of staff and students.

Macfarlane (2009: 221) points out that "The importance of trust to 'good' teaching in higher education is comparatively neglected compared to work focused on the use of techniques to develop active learning and reflective processes." One of the reasons for this may lie in the difficulty of measuring and evaluating levels of trust within a classroom. By way of exploring how trust can be formed and negotiated within a university classroom it may be helpful to view the student/teacher/trust relationship in terms of a spectrum. At one end is the assumed professional trust which comes with the authoritative and knowledgeable role of the teacher. This professional trust exists before the student has got to know the teacher as this degree of trust is one that accompanies the teacher's position in the institution. The payment of student fees is accompanied by the expectation that the university will provide a high standard of teaching. The trust which the university has given the teacher through their appointment is hereby implicitly passed on to the student.

However, a student's professional trust in the teacher does not necessarily mean that they will feel comfortable responding to or asking questions in class. This professional trust at its basic level means the student is accepting of the teacher's expert knowledge and willing to listen to the communication of this knowledge in class. Teachers usually expect to receive this professional trust immediately from their students due to their role. But depending on the length of their teaching experience, some teachers may feel confident or nervous about having this instant level of trust. Fluctuating trust may be used to describe the part of the spectrum when a student's trust toward their teacher is either increased or decreased depending on the comments or behavior of a teacher inside or outside of the classroom. Mutual trust is when both parties feel comfortable with one another. The way a teacher is perceived influences the levels of trust students feel toward them. Consequently, this affects how information is received. The level of trust which a teacher has in their students to remain committed to their independent learning can also affect the way in which they teach. Feelings of trust are therefore tied to delivery and dynamics.

If a teacher feels distrust toward their students in the form of underconfidence in student commitment to a program, they may react by taking firmer control over student learning through the formation of a more structured and hierarchical classroom. Such a reaction creates a learning environment where power dynamics seem fixed with the teacher. Hook (2007: 96) advises to "not fix the flow of power in a single direction; look for bi-directionality; attempt to grasp the reciprocation of passive and active positions in the conduction of power, trace the joint productions of 'top-down' and 'bottom-up' flows." Rather than trying to control the power dynamics in a classroom, allow space for them to settle naturally and evaluate what they say about the learning environment. From this, they can be negotiated as appropriate in light of student needs.

It is also important to encourage the development of trust among students to enhance the community spirit within the classroom during critical discussions, peer learning, and peer feedback. Pawlina et al. (2018: 5) suggest that

> Trust may be earned by demonstrating a student-centered approach in the learning environment. [. . .A]t the same time show commitment to active participation in course related activities as a partner in the process of learning, engaging with both the subject matter and learners at hand. [. . .] Trust could also be demonstrated through awarding accountability to students for their own learning.

Trust and respect can therefore be given by the teacher to the student. Returning briefly to our earlier discussion of assessment, offering students the choice to choose their own focus or formulate their own assignment question is another example of giving students trust and the opportunity to be independent in leading their own learning. Building trust often takes time and for colleagues who have limited, infrequent, contact time with their students (as is the case for part-time, temporary contracted, or hourly paid staff) there lacks opportunity to develop high levels of trust which would lay a supportive groundwork for initiating discussions on decolonizing. But high levels of trust between staff and students are not prerequisite for showing respect and openness to differing positions, perspectives, and contexts, which are vital to developmental decolonizing discussions.

Power Dynamics as a Product of Teaching Approaches

The clear structure and boundaries which come with a traditionally hierarchical classroom can for some students offer a sense of clarification and order. Approaches to teaching which go against this tradition can thus come across as confusing and jarring for some students. An example is given by Paul Breen in his Chapter 8 contribution when discussion turns to Chinese students in English for Academic Purposes (EAP) contexts. Paul notes, "These students come to the UK from a culture shaped by Confucianism which downplays the importance of forming individual opinions. [. . .] It is more about acquiring wisdom than questioning that knowledge." Depending on how power dynamics are created and negotiated, they can enhance or inhibit the connection between staff and students. The following section briefly considers different approaches to delivery: team teaching and online teaching.

Team teaching involves two or more colleagues working together "with mutual concern, the teachers work to impart course content: knowledge, values, and skills. [. . .] They model the competence they try to impart, forming the students by their example of interaction as much as by their words" (Buckley 2000: 4). The relationship between the teachers therefore needs to be respectful and fluid as they share the teaching space with each other. The process is also an opportunity for the teachers to observe one another and reflect on individual practice as part of their own development. For Tajino and Tajino (2000: 6), looking at the practice of team teaching in the context of Japanese secondary school EFL classrooms, they argue that "reinterpreted as team-learning [. . . this approach] encourages all the participants, teachers as well as students, to interact with one another by creating more opportunities for them to exchange ideas or cultural values and learn from other 'team members.'" Similarly, Perry and Stewart (2005: 568) found that the practicing team teachers they interviewed "indicated that because of the communication demands implicit in the team teaching process, teachers can become more creative and insightful."

The power dynamics generated from a team-teaching approach is often one that encourages student participation. As the teachers offer up personal perspectives, an environment for sharing opinions is formed. "Increased student participation naturally follows when teachers encourage the expression of multiple perspectives by model[l]ing learning and mutual respect" (Anderson and Speck 1998: 673). Through this dialogue of sharing, connections are formed among students and between staff and students. As a result, while there are more teachers in the room during a team-taught session, the increase in the number of authority figures can in fact help create a more relaxed atmosphere. The teachers involved in the classes can also choose to play different roles or allocate responsibility for distinct aspects of the class.

When classes are delivered online, staff and students are faced with several challenges before the class has even started. Teachers are immediately located in the position of control as online hosts. There tends to be limited or no formal training given to students in using webinar tools as their skills of employing technology are often assumed. Any form of general assumption in a classroom can lead to unintentional carelessness and a lack of appropriate support for students. While webinars are designed to increase opportunities for students to connect with staff and one another, if sessions are not planned and delivered appropriately, they can result in increasing levels of disconnect. Due to delays in sound or unreliable wireless connections, communication between staff and students can sometimes be made more challenging. Shyer students may find the learning environment off-putting and retreat into silence, while the choice of whether or not to share their web cameras may be another area of concern. Consequently, students may struggle to find space to interact with one another or with the teachers in a meaningful way. The power dynamics in such a situation can go into a state of flux. All of these considerations have recently been heightened as a result of the Covid-19 pandemic causing university teaching to move online.

However, some students may find the increased choices in modes of communication through online classes to be empowering. In some ways, online classes make it easier to engage and disengage from conversation. Students are able to close their webcams, mute their microphone, or choose to type messages to the teachers or other students either individually or as a whole group. Options for how they can engage are opened up, and this can give students a sense of agency and control over what they say, how, and when. When delivering a class online, teachers are responsible not only for the class but the management of the environment too. Responding to challenges relating to audio, video, screen sharing, break-out groups, chat threads, and more can potentially disrupt the flow of a class. This may lead to staff feeling a lack of control over the situation.

In many ways, the delivery of an online class is very similar to the delivery of an in-person session. The teacher may choose to take the lead or have a student-led discussion. The teacher may choose to employ the position of a facilitator. Such a position should not involve less work but a different kind of work when it comes to navigating the class. The teacher is still going to be viewed as the subject expert, and students will continue to look to the teacher for reassurance and steer. Furthermore, opportunities for the development of meaningful connections between staff and students and among students remain the responsibility of the teacher.

The Production of Knowledge: By Whom and for Whom?

The language which teachers employ in class can directly affect the sense of belonging among students. Particular words or phrases may cause some students to feel side-lined or disempowered in the classroom. This creates an environment where they feel immediately less involved. As a result, students may perceive teachers as either being ignorant, unaware, or disinterested in how their speech may be impacting on their learning experience. Consideration of the language used in teaching can help to create a participatory learning environment, thereby forming developmental connections with students.

One of the ways in which language can play a divisive or more inclusive role in teaching and learning is how gender is considered in language use. Prior (2017) describes how "gendered language is commonly understood as language that has a bias towards a particular sex or social gender." There has been a tradition that favors "he" as a generic pronoun in scholarship and academia. Discussing feminist language reform, Pauwels and Winter (2006: 128) note how "The dual function of the pronoun *he* as epicene (generic) and masculine-specific pronoun is seen as a major contributor to the gender bias in language. Its elimination has been high on the agenda of feminist linguistic activism." Such gender bias can be argued to be evidence of ongoing patriarchal structures that have yet to be erased from society. Similarly, Menegatti and Rubini (2017) note how "language subtly reproduces the societal asymmetries of status and power in favor of men [. . . and . . .] linguistic forms have the negative effects of making women disappear in mental representations." The persistence of gender bias in language means our lexicon continues to play a role in perpetuating this bias in society. In an article by Katayoun Jalilipour (2017: 20–1) discussing pronouns in the publication "Queer Bodies" by Shades of Noir, it is noted that the "Singular they is a gender neutral pronoun. [. . .] Non-traditional Pronouns and gender identities need to be taken seriously and to do that we need to decolonise our mind."

The language employed by university staff can also influence how students begin to reflect on their own identity. Nelly Kibirige's contribution in Chapter 2 describes the time when a member of staff raised a conversation about the difference between "being born British, being English and being a British citizen." Nelly comments, "what I saw, was an individual trying to put people in their place: If you had 'acquired' British citizenship, you would never be English and it was very special to be English, a privilege which apparently a small number in the class possessed." The language which teachers employ, and the discussion topics raised by staff, plays a role in the development of the classroom culture. This has an impact of levels of student belonging and interaction. In the example Nelly reflects on, the teacher's comments led to "groups of people slowly start[ing] to form based on who they identified with." In Ryan Carty's contribution in Chapter 6, Ryan also reflects on how comments made by teachers had an impact on his sense of well-being, identity, and belonging. Language used in the classroom sets the tone for what is considered acceptable and conventional. As a result, an interrogation of language is necessary if we are to review how language used in teaching can enhance connections or cause disconnect within a class. Cushman (2016: 1) is "interested in understanding the ways in which language and meaning making relate to power in the everyday lived realities of peoples in communities, classrooms, and Nations. [. . . Cushman's] efforts have been to better understand where, how, for what reasons and with what outcomes knowledge can be made with peoples."

Hall (2019: 11) argues that "within HE, complex hierarchies of value ascribe greater worth to some disciplines than to others. Such value-based judgements have impact on the experience of students and staff in terms of identity and belonging." Some subject areas have become associated with being more intellectual, having greater earning potential, or receiving more respect. This hierarchy of disciplines connected to a sense of value might be internalized or experienced by staff and students. An individual's engagement with a program can therefore be significantly influenced by external perceptions of the discipline. Coate (2006: 408) comments, "To gain legitimacy as an academic subject area in higher education is to gain power, and so an exploration of those knowledge domains that remain illegitimate is to reveal the processes of power at work." Although Coate's article focuses on the history of women's studies, the points raised are also relevant to the wider socially created hierarchies at play that influence the educational sphere.

These social hierarchies have led to categorizations of peoples where certain groups have been able to create dominant narratives about others. Consequently, as Cushman (2016: 5) describes, "The problem becomes when what counts as valid is always judged against a baseline that privileges one group of people's knowledge and forms of expression to the necessary exclusion of others." Ball (2013: 5) points to how this is revealing of power relations "in the sense that some groups or institutions have been able to speak knowledgeably about 'others,' subaltern groups, who were concomitantly rendered silent—men speak about women, deracialized whites about racialized others, heterosexuals about homosexuals, the West about the Orient." The tensions around privileging dominant social narratives are also raised by a philosophy student taking part in Bernadine Idowu-Onibokun's focus group (Chapter 2), who similarly discusses the "tendency to maintain European ideological conventions and 'other' everything outside of the normalcy of our domestic context. This manifests itself in disrespectful and often racist, sexist, or classist remarks which reinforces, and sometimes justifies, the inequality experienced by those disadvantaged by society." If the above is experienced among students at an institution, feelings of unbelonging are likely to grow.

For a more connected staff and student community to develop, and in light of growing calls for anti-racist work to be prioritized, white colleagues must play an active role in progressing the decolonizing agenda so that white allyship can develop effectively across an institution. For the decolonizing agenda to progress, shared responsibility and accountability is required. The work cannot be intentionally or unintentionally delegated. Conversations and decolonizing work led by staff and students will differ, each bringing up a range of complex questions for further exploration. Colleagues who belong to BAME and/or LGBTQ communities, and/or who are disabled, should not be expected to lead or be pressured to lead on particular areas of work simply because they identify with a specific group. All staff and students should be involved in conversations concerning decolonizing teaching and learning and encouraged to initiate respectful and developmental discussions.

Chapter Summary

This chapter has considered the ways in which different teaching approaches can affect the relationship between and among staff and students. This then has an impact on the power dynamics that are formed in the classroom. Power dynamics always exist in some form or other in a classroom. But they can be negotiated and changed. By reflecting on the dynamics created, who is leading on the creation of them, how they are being produced and their outcomes, a greater understanding of the ways in which power dynamics can be made productive can be achieved. It is also worth examining both explicit and implicit manifestations of power.

The issue of trust can be a significant factor in the formation of developmental relationships between and among staff and students. This chapter put forth the idea of trust in the classroom as being located across a movable spectrum. Approaching trust in this way draws attention to how trust can be shown, given, and received. Another way of creating a rapport and inclusive teaching environment is through being conscious of our language of delivery. Being mindful of who is speaking, about whom, to whom, and for whom helps raise awareness of how these factors can affect the power dynamics in a classroom. The way information is received is directly affected by the way it is communicated. As a result, the delivery of messages or "how" something is taught and talked about plays a key role in learning and teaching. The way a learning environment has been cultivated by those within it will also affect the levels of openness and trust for more challenging discussions to take place. Furthermore, the power of seeing diversity is significant but approaches to enhancing diversity should not be tokenistic.

8

Implementing the TRAAC Model across Disciplines

With Contributions from Paul Breen, Anthony Cullen, Rahma Elmahdi, Peter Jones, Savvas Michael, and Dawn Reilly

This chapter is made up of contributions from Paul Breen, Anthony Cullen, Rahma Elmahdi, Peter Jones, Savvas Michael, and Dawn Reilly. The contributors are based across different institutions and comment on how decolonizing teaching and learning has affected their work within their discipline. Although their roles and areas of expertise differ, the contributions highlight how discussions on decolonizing teaching and learning are affecting staff and students across subject areas. These contributions help to evidence the need to extend conversations around decolonizing across disciplines. The topic is not one which should be steered by a small group of staff within a university. The contributors emphasize differing issues relating to decolonizing, pointing to the complexity of the work and the wide-ranging impact that the work can have. Many students and staff express a desire to understand and engage with conversations around decolonizing but are unsure how to approach the topic authentically.

The TRAAC model is not intended to force the subject of decolonizing into a ridged space or confine the discussion to set topics. But it is aimed at offering an entry point for reflective and reflexive discussion on decolonizing teaching and learning. All of the contributions have been influenced in some way by the use of the TRAAC model. It has at times been used as an overarching framework which is referred to by way of instigating reflective thoughts and ideas about decolonizing teaching and learning. At other times, selective segments of the model have been focused on as areas for review when trying to enhance levels of inclusivity and work toward decolonizing a particular course. The contributions in this chapter are followed by a general discussion of the themes raised across the writings and the ways in which they help to extend both the use of the TRAAC model and wider discussions on decolonizing.

Implementing the TRAAC Model in an Academic English Context

Paul Breen

Taken at first impression, English for Academic Purposes (EAP) appears to be a subject at odds with an aim of decolonizing teaching and learning. Partly that is due to the prioritization of "English" in the title of a subject that actually involves "grounding instruction in an understanding of the cognitive, social and linguistic demands of specific academic disciplines" (Hyland and Hamp-Lyons 2002: 2). EAP then is not just about viewing "language as a neutral medium through which meanings pass" (Pennycook 1997: 257) but about using language as a means of familiarizing students with the social practices of their academic disciplines. Increasingly, those disciplines are shifting away from "a western genealogy" of teaching and learning (Icaza and Vázquez 2018: 111) toward "decentring" or "deterritorialising" (Le Grange 2016: 6) the terrain of higher education (HE).

EAP too has made significant shifts in past decades from having "a vulnerability to claims that it ignores students' cultures" (Hyland and Hamp-Lyons 2002: 4) toward a greater awareness of a need to "facilitate the discussion and practice of decolonizing EAP material" (Ewing and Reece 2019). Other scholars such as Gimenez (2020) have advanced a tradition of bringing EAP out of relative isolation into the broader social practices of the university as also advocated in earlier studies such as Gimenez and Thomas (2015). The latest manifestation of this comes in the form of a new theory of "Edulingualism" which strives to capture a sense of how students use their existing "linguistic capital" as a means of "negotiating with, rather than accommodating to, a particular context or social structure where English is the dominant language" (Gimenez 2020: 4).

Though often playing the part of "chameleon discipline" within HE (Breen 2018: 1), EAP can be quite conservative and rule-bound. Even the ways in which we teach our students to write often assume a sense of rightness and perhaps also a righteousness about the conventions they must follow. Within UK HE at present, a substantial majority of EAP students (*international students*) are Chinese. If such students are to be treated as more than simply a "cash cow" for universities (Hackett 2017: 8), Liao (2019) has argued for a greater emphasis upon understanding and development of their cultural literacy rather than simply academic literacy or language acquisition. Presently within some EAP contexts, there is a sense that the onus is upon students to adapt to Western ways of thinking, writing, and presenting.

Yet in assuming this need for change on the part of students alone we, as EAP practitioners, are often guilty of the "unconscious bias" that Tran (2020) speaks of in outlining the Relationship segment of her TRAAC model. The idea is that such students must adapt to *our* ways of teaching and learning and *our* perceptions of what Lea and Street (1998: 158) term as "academic skills" and "academic socialization." Inherent to this is a sense of *our* Socratic and *our* socio-constructivist approaches to teaching being the right way of doing things. Divergence from the Western idea of how things should be done is often most apparent in the case of the aforementioned Chinese students in EAP contexts. These students come to the UK from a culture shaped by Confucianism which downplays the importance of forming individual opinions in favor of developing awareness of the great body of knowledge and thought that has gone before. It is more about acquiring wisdom than questioning that knowledge. Thus echoing Hyland and Hamp-Lyons (2002), there is an EAP ignorance to expecting instant adaptation to Socratic and socio-constructivist approaches.

As far as I am concerned, there is equal ignorance in the idea that decolonizing the curriculum simply necessitates the removal of Western-centric materials. Even the use of terminology such as "whiteness" as a blanket to describe colonization faces a challenge in certain EAP teaching situations. One example might be a discussion of political colonization with History students, examining such cases as Ireland, Kashmir, Kurdistan, Poland, Tibet, or the Soviet Republics. To a large extent these cases challenge reductionist ideas about colonization and suggest need for movement beyond binary narratives of black and white.

Real change occurs at philosophical rather than cosmetic levels as recognized two decades ago in Pennycook's demand for EAP adopting a broader philosophy than simply "the local and the everyday defining what we do" (1997: 255). This then is where Tran's (2020) TRAAC model could serve a positive purpose within EAP in the sense of providing an overarching philosophical framework for decolonizing curricula within EAP contexts. That is because this TRAAC framework draws together relationship with students, course content, activity/

assessment, and most importantly from my perspective, teaching approach which might also be labeled personal philosophy of practice (Warschauer 1996; Breen 2018). Each of these is crucial within any teaching situation and particularly within the assessment-heavy context of EAP.

The ways in which the TRAAC framework might be applied to EAP begin with the aspect of an overarching philosophy. Presently as suggested by Liao (2019), there is a mismatch between Socratic and Confucian ideology in the minds of students. Vygotskian approaches might work well in bridging this gap, providing synergy between eastern ideas about the role of expert (teacher) and constructivist approaches to the responsibilities of the autonomous learner (student). To my mind, many EAP practitioners have fallen into a pitfall of constructivism with teachers reduced to facilitators rather than experts. Consequently, EAP lessons are driven by reflection and recycling of knowledge rather than a learning of the strategies that they need to navigate the social practices of their disciplines. International students at best find this a struggle and at worst, as evidenced in my course's feedback, see this as an abdication of teaching responsibilities.

What happens then as a consequence of this disparity in expectations about teaching is that there is a knock-on effect for other TRAAC components. First, the choice of content and materials is going to be shaped by teachers having a false sense of what students need. Materials that lend themselves to reflection, discussion, and recycling of knowledge have more in common with generic English Language Teaching approaches than with providing the strategic knowledge that students of EAP require. Second, relationships are impacted as evidenced in Liao's (2019) study of Chinese students' attitudes to the teaching of academic writing within EAP courses. Recurringly, these students expected teachers to be their educators and advisers rather than their facilitators or their guides. However, it is also important to ensure that expectations about the teacher's role are managed properly so as to enact Chang and Beaumont's (2004) emphasis on bottom-up approaches that are both context sensitive and guided by belief in the benefits of persuasion over imperialistic forms of direct imposition.

One way of guiding students along this pathway between learning from an expert and learning for themselves is to prioritize activity and assessment. Within my own EAP teaching context, we have shaped our curriculum based on a "backwards design" process (Wiggins and McTighe 2005; Fink 2007). This means that assessment shapes the curriculum rather than vice versa, and the assessments are shaped taking into consideration the direct needs of students.

On our EAP courses in Westminster we have done this by increasing the discipline-specificity of assessment to reflect a similar disciplinary emphasis within courses themselves. Students now work on assessment tasks that will allow them to become more empowered by the knowledge of their disciplinary practices and a greater understanding of how discourse is constructed and reconstructed within those disciplines. At the same time, this is not yet perfected because our teaching still retains dogma that lends itself to de facto colonization. Foremost among these across disciplines and not just within EAP is the idea that study must always be conducted and all sources evidenced through the medium of English. As such, on our EAP courses, there is often a reluctance on the part of teachers to allow their students to make use of resources not provided through the medium of English. However, Gimenez's aforementioned theory of "Edulingualism" challenges this idea by supporting international students' right to access information in their own language and to use that as part of their knowledge base (2020).

On the whole then there has been significant recent progress at both practical and theoretical levels of English Language Teaching and Academic English teaching in recent times. There is still a lot of work to do though, particularly in wider acceptance of edulingual approaches and other philosophies that lend themselves to giving credence to students' voices, expectations, and perceptions. Throughout its history, English Language Teaching has often been at the forefront of exciting developments within education. The newer subject of EAP, in the half dozen decades or so that it has existed, has also been active in reshaping the experience and education of international students. Now once again it can come to the forefront within HE by serving as a bridge for students to take part in helping shape or reshape the social practices of disciplines in today's rapidly changing internationalized environment.

Decolonizing Public Law

Anthony Cullen

This case study focuses on the application of the TRAAC model to the teaching of Public Law at Middlesex University, London. As a core undergraduate module on BA and LLB law programs, Public Law is taught across three campuses of Middlesex University (London, Mauritius, and Dubai). The module covers the area of law which relates to the constitution of the UK and the administration of the state. The majority of those enrolled from year to year are BAME students. The TRAAC model is utilized here as a tool to reflect on issues pertaining to the decolonization of the subject and its delivery.

The motivation underlying the decolonization is one that is influenced by my experience as an immigrant and as a national of a state partitioned as a result of colonization. It is also influenced by the experience of living and working in former UK colonies in India, Africa, and the Middle East, and by the work of anti-colonial figures such as Frantz Fanon (1986), Mahatma Gandhi (2001), and Nelson Mandela (2004). Conceived in terms of "a paradigm shift from a culture of exclusion and denial to the making of space for other political philosophies and knowledge systems" (Keele University: 1), decolonization demands a radical approach to both the content of the curriculum and its delivery.

Teaching Approach

The transition into HE is often a particularly challenging one for students who work, have caring responsibilities, or have a long commute to university. A significant proportion of first-year law students at Middlesex University fall into this category and are affected by one or more of these factors. This impacts on class attendance, levels of engagement, and participation in both formative and summative assessments at different stages of the academic year. While teaching approaches vary, it is foreseeable that the incorporation of measures addressing more holistically the experience of students would impact positively on rates of continuation, progression, and achievement. However, for such measures to succeed—for decolonization to be effective—the nature of the relationship between students, staff, and the institution itself needs to be taken into account.

Relationship

Relationships between staff and students at Middlesex University are shaped by different factors. These include not only the power dynamics of the classroom but also that which takes place outside the classroom, including pastoral and academic support, the grading of assessments, and writing references for purposes of employment or further studies. The importance of decolonizing this aspect of the student experience is underlined by increasing recognition of the need for greater inclusivity in the legal profession. Traditional inherited hierarchies of power—reflected in the dominance of Oxford and Cambridge training contract recruitment—have (and continue to be) a source of alienation for many law students. Decolonization requires recognition of this. According to Icaza and Vázquez (2018: 119), "decolonisation of the university should include a transformation of the relationships established in the classroom and across the university. The classroom is a space in which power hierarchies and forms of exclusion often get reproduced." To counter the reproduction of "inherited hierarchies of power and patterns of exclusion" (El-Enany: 46), a reflective approach must be taken to how such relationships are cultivated, considering ways and means of empowering students to exercise control and ownership over their own learning.

Activity and Assessment

Although there is little choice over the format of assessment for Public Law, choices do exist regarding activities to support success in relation to assessment. Given issues with attendance that reoccur from year to year—and the importance of empowering students to exercise control and ownership over their learning—flexibility is needed in terms of extending the possibilities that exist to support student learning. In this context, the enhancement of online learning is essential. Although not a substitute for other forms of interaction, it is important to address the situation of students who are unable to attend for whatever reason.

As a core first-year module, Public Law is delivered through a series of lectures, workshops, and seminars. Both the lectures and workshops involve large group teaching while the seminars involve small groups. While activities are constrained by the space utilized for teaching, a creative approach must be taken to possibilities for interaction. Mindful of the diversity of the class, and the fact that many students (or their parents or grandparents) would come from countries that are former colonies of the UK, activities focusing on the constitutions such states would be helpful in cultivating a sense of ownership and belonging among students.

Though guest speakers who reflect the diversity of student cohort are regularly invited, the majority of these have been UK based with affiliations with academic institutions in London. Inviting speakers from further afield (in particular from countries in the Global South) would enrich the diversity of knowledge and voices that students are exposed to. This could be facilitated though the use of videoconferencing and where possible arrangements made through networks for scholars visiting the UK.

Constraints on students' time, and the strain resulting from workload, should also be taken into consideration. At the start of the academic year the students exude energy and enthusiasm. Toward the end, all too often the weariness and despondency are palpable. While it is natural for energy levels to fluctuate, the difference between the two extremes in first-year law students is striking. As noted by Teresa Brostoff (2017: 157), "Research, statistical, and anecdotal data have established that the study and practice of law are stressful. [. . .] Law students seem to grow less happy as they proceed through law school." If the process of decolonization is to be meaningful, the activities and assessments employed must in some way address how they affect well-being of law students. This requires radical rethinking of legal education and the underlying culture of institutions where law is taught (Larcombe 2016; Cullen and Kerin 2019: 165–8).

Content

Perhaps the most obvious point of focus for the decolonization of Public Law is the content of the module. Although rarely alluded to in textbooks, the constitutional framework for the administration of the UK State has historically facilitated the practice of colonization. Standards of value associated with human rights—including principles equality and nondiscrimination—exist only insofar as they are permitted by the Supremacy of Parliament. As matter of UK constitutional law, Parliament is sovereign. This negates the possibility of entrenched guarantees protecting human rights.

To decolonize Public Law is to deconstruct the role that the constitution has played and continues to play in practices of colonization. Insofar as it is possible to do so, delivery must engage the lived experience of students. One approach to this would be to explore how distinctions between persons based on characteristics such as class, color, religion, ethnicity, and sexual orientation have been utilized to maintain the status quo in the administration of the state. Another approach could be to highlight tensions between the different parts of the constitution and their role in defining the national and international context for furthering social justice, equality, and nondiscrimination. Irrespective of the approach adopted, the decolonization of the subject matter would not be complete without considering the role of Public Law in the state's appropriation and exploitation of overseas territories.

If consideration of the state's colonial past is to be meaningful, it is essential that it be linked to the colonial present. As Regan (2010: 11) points out, "how people learn about historical injustices is as important as learning truths about what happened." The state's treatment of migrants—and the law relating to citizenship—provides a concrete example of how the UK's past has to a large extent shaped current position on such matters. As the content of Public Law defines the relationship between the citizens and the state, decolonization demands the current state of law be put in context.

To conclude, the decolonization of Public Law requires a process of self-reflection on the past, present, and future of the subject. Toward this end, the TRAAC model provides an invaluable framework not only for the enhancement of teaching and learning, but also for the personal and professional development of the educational practitioner. As a field of study, Public Law defines virtually all aspects of the legal relationship between the individual and the state. For the vast majority of former colonies, the process of decolonization has resulted in the codification of a constitution: the drafting of a document containing rules that regulate the different institutions of the state and laws governing the relationship between the state and the individual. The UK does not have a codified constitution, and there are currently no plans for a process that would culminate in one (Doherty: 109). There are two consequences to this. First, an era characterized by constitutional crisis; second, the erosion of the protection for human rights, in particular the rights of Black, Asian, and Minority Ethnic persons. The decolonization of Public Law arguably serves as best possible antidote to such issues. In this context, the codification of a constitution could address the sense of belonging that is absent for many, in particular in terms of national identity. It would also realize the constitutional entrenchment of fundamental rights and freedoms, including principles of equality and nondiscrimination.

Social Constructivism for a Decolonized Classroom

Rahma Elmahdi

In 1954, Sir Roger Bannister became the first person to run a mile in under four minutes. I enter the Sir Roger Bannister lecture theater. In fifteen minutes, I am due to meet for the first time the batch of medical students I will be teaching for the rest of the academic year. My new cohort will have spent the last three years in the early stages of their medical training. It is only in this year that they can be introduced to a different learning style or worldview from the one they have experienced up until now in the course of their medical education (and will be returning to for the rest of their medical education). I pause to look at the large gold stopwatch encased in a glass cabinet by the entrance to the lecture theater, its minute hand at four and second hand suspended at fifty-nine. At the back of the room hangs a painted portrait of the man the lecture theater is named after, the renowned clinical neurologist, research scientist, record-breaking athlete, and celebrated alumnus of St. Mary's Medical School. In the portrait, he stands in a dimly lit laboratory, the only light, coming from a window above his head, beams down on him, highlighting the pallor of his skin and his grey hair. He stands alone to be celebrated and revered.

In attempting to address the TRAAC model questions of "What perspectives of content have been considered?" and "How inclusive are your learning activities?" one should consider the adoption of a social constructivist perspective in their approach to decolonizing teaching and learning. The social constructivist perspective of teaching and learning is grounded in the cognitive development theories of Piaget (1970, 1977), which suggest that cognitive growth occurs due to social interaction. Knowledge is initially gained from interactions with the world, which are external to ourselves (particularly social interactions) and that this knowledge, gained from collaborative interactions, is internalized, becoming individual knowledge as part of the learning process. According to Di Vesta (1987), this process, which is a crucial part of learning in early life, allows us to relate ourselves to one another and the wider world through sociocultural interaction but is normally forgotten after it is internalized as individual knowledge. In a decolonized classroom, therefore, one might begin to use the social constructivist process of collaborative elaboration (Van Meter and Stevens 2000) in an attempt to teach and support learners as they create inclusive knowledge. The benefit of adopting a social constructivist perspective and process in the classroom is that it can serve as an explanatory framework for the critique of existing systems of colonial knowledge creation, framing them in the context of their sociocultural origins and thereby allowing learners to understand the structural basis of colonial forms of knowledge. This simultaneously provides learners with the tool by which to interrogate existing systems of knowledge, while creating new, equally legitimate, and real knowledge forms that can be compared and again interrogated using the same method of collaborative elaboration in a social constructivist classroom.

At its core, social constructivism is based on idea that human beings rationalize their experiences by creating a model of the world through social interaction. Vygotsky's (1978) theory of social constructivism expanded from the cognitive constructivist theories of Piaget requires us to make particular assumptions about reality, knowledge, and learning. Namely, we should assume that reality does not exist in advance of our creation of it. It is instead constructed through human activity, and therefore history, science and all knowledge are in fact the product of our shared understanding of one another and the world. Kukla (2000) further explains social constructivism as members of a society or group *together* "inventing the properties of that group and the world." If we subscribe to this perspective and consider knowledge as a human product that is socially and culturally constructed, it stands to reason that in order to learn "one must engage with social and cultural sources of knowledge" themselves (Kim 2001: 55). Social constructivism therefore calls for the creation of learners' knowledge through collaboration with others and suggests that the more interactive the collaboration is, the more meaningful the learning becomes and *real* the knowledge created. Derry (1999: 197) particularly emphasizes the central role of culture and context in understanding that "the knowledge we develop doesn't stand in isolation, it is the product of systems of influence, that we as humans, due to our highly social nature, are hard-wired to learn through" and can be most effectively utilized when learners find themselves most at odds with their new environment and the knowledge presented there.

In deciding on the content, activities, and assessments of your decolonized classroom, you should therefore start by exploring the sociocultural makeup of the student group. Often, the simplest way to do so is to set aside a session to ask the students, together or individually, who they are, how they learn, and who they feel they have previously learned successfully from. The answers to these questions might be surprising, and so they are worth asking before deciding on the activities and assessments they will undertake. Often students cite school teachers but also family members, close friends, and cultural figures as their inspiration for learning, with environments such as their homes and shared resources from friends and acquaintances via social media being the places where they have found they have learned most successfully, and not necessarily in the classroom environment. This is essential information for designing activities and assessments which are inclusive of different learning approaches and styles. It is often the case that the people and places that have successfully informed a students' development and learning as a child will continue to be the best way to inform their learning and development as a young adult.

The benefit of this approach for a decolonized classroom is multilayered. It calls for the framing of individual knowledge or beliefs in the context of their sociocultural origin, allowing students to question the systems and structures where this knowledge has come from, while also allowing learners to construct alternative, and equally valid, knowledge forms based on the makeup of classroom itself, and the current sociocultural context that is created by the learners. Within this perspective, even the most colonial content and expression of knowledge can be interrogated critically as they are put into their proper context, that is to say, in light of their Eurocentric and often repressive sociocultural origin. Vygotsky also emphasizes that human mental activity is a particular case of social experience. We cannot achieve our best thinking in isolation of one another, and we cannot achieve a rational knowledge of reality if the social and cultural diversity of our world is not fully utilized. Inclusive learning activities therefore are not just preferable for decolonizing teaching and learning but necessary for all learners, not just those who have historically been culturally and socially excluded from academic knowledge creation. The decolonized classroom therefore becomes a space for a social construction of reality (Leeds-Hurwitz 2009).

In 2019, Eluid Kipchoge became the first person to run a marathon in under two hours. He managed to complete this feat with the help of forty-two of his fellow world-class distance runners acting as pacers. This achievement was therefore not simply the product of one man's athleticism in isolation but rather a complex physical and psychosocial interaction of multiple players. As the new cohort of students enter the Sir Roger Bannister lecture theater, I introduce myself and tell them about the celebrated academic immortalized on the wall. I also remind them of a fact never shared with me during my time being taught in the same lecture theater, that Sir Roger Bannister, like Eluid Kipchoge, also had two of his fellow track team mates providing the pacing that allowed him to run a mile in record-breaking time. I explain that these two feats of human attainment, never before thought possible until they occurred, were reliant on the interaction of the individual with their peers and that this will form the basis for the social constructivist learning they will be undertaking in the coming year. Through their collaboration with each other, they will create new knowledge that will become reality. At the finish line of his record-breaking run, Kipchoge declared that "Together, when we run, we can make this world a beautiful world" (quoted in Keh 2019: 5), and the same can be achieved through social constructivist methods for a decolonized classroom.

Responding to Student Diversity in "Mass Participation" Universities: Decolonizing and "Declassifying" Learning, Teaching, and Assessment in Sociology

Peter Jones

In the UK, initiatives and campaigns aimed at decolonizing HE emanate mainly from "selective" or "elite" universities—albeit often portrayed, at least by implication, as reflecting the British HE sector in its entirety.[1] The exclusivities and privileges they challenge are those associated with "whiteness" and "Eurocentricity," especially as experienced by students in such universities who do not identify as white and European. In contrast, this case study considers the "post-1992" or "mass participation" university subsector and *its* students, with reference to learning, teaching, and assessment in Sociology. It is argued here that decolonization in mass participation universities should reflect their distinctive institutional and student characteristics—the latter including "intersectionalities" of ethnicity *and class*. This analysis draws on the TRAAC model, mainly with respect to "content," "activity," and "assessment." In a longer exposition, the "teaching approach" and "relationship" dimensions of TRAAC would merit fuller attention—including the permutations of ethnicity and class that apply to student-staff, as well as to student-student, relationships in this subsector of British HE.

Data from the Higher Education Statistics Agency (HESA) suggest that while HE students *in aggregate* divide approximately 50:50 between selective and mass participation universities,

- BAME students divide nearer 60:40 in favor of mass participation universities;
- Those from "low participation neighbourhoods" divide approximately 65:35 in favor of mass participation universities; and
- Private school-educated students divide nearer 85:15 in favor of selective universities.[2]

---

[1] For example, Roseanne Chantiluke et al. (Eds.) (2018) provide case studies of five elite universities, while the mass participation subsector is conspicuous only by its neglect, beyond the book's "Preface." Equally, around 90 percent of participants at the inaugural meeting of the British Sociological Association's "Postcolonial and Decolonial Transformations Study Group" in November 2019 were from elite universities.

[2] These are merely indicative differences between two internally diverse and imperfectly defined clusters of HE institutions. For details, see the HESA website at https://www.hesa.ac.uk/.

It therefore appears that British HE is even more segregated in terms of class than ethnicity (see Clarke and Beech 2018 for a related analysis). Indeed, other sources confirm that mass participation students *in general* are not privileged, are overwhelmingly state- (and usually comprehensive-) school educated, are often from the first generation in their families to go to university, commonly choose a university within their own region, and may well be living at home (see, for example, Metcalf 2003; Moreau and Leathwood 2006; and NUS 2015); and these characteristics are thought broadly to apply to BAME as well as to white British students.[3] However much HE may fulfill these students' intrinsic desires for learning, it is also crucial for their social mobility and employability in ways that don't obviously apply to many of those from selective universities. What else characterizes such students? Not much sense of "entitlement," not self-confident essay writers, and not risk-takers. It's less easy to envisage these kinds of students campaigning for changes in HE, compared with those who have taken a lead at numerous selective universities. Many of these characteristics play into questions of learning, teaching, and assessment, as will be shown later in the chapter.

A further broad distinction, between metropolitan and nonmetropolitan universities, crosscuts that of selective versus mass participation HE and suggests a wider range of scenarios. For example, BAME students constitute a very small numerical minority in some nonmetropolitan mass participation universities, and their educational and social experiences may reflect an overwhelming concern to "fit in" and "play down" their differences (see, for example, Davies and Garrett 2012). By contrast, students in metropolitan mass participation universities, with much greater ethnic diversity, may be familiar and comfortable with multicultural educational and social situations *and* able and willing to bring awareness of diversity, and of global (e.g., diasporic) relationships, to their learning. In further contrast, selective universities—particularly in metropolitan regions, where student ethnic diversity tends to be greatest—may bring together BAME and white middle-class students with limited prior experience of educational and social diversity. This latter scenario may go some way to account for the negative experiences of many BAME students identified in Akel (2019)—in contrast with those reported by Gulnaz Ahmed (2020) in a neighboring mass participation university. In this respect, it is notable that Sally Weale et al. (2019) repeatedly reference complaints of racism at "elite," "leading," "Russell Group," "select," and "top" universities—while nonetheless maintaining that "the issues

---

[3] This is not, of course, to deny that BAME students face additional challenges that do not apply to their white British counterparts, especially in terms of relationships and curriculum content.

are clearly sector-wide." The argument here is not that racism is confined to selective universities, but rather that its nature and extent are not everywhere the same—and that all aspects of decolonization merit more "scenario-specific" analysis.[4]

Selective and mass participation institutions themselves are also quite different, in ways that extend beyond the characteristics of their students. Few of the latter exhibit colonial legacies of the kind that have provided a lightning rod for "Rhodes Must Fall in Oxford" and the decolonization campaign at London University's School of Oriental and African Studies (though many doubtless have less visible colonial histories, typically of a more mundane nature). Mass participation universities are also less "research intensive," arguably more student-centered, and probably more "applied" in their teaching and scholarship. But there's also something of the "post-1992 syndrome" at work—that is, institutions torn between aspiring to emulate the selective university model of research-led teaching, etc. and wishing to retain their applied and student-oriented traditions. Again, these characteristics are relevant to questions of learning and teaching, as will be shown later. Before doing so, however, a word about Sociology as a discipline.

Sociology is first and foremost the study of "modern" societies. Its origins lie in the European "Enlightenment" and revolutions (scientific, political, and industrial) of the eighteenth and nineteenth centuries, which gave rise to ideas of liberty, equality, reason, science, and "progress" that were claimed to distinguish these emerging societies in Europe from their feudal predecessors, as well as from "pre-modern" societies elsewhere. In other words, Sociology's roots are inherently Eurocentric—and particularly so, to the extent that its founding figures saw European "modernization" as a mainly endogenous affair; and in so far as important strands of thought have judged non-European societies by criteria derived from the European experience (especially those pertaining to material wealth) and looked for evidence of the diffusion of "modernity" from more to less "developed" realms.

Critics of these views have argued that

1. European material enrichment is far from an endogenous affair: it has been achieved at the expense of enslaved, colonized, and dispossessed non-European peoples, including ongoing exploitation of labor and resources.

---

[4] For evidence that concerns about racism extend across the mass participation-selective university spectrum, see Batty 2019; and EHRC 2019: 14–15.

2. Similarly, in the cultural realm, a sense of "modern" identity has been formed in explicit opposition to the (mainly European) construction of "other" (including so-called "Oriental") identities.
3. Modernity itself has a dark side—or, rather, dark sides—as revealed, not only in genocidal applications of science and "industrialized" systems of slavery, but also in "risks" such as those associated with anthropogenic environmental degradation, which represent unanticipated downsides of the "modern" drive to exploit nature for human ends.

Particularly in relation to (1) and (2), opportunities for decolonization of Sociology are obvious—and reflected in the work of, for example, Walter Rodney (see *How Europe Underdeveloped Africa* 1972), Edward Said (see *Orientalism* 1978), Stuart Hall (see "The West and the Rest" 1992), and Gurminder Bhambra (see *Rethinking Modernity* 2007). It's less evident that ideas associated with (3) are all directly compatible with decolonial thinking, though their relevance to students' learning about contemporary issues—and potentially, their employability—hardly needs spelling out.

Non-Eurocentric perspectives and contemporary issues are now, of course, more widely represented in Sociology—with diversity-related questions frequently embraced by white British as well as BAME students. Nonetheless, the "canon" remains deeply entrenched and stoutly defended: it is institutionalized in, for example, introductory textbooks (see, for example, Giddens and Sutton 2017) and the national Subject Benchmark Statement for Sociology (QAA 2019). Students cannot graduate without a firm grasp of the founding theories of European industrialization, though it would appear that knowledge of European colonialism—and of twenty-first-century issues such as automation, biotechnology, and environmental degradation—remains of lesser priority. And paradoxically, risk-averse mass participation students who have been acculturated into thinking of sociological knowledge as largely external to themselves—to be "learned from the textbook" and wrapped in "grand theory"—may be ambivalent about attempts to challenge the received wisdom. However, "epistemic dissent" is, according to CK Raju (2018: 269), "central to decolonisation." Hence, this case study proceeds to offer some critical reflections on established "ways of knowing and doing" in Sociology—beginning with "the essay," which embodies the discipline's self-proclaimed "gold standard" of argumentative exposition, and remains the default assessment genre (either as coursework or as examination); and concluding with some pointers toward possible "decolonizing" *and "declassifying"* transformations of learning, teaching, and assessment.

Peter Womack (1993: 43) has characterized the essay as a *"culturally specific form of communication which has not always existed, and which depends for its existence now on some quite definite institutional contexts"* (emphasis added). He traces its current form to the nineteenth-century introduction of public examination for entry to, in particular, the Indian Civil Service—noting that "there was an urgent need to turn the commercial rapacity of the East India Company into something like an imperial *mission civilisatrice*" (1993: 45); and that the essay was considered to provide "an appropriate medium for assessing ... [candidates'] intellectual, moral and cultural qualities" (1993). Its supposed "functional innocence" and "pure embodiment of writing" (Womack 1993: 46), along with the self-ascribed superiority of "contrastive argumentation" as a core "epistemological stance" (on which, see Barton 1993), may go some way to accounting for the essay's survival in contemporary education systems which owe so much to the history and continuing primacy of elite universities. However, this rather exclusive way of "knowing and doing" arguably favors those coming from selective schools (who are more likely to be versed in the mysterious arts of essay writing); those who envisage an academic career (for whom exhaustive exposure to this genre may be a valuable investment); and those for whom employability is not a major anxiety (given that few outside HE greatly value the ability to write a good essay!). It is less obviously relevant, to BAME *and other* mass participation students, compared with more applied forms of "knowing and doing."

The essay's insistence on an "appropriate" language register, including a particular style and tone, grammar and vocabulary, raises further questions about its "diversity" credentials. Constant Leung (2013) has argued that in an age where people from all kinds of language backgrounds communicate successfully in English, universities' insistence on a singular "Standard English," modeled on what he describes as the "putative native speaker who is usually imagined to be middle class ... and from the ... (Global) north" (2013: 305), amounts to a form of "censorious parochialism" (2013: 309). Leung is thinking mainly about the learning of English as an additional language, and in particular about its spoken forms; but the same might well apply to writing requirements and to diverse "native" users of English, including multilingual BAME users (on which, see Block 2008) as well as to white British users of "non-Standard" English.

All of this is not to suggest that sociological exposition should neglect grammar, punctuation, and spelling—but rather that a lesser degree of "censorious parochialism," and greater diversity of written and non-written forms of expression, may be relevant to the circumstances and needs of BAME and other mass participation students. Nor is it to suggest that theory-informed reasoning should be abandoned. However, most nonacademic applications of Sociology rely on issue-led analysis, involving the deployment of concepts, methods, and evidence which may be shared among alternative theoretical positions, rather than "contrastive argumentation" based on a preference for one or another rival theory. And many Sociology students doubtless aspire to apply their learning, in a professional and/or civic capacity—for example with third sector organizations, including those who have come to recognize a need for diversification of their own staffing. Learning, teaching, and assessment in Sociology that more closely mirrors this "issue-led" approach, and which nurtures the ability to deliver a well-informed and thoughtful research report, news release, blog, poster, presentation, film, portfolio, or exhibition, may be an appropriate response to student diversity in mass participation universities and possibly beyond.[5]

Are BAME Students on TRAAC for Success in Law?

Savvas Michael

The statistics involved in understanding the awarding gap between BAME and white students in the field of law are a little more complex than for other subjects. There are many available educational routes and a large amount of data from BAME and white students from both law and non-law degree backgrounds which would need to be reviewed in order to get a true and accurate idea of the attainment gap in law. Nevertheless, there is an attainment gap at university which continues into employment as a lawyer. This contribution considers how the application of the TRAAC model assists in reviewing issues of the awarding gaps of BAME law students and the underrepresentation of BAME lawyers.

I will be using public data from the University of Law to illustrate the attainment gap such as the 2019–20 Access and Participation Plan. This data should not be taken as an overall study on the achievement of BAME and white students in law nationally. Of those who graduated from the law degree in 2015–17, 92.3 percent of white students passed and 62.2 percent achieved a 1st or

---

[5] Examples of currently popular issues among my own students are "fast fashion," global supply chains, and "modern slavery"; and transnational organized crime, including human trafficking and people smuggling.

2.1—the highest in both categories by far. Asian or Asian British students had a similar pass rate at 90.4 percent; however, strikingly just 37.6 percent of these students achieved a 1st or 2.1, almost 25 percent below white students, and the lowest of all ethnicities. Black or Black British students did better in terms of achieving a 1st or 2.1 at 47.4 percent, but over 20 percent failed with a pass rate of just 79.2 percent. Mixed students had the lowest pass rate of 75 percent and only 38.9 percent gaining a 1st or 2.1. Furthermore, when looking at the Asian and Black student withdrawals, they are the most likely to have withdrawn after Year 1. University of Law's 2020–21 Access and Participation Plan has picked up on the awarding gaps of BAME students and made it a priority for the years ahead.

The Solicitor Regulation Authority also released figures in 2017 on BAME solicitors. The initial data seems positive, on the surface at least: 21 percent of solicitors in the UK are BAME with 14 percent being Asian solicitors (they are largely over-represented in law given that Asians make up just 6 percent of the overall workforce in the UK) and 3 percent being Black solicitors (the same as their representation in the overall workforce). In terms of partners in law firms (a highly senior role), 20 percent of partners are BAME. Thus, it would seem there is no problem in law—BAME lawyers are pretty fairly represented in comparison to their overall representation in the workforce. However, when these figures are analyzed at a deeper level, the outlook is less promising for BAME solicitors.

Criminal and private client work tends to be associated with "high street" firms—small, family-owned firms where solicitors tend to be overworked but unprotected and underpaid, in an at times disorganized, unprofessional, and exploitative environment. Thirty-three percent of solicitors in these criminal law firms are BAME, while 37 percent of solicitors in private client firms are BAME. By contrast, medium-sized firms and large firms doing mainly corporate work tend to be those located in offices in the City of London, the "magic circle," and "silver circle" firms as they are known. Here, solicitors are worked hard but are part of a large corporate organization with HR policies and protection, and rewarded with huge six-figure salaries and a prestigious legal brand for their CV. Within these firms, just 12–19 percent of solicitors are BAME. Furthermore, the largest firms have the lowest proportion of BAME partners at just 8 percent, while incredibly 34 percent of partners at one partner (small) firms are BAME. This gives an indication of how the 20 percent BAME partner figure is highly misleading. Thus, BAME solicitors and partners in the more prestigious, highly paid, City of London firms are grossly underrepresented.

The BBC documentary "How to Break into the Elite" (2019) provides a good analysis on the class and potential race struggles in London. It argued that there is still very much a culture of recruiting middle- and upper-class white graduates for roles in large companies in the city including corporate law firms. This is further exemplified by the case of Kate Norfolk, a student whose A Level Latin E grade was deemed as likely resulting in city law firms not even placing her on an interview shortlist, which caused her family to sue her school (Smithers 2001). This shows that Latin A Levels, arguably not associated with state school students, would be used to filter out these students from becoming lawyers. Thus, BAME underrepresentation as solicitors may derive partly from this British class system and implicit racism engrained in society. However, I will discuss the possible reasons behind the grades of BAME students in law at university level, which then have a knock-on effect on their ability to become a lawyer at a large firm.

In response to the first quartile of the TRAAC model, I encourage a two-stage teaching approach when teaching law—stage one: ensuring that the students understand and have good knowledge of the law itself; and stage two: ensuring that students are comfortable in applying that law to a factual scenario, whether it be to a real or hypothetical case. The first stage is often a step-by-step, almost mathematical approach. It would be easy for this first stage to create a hierarchical learning environment. The format of this first stage may consequently discourage discussion, which is important in a student's development. There thus needs to be a balance and variety between this participatory approach and the expectation on teachers to teach concrete, somewhat certain, legal principles. Indeed, there will be times when a teacher-focused approach may be appreciated by students, but they should feel able to ask any questions without judgment in a safe environment. The legal knowledge of a teacher should generate respect and direction rather than power and authority, enabling students to feel part of a productive discussion with a competent and supportive teacher, but not excluded.

It may seem as though none of this directly relates to BAME students. However, in fact, it is completely relevant, as the key is to create a level playing field among students. BAME students may be less likely to be part of families of lawyers with role models or part of a group of friends of lawyers, thus not have grown up engaging in any legal conversations, compared to a student whose parents are lawyers for example. They may therefore feel less confident in class—this is no reflection of their intellect in any way, but the sight of other students articulating themselves well on legal issues may on the surface be threatening to these BAME students and discourage them from participating. This can be resolved by an open, encouraging teacher who promotes a comfortable setting where any question is treated with respect. The more a student realizes their questions are relevant, the more they will ask and the better their learning experience will be. In contrast, if they are faced with an authoritative teacher who seems as though they would judge or even embarrass a student if they raise a question which may not be wholly relevant, the less likely they will participate.

Some aspects of the teacher-student relationship, the second TRAAC quartile, are somewhat out of a teacher's control, but within the control of an employer. Most lecturers in legal education are ex-lawyers. And as stated earlier, figures suggest that top lawyers mainly come from white middle- to upper-class backgrounds. Furthermore, BAME students will unfortunately see very few nonwhite teachers in law. Seeing how BAME lawyers are underrepresented in the silver circle may also have a subliminal impact on the confidence levels of BAME students in pursuing a career in law. Universities can begin to address this by inviting special guest lecturers from diverse backgrounds to discuss areas of expertise, but I would suggest that this should be resolved on a more permanent basis.

I am a thirty-one-year-old white European man from a working- to middle-class background who studied at a failed state school but also at the University of Cambridge. In this sense, by my diverse experiences and nature, I attempt to make myself aware of any unconscious biases that may exist and ensure I do my best not to alienate students of any background, which I believe I am able to do well due to my age and class. Of course, there will be older teachers who communicate wonderfully with students, while there will be inept young teachers. Furthermore, my age may also cause students to view me as young and inexperienced; thus I must rely on my knowledge and efforts to gain respect and trust. However, BAME students will be encouraged from being taught by teachers from a nontraditional background; thus a permanent recruitment of more diverse teachers in law, although of course appropriately qualified and competent, may create a better learning environment for BAME students.

The third quartile of TRAAC on activity and assessment techniques are perhaps the most noticeable in law when looking at ways in which the attainment gap could potentially be closed. As stated earlier, the second stage of teaching law is ensuring students can apply the law to hypothetical scenarios formulated via problem questions, which essentially tests their ability to give advice in a practical scenario. Problem scenarios in exams and activities are still immensely guilty of using archaic and outdated sets of facts and circumstances, which fail to reflect 2020 multicultural London and the UK. They draw on situations that are simply not relatable to students, particularly of working classes but even less so to students of BAME backgrounds. The use of nonlegal quintessentially "British" words or phrases in these problem questions can severely impact a BAME student's performance even if their knowledge of the law is good. They are not connected to the law in any way and are thus simply unnecessary. Even the use of non-English names may help BAME students—of course this will not impact their understanding of a scenario, but it may have a subliminal impact on lessening the alienation they may feel and in turn distance law with its traditional white upper-class connotations.

In terms of the fourth quartile, Content, law is arguably one of the hardest disciplines to change in line with decolonizing the curriculum. In accordance with regulations, students must complete seven core modules (Contract, Tort, Land, Equity, Criminal, Public, and EU) and only EU law takes an international nature, although this is only as EU law has an impact on UK law and this may change following Brexit. There are optional modules which draw on International Law (Private and Public) and perhaps some modules which compare the law of different jurisdictions. However, it is likely a student will not encounter too many at undergraduate level. There is thus the argument that there should be more international optional modules as part of a law degree, alongside the core ones, and this may generate interest from BAME students.

For example, I teach an International Human Rights Law module as part of the master's degree (LLM). The starting point of this course discusses the Universal Declaration of Human Rights (UDHR), an international treaty signed and ratified by many states, which was created by the United Nations (UN) in 1948. However, when teaching this topic, I immediately ensured that students questioned the notion of a Convention setting out Human Rights Law universally, created by the UN, a somewhat Western-influenced organization. Considering the year and context in which it was created, during a time when Britain and the West were starting to let go of their colonies but finding ways to retain some form of influence over them (political, economic, social, cultural), the Convention is not too dissimilar to the colonial idea of the West "civilizing" these countries. I thus emphasized the need to be aware of "cultural relativism," the concept that it may not be so simplistic to apply a "universal" form of Human Rights Law, as cultural differences may mean that certain "universal" or Western ideals of human rights may not be suitable for many countries, and even have ulterior motives behind their imposition. The syllabus of this module also included topics on the human rights systems in the Americas (Central and South), and Africa, which provided good coverage of Human Rights Law on a regional scale.

International Law in general follows this theme—UN treaties and conventions often form part of codified international law. Furthermore, customary international law is a set of unwritten rules, developed through so-called customs and norms, but arguably Western, which are even more dangerous as they require no ratification. This entire body of law must be seen with caution given that it may be able to be enforced "universally" even if not appropriate to do so. If International Law is taught with skepticism and critique of this law, then it can be an excellent way of decolonizing the teaching of legal content. However, if taught with acceptance of these "international" UN conventions and treaties, it could exacerbate the problem.

Furthermore, in the mandatory EU law module, for example, one small part of the syllabus is on antidiscrimination laws; however, following the Black Lives Matter protests, there has been a move by many universities to highlight and place more focus on race discrimination laws in Europe, both in the context of the European Union and the European Convention of Human Rights. Even within UK law, more emphasis could also be placed on the Equality Act 2010, which incorporates many EU directives. As the TRAAC model suggests, it may be worth considering the student group and level of demand for both of these. Including such modules and amendments to syllabuses may help to promote a multicultural society whereby students may be encouraged to broaden their knowledge by qualifying as a lawyer and practice law in different countries and jurisdictions, for example (certainly an aim of mine), or raise awareness of Human Rights Laws in Europe and beyond.

University of Law data shows that fewer Asian students are getting 1st's and 2.1's while Black students are failing more than others. Can this all be explained and changed by decolonizing education? Perhaps not, societal factors play a part—fewer opportunities due to BAME students' social status from a young age for example. But this simply points to how the decolonizing agenda actually looks at wider issues both within and outside of the university setting. The TRAAC model helps to encourage consideration of connected issues that can have a significant impact on diminishing power dynamics and a hierarchical learning environment (teaching approach), diversifying employees (relationship), and changing the nature of problem questions (assessment and activities). As argued, content in law is harder to change than some other disciplines, so not all segments of TRAAC necessarily need to have equal focus, but the model could instead be used holistically. So does the TRAAC model offer an entry point for critical reflections and developmental dialogue? Unquestionably. Objection? Overruled.

A Phased Implementation of the TRAAC Model in an Accounting Module

Dawn Reilly

Introduction

The context for this case study is an accounting module at a UK university with a commitment to widening participation in HE for underrepresented groups. Our students come from a diverse range of backgrounds, so within the class, we had students from a number of different ethnicities. The class included students who joined the university via one of our extended four-year programs, as well as students who belong to the group which has come to be termed "commuter students," meaning that they live at home and not in halls of residence. This is so that they can continue with their part-time jobs, or they have other responsibilities to manage outside of the university, at the same time as they are studying. It is extremely important that any attempt to make the curriculum more inclusive considers the needs of these different groups, which, of course, are not mutually exclusive. While the TRAAC model is useful across a range of inclusion issues, its main purpose is to assist in decolonizing the curriculum. The university has a strategic focus on addressing the attainment gap for BAME students, and we have started to see some success in this area within the faculty (Warren and Reilly 2019). The TRAAC model has provided a way to operationalize that strategy at the module level in order to contribute to efforts across the faculty and wider institution to shrink and ultimately eliminate the gap.

I have found the TRAAC model to be very useful because it provides prompts in relation to particular areas where the inclusivity of my practice might be enhanced. Although the model highlights four main areas with corresponding questions for consideration, this case study shows how it is not a requirement to review all areas concurrently the first time the model is used in order to start to apply it. I have also learned that it is unnecessary to make huge changes in order to gain benefits from using the model. Personally, I have found it helpful to focus on two areas initially: Teaching approach; and Activity and Assessment. Having used the model to guide me as I consider the various facets of an inclusive curriculum in these areas, next year I shall concentrate on how the model can help me to improve my practice in relation to the remaining areas of Content and Relationship.

Teaching Approach

The technical nature of accounting lends itself to a teaching style where a lecturer explains a topic and demonstrates how to perform a particular calculation in order to answer a question. Therefore, as an accounting lecturer, my favored teaching approach has been to use a front-led lecture style. However, the TRAAC model highlights the benefit of a participatory learning environment. Therefore, I designed the module's sessions so that a main learning activity was a research project, conducted in groups, enabling students to learn from one another in order to create knowledge together. To introduce this type of activity necessitated arranging for the provision of laptops for students to use because very few bring their own. The provision of laptops in this way made the sessions very inclusive and considered the needs of students who cannot afford to buy a laptop.

I was able to move around the room and sit with students in their groups to discuss their ideas and progress made on the project, thereby using dialogue to alter the perceived imbalance of power between lecturer and student. Many sessions start with a short introductory talk from the lecturer before students work in their research groups which is when I circulate among them. However, an honest application of the model has highlighted a lack of variety in my teaching approach. Next year, we shall use video clips to reinforce some of the module content. We shall look for videos which (a) are short; (b) are on a relevant topic; and, if possible, (c) have a presenter or focus which reflects the diversity of the students in the class. The final point is important because this is a small module with only two people on the teaching team, both of whom are white and female. I hope that we can use a few videos to provide different voices which more students can identify with in order to enhance the sense of belonging within the academic community for all students.

Activity and Assessment

The TRAAC model points to the importance of considering the needs of the student body in designing assessment because different methods of assessment and support can favor particular groups over others. For example, in a joint research project, the Institute for Policy Studies in Education and London Metropolitan University (2011) suggest that assessment by examination disadvantages BAME students compared to their white peers. There is no exam in the module being discussed, but it remains relevant to consider how we assess and support students. For example, as "commuter students," many of the class can find it a challenge to set aside time for their studies. Some students lack confidence in asking for feedback, especially if they have not done as much work as they think we are expecting to see ahead of that kind of request. To respond to this, we introduced a comprehensive process of verbal feedback into the module. The assessment structure was set up with a linked series of assignments being an initial individual report, a group presentation and a final individual report.

On reflection, the role which feedforward had in one assignment to help students apply comments in their subsequent assignment was subtle, and I wanted to give more specific feedforward comments ahead of each assignment. At this point, I must say that not everything which we planned was successful. Specifically, I offered written feedback on the draft initial report but very few students engaged with that. Straight away, we changed our plans, rather than waiting for the next academic year, and offered dialogic feedback on both the mock presentation and draft final report through conversations at scheduled appointments. There were still some students who did not engage with those meetings, but many did. Some students came with no draft final report but wanted to join in, and a conversation provided an inclusive approach to formative feedback because we could discuss their ideas and I could answer questions.

Content

Looking forward to the coming academic year, I am using the TRAAC model to reflect on the Content of the module and on my Relationship with students. Last year I allowed students to select their own choice of company for the research activity, enabling them to participate in designing their own curriculum. I had intended this to make students feel included and thereby maximize engagement with the research exercise, but their choice of companies had a strong UK focus. This may have been because it is easier to find information on UK companies for students who are doing web-based research in the UK. However, next year I shall try to offer suggestions of companies with boards of directors made up of diverse ethnicities in order to enhance the international perspective on the module and to take the opportunity to provide aspirational role models to our BAME students.

Relationship

Approximately, a third to half of the students in the class have been taught by me before through their participation in the initial "foundation" year of their extended program. This certainly aids the relationship between the lecturer and some of the students in the class. However, the TRAAC model has caused me to reflect on the alternative perspective which is how the other students view their relationship with me. This is something to be mindful of, especially in the first few weeks of the module when I need to be active in trying to find shared connections with all students.

Conclusion

I have found the TRAAC model to be an extremely useful guide in helping me start to make my module more inclusive both for students with different ethnicities and commuter students. The model has therefore helped me to consider multiple perspectives which have an impact on the experience and attainment of students. In the context of the module in this short case study, it has been helpful to use a phased adoption by prioritizing Teaching approach, and Activity and Assessment in the first year and then moving to focus on Content and Relationship for the second year. I also plan to return regularly to the model to undertake an "inclusivity health check" in the future. Indeed, I have already done so in the area of Teaching approach.

Chapter Summary

All the contributions in this chapter highlight the importance of being aware of the needs of our students. Responding to student needs involves being mindful of the different lived experiences which students bring with them on entering university and which influences the ways in which they engage with teaching and learning. This affects the types of support that need to be offered and the adjustments that can be made to ensure that teaching practice is inclusive. This reflective summary of the contributions explores the shared themes and issues that are touched upon by the authors. These are used to consider the ways in which the contributions have helped to develop the use of the TRAAC model and extend wider discussions on decolonizing teaching and learning. Each of the contributions makes efforts to highlight the particular disciplinary area in which the author is rooted in. By doing so, the importance of understanding and approaching the discussion of decolonizing in light of disciplinary context is underlined. The particular context(s) under consideration affects what issues are prioritized and how they may be engaged with when trying to decolonize teaching and learning. As the different contributions have shown, some authors have prioritized the issue of content as being a key challenge to decolonizing their subject area. Others have placed emphasis on problematizing the issue of assessment, language, or wider social structures.

What the TRAAC model has been able to assist with is encouraging the contributors to reflect upon their individual educational settings and experiences so that their discussion of decolonizing is focused on their specific context. Many of the contributors in and outside of this chapter have made efforts to reflect upon their own identity and experiences. The subject of decolonizing is often one that is located within a space that is perceived as being only relevant and beneficial for BAME students and staff. The contributions in this book have underlined the accessibility and relatability of the decolonizing topic to anyone with a commitment to enhancing teaching and learning for everyone. They have shown that the topic of decolonizing should not be viewed as a competing agenda but one that should be considered as relevant to all core university agendas due to its influence on wider discussions relating to inclusivity, access, equality, and education.

For a few of the contributors, it is the content of their curriculum that is often seen as the biggest challenge to decolonizing. This leads to an interrogation of the origins of canons, the influences behind them, and a questioning of their continued authority. In these contributions, authors have already begun to explore ways in which changes might begin to occur through approaches to content, the delivery of material, and the ways in which knowledge is discussed. This may also involve questioning the connections between content and wider social issues, structures, and institutions. The contributions have helped to extend the TRAAC model by evidencing its usability. The questions raised within TRAAC have been approached in differing ways among the authors. Each contribution has underscored particular issues relating to their discipline while all share similar concerns and values. As a result, the contributions help to evidence the transferability of the model across disciplines and roles.

Conclusion

This book began with an outline of the recent renewed interest surrounding the topic of decolonizing teaching and learning within higher education (HE). Students have played a key role in bringing the decolonizing agenda to wider attention. The Rhodes Must Fall campaign and other student-led university movements that have centered on the decolonizing agenda point to ongoing tensions between past and present that continue to exist within all areas of the institution. Hayes (2016: 39) comments,

> Our ability to decolonize our educational spaces depends on our willingness to decenter white supremacist culture, this is often a struggle itself due to how normalized its indoctrination is in our society. [. . .] We must find it in ourselves to have the courage to take the steps and make the necessary changes in expanding our perspectives of learning and knowledge.

Keeping the conversation and efforts going around the decolonizing movement is vital to keep the topic from being relegated to that of a passing trend. As Tuhiwai Smith stresses, "There is a sustainability issue in terms of a decolonising agenda. We have to sustain it inter-generationally because there is no end point" (Sociological Review Podcast 2020).

The continued privileging of the West has manifested itself in various forms throughout the university. This has created an institutional environment which appears to support a hierarchy of knowledge that assigns greater authority and value to Western perspectives and contexts. Such coloniality (Quijano 2000) impacts on the culture of the university and culture more widely. "Culture pervades learning, and in designing instructional environments there needs to be serious debate about issues concerning the social and cultural dimensions of task design, communication channels and structuring of information if the needs of culturally diverse learners are to be met" (McLoughlin 2001: 9). wa Thing'o (2009: xi) comments that "modernity can be considered a product of colonialism." Brew (2013: 603) describes it as "a postcolonial, pluralistic context in which people are required to deal with constantly changing knowledge; where every day people come across ideas that are not only different but radically different to their own."

Engaging with the decolonizing process can be personally and intellectually dislocating. But challenging conversations should be viewed as learning opportunities, and it is important to see the potential productiveness for teaching and learning in being dislocated. Participating in the process of reflection is a vital part of engaging fully in these challenging conversations. Critical reflection that informs action can lead to effective changes in our teaching that positively impact on student learning. As Rahma Elmahdi states in the Chapter 6 contribution, "In short, if a teacher brings into the classroom the unresolved, Eurocentric structures of their previous experience, not having interrogated what this might mean for them and their students, achieving the environment of the decolonized classroom, that is, facilitating access to voices and visibility of knowledge forms which are normally unseen and unheard, becomes even more challenging."

The issues that lie at the heart of the decolonizing movement are often misunderstood. When this happens, conversations around decolonizing are framed within extremes—as an attack on white authors, as a call to replace all texts that have some sort of focus on the West, or as a movement which incites racial tensions. These misunderstandings lead to miscommunications on the topic, so it's unsurprising when not everyone wishes to engage with such conversations. Ryan and Tilbury (2013) outline, "The idea of 'decolonising education' is concerned with deconstructing dominant pedagogical frames which promote singular worldviews to extend the intercultural understanding and experiences of students, plus their ability to think and work using globally sensitive frames and methods." Raising the profile of decolonizing teaching and learning will play a role in developing the culture of an institution.

Morrison (2017) states, "Inclusivity isn't soft, it isn't passive, it isn't a polite middle class way of addressing the needs of society. It is real and gritty and challenging and meaningful. It requires us all to assess our own role and contribution." This book has understood decolonizing as extending discussions around inclusivity. Considerations for decolonizing include reviewing curriculum design, pedagogy, strategies for enhancing engagement, and an examination of institutional structures. The latter includes addressing levels of diversity among staff and the extent to which these mirror the diversity of the student body, particularly at senior levels. Decolonizing work also involves reflecting on one's own position, perspectives, and those of other peoples. The perceptions among and between staff and students can be influenced by unconscious bias. This can affect levels of trust and the type of relationships that are formed, the levels of student belonging and the power dynamics within a classroom. Unconscious bias training can help individuals to become more aware of their biases and learn strategies for responding to these biases so that they might be reduced. However, as new biases may occur, it is important that staff and students engage in the process of being responsive to unconscious bias in the same way they should engage in reflective practice, in that commitment should be continual rather than momentary to be effective.

The recent renewal of interest around the decolonizing agenda has been fuelled by high-profile student campaigns. Although it cannot be assumed that all students are supportive of the calls to decolonize, just as it cannot be assumed that all staff are supportive. Nevertheless, the decolonizing agenda aims to benefit all students and staff by interrogating hegemonic narratives and drawing attention to the positions, perspectives, voices, and contexts of marginalized groups who have been historically oppressed. In order to help achieve an equally positive learning experience for all students, diverse experiences, cultures, and histories need to be considered in curriculum and pedagogy. As Killick (2017: 14) notes, "For diverse students at home and overseas, in virtual or physical learning spaces, socioculturally appropriate and relevant learning, teaching, and assessment practices are the roots of equitable learning experiences. This means, above all else, attending to the voices of all our students, and of all the faculty who shape and deliver their experiences."

University strategies and policies play a key role in affecting change. Smolicz (2006: 18) raises the following: "Once different ethnic groups have appeared within a given society, be it through conquest or other movements of population, the question arises as to their ultimate fate in relation to the majority group. Does government policy generally, and the education system in particular, work to eliminate, modify or encourage the cultural diversity they introduce?" Dowling and Flintoff (2018: 4) recognize that "Policies can change, but we also know that practice can seemingly remain the same. The crucial point is that policies are *acted* on in some way." The words of policy need to manifest into practical actions. Beaty (1995: 148) comments, "Policy-led staff development takes account of pressures from outside and from the powerful within but it does not harness and support innovation from the grass roots." At an academic level, decolonized teaching and learning would be evidenced through changes (macro and micro) to curriculum and pedagogy. What we are most used to is not necessarily what will be of most benefit. Seeking knowledge and feedback from past and present students can be invaluable in pinpointing particular strengths and areas for development. This can include exploring with students what they learned, did not learn, their lived experience, and the extent to which the program of study met their expectations.

At the heart of the decolonizing discussion is people: people's histories, whether individual, shared, or conflicting; people's experiences, the extent to which these are affected by manifestations of colonial history; people's relationships, the power dynamics which exist and are created within learning environments between and among staff and students; and how the presence of unconscious bias within us all can influence these dynamics. The importance of valuing and nurturing the relationship between people and education within a university setting should be obvious. People educate other people about different subjects within an institution. People debate and learn from one another. Without people, there would be no education, and universities would not exist. Yet, the subject of decolonizing teaching and learning calls into question the existing relationship between people and education within a university. Anthony Cullen, in his contribution in Chapter 8, similarly comments, "for decolonization to be effective—the nature of relationship between students, staff, and the institution itself needs to be taken into account."

Rather than offering up answers or resolutions, the purpose of this book has been to highlight the benefits of decolonizing teaching and learning for all staff and students and encourage discussion on the topic. By bringing together questions raised within existing scholarly discussions on decolonizing teaching and learning, the TRAAC model provides an entry point to deeper conversations by way of supporting colleagues to start a productive dialogue. The four segments and corresponding questions were discussed in greater detail in the earlier chapters of the book. This helped to explore the questions in light of decolonizing issues. The contributions spread throughout relevant chapters from colleagues holding a range of roles across different universities point to the accessibility and usability of the TRAAC model.

Users can engage with the TRAAC model in whatever way is most productive for them and their needs. Some authors engaged with the model on a personal note, while others used it to instigate conversations. Some contributors used the model to reflect more generally on decolonizing issues affecting their universities, their disciplines, or the sector more widely. While it is recommended that the model be used holistically to review core aspects of a curriculum in a connected way, individuals may choose to place emphasis on particular segments in light of specific needs at different times. This is similar to the approach Dawn Reilly describes in Chapter 8; he outlines the use of a "phased adoption" where certain segments were prioritized over the course of a program. Or as Paul Breen describes in his contribution, the model was used as an "overarching philosophical framework for decolonizing curricula." The different ways in which the TRAAC model has been employed underlines that there are no rules or instructions for how it should be accessed or approached. Through these critically reflective and reflexive conversations, action-oriented discussions can simultaneously take place.

The process of decolonizing has the potential of changing a culture of an institution. The outcomes of a university engaging authentically in the decolonizing process could be evidenced in changes to strategy, policy, institutional direction, and structural dynamics, to name some examples. This should not result in minimal amendments to policy where issues around decolonizing are tagged on as supplementary points. The decolonizing agenda should be promoted and modeled as good practice. Senior management teams need to work with academic, professional services, and technical staff if decolonizing plans are to be successfully implemented across the university. Carr (2007: 24) similarly comments, "Connecting the educational policy process with what takes place in the classroom is key to increasing the quality of the educational experience." Colleagues looking to review their teaching practice and curriculum in support of decolonizing efforts should be encouraged to share their intentions, plans, and experiences with their teams.

Any local shifts in practice toward decolonizing can have significant impact on the student learning experience. Lessons learned from what works and what does not work should be shared so that successful interventions can be scaled up more widely as appropriate. Decolonizing interventions should not be limited to one-off events or small-scale, time-limited projects. Resource, capacity, and time are needed to support staff and students to carry out long-term projects and approaches that become embedded in an institution to help achieve long-term change. Changes in staff practices can also lead to changes in communication with students. A more connected community of staff and students might be evidenced by improved student feedback and levels of engagement. For the decolonizing agenda to progress, the work toward change cannot be delegated to individuals or groups of people.

The accountability and responsibility of decolonizing work lies with us all. It requires support and engagement at all levels of the university. Without strong university-wide support, the work can become marginalized and deprioritized. "A change in culture is needed alongside a clear institutional message that issues of race will be dealt with as part of wider, strategic, organisational practice. Not as an 'add on'" (Universities UK: 2019). By being reflexive and reviewing the approaches and choices behind curriculum design and pedagogy in light of decolonizing issues, more students will be able to experience an enhanced teaching and learning environment. This will be an environment which takes into consideration their needs both within and outside of the classroom, a setting that is mindful of the multicultural society we live in and the global world in which HE operates. The decolonizing agenda offers all university stakeholders an opportunity to work together in leading the sector into another stage of development, an agenda that should appeal to anyone committed to enhancing the student experience. Without genuine support at all levels and authentic collaboration between staff and students, the decolonizing movement risks becoming a passing trend.

While more universities begin to allocate attention to the decolonizing agenda, the levels of buy-in from staff are varied. One of the reasons for this hesitancy among staff toward engaging in this area of discussion has been due to the topic being perceived as a racialized conversation and/or one that appears to be only relevant to a niche area of subjects. But as discussed in previous chapters and highlighted by the contributions in this book, decolonizing issues are relevant to everyone. This is because the decolonizing agenda looks to enhance the student experience for all. Universities will each have their own particular challenges, strengths, and contexts. Decolonizing teaching and learning should explore how the decolonizing agenda can help to address these specific challenges within one's own contextual setting. There is no one-size-fits-all solution to decolonizing a university, curriculum, campus, or classroom. The discussion is very context based; therefore, a bespoke approach to decolonizing is required for each university. While one university may struggle to resolve their BAME awarding gap, another institution may be more focused on addressing the gap between students from different socioeconomic classes. Others might need to focus more on gender-related gaps or issues relating to staff and student diversity. Discussions on decolonizing are not aimed to be divisive or increase existing tensions.

A growth in interest and action around work to decolonize teaching and learning can play a part in influencing the areas of interest for publishers too. This can lead to more research in the area, case studies being produced, alongside more critical discussion on ways of approaching and navigating discussions on decolonizing. Collaboration between academic staff and Library colleagues can help to bring together materials for a more decolonized curriculum. The work that students and staff undertake in the process of decolonizing is often evidenced through visible outputs and demonstrative examples of engagement.

Examples include demonstrations, articles, exhibitions, seminars, artwork, and videos which highlight issues around decolonizing teaching and learning. These all underline student and staff engagement with decolonizing conversations and help to increase awareness of the subject for all stakeholders.

However, when trying to evaluate the extent to which a university is successfully engaging with the decolonizing process, it is important to look beyond the products and outputs and to examine the changes that are unseen but experienced. This includes changes in attitude toward challenging conversations and more direct efforts to address issues regarding inequality at all levels. A change in university culture can also be explored in terms of the extent to which there are spaces and opportunities for students and staff to voice feelings around identity and belonging in a supportive environment that responds mindfully to concerns raised. These impacts are hard to quantify, creating challenges for institutions under constant pressure to evidence progress through metrics. But these are some of the impacts that evidence authentic and meaningful change.

Changes in support of decolonizing work may also occur at the operational level with enhanced teaching and learning practices. Longer-term changes may include a more connected staff network where all colleagues are actively playing a role to progress the decolonizing agenda within their spheres of influence. While this book is not a handbook for decolonizing, it offers an initial steer through the TRAAC model toward core areas of consideration and questions relating to decolonizing that should be interrogated. The text has been written by colleagues passionate about the subject and who have approached the conversation around decolonizing in various ways. This book raises more questions than it does suggestions, encourages further debate than it provides focus, which is reflective of the stage the sector is in regarding the decolonizing agenda. The process of decolonizing continues to be complex and disorientating. Decolonizing calls for an embracing of this discomfort as it is within this space that significant, long-lasting developmental change can occur.

References

Preface

Inc Arts UK (2020) "#BAMEOver—A Statement for the UK." Available at: https://incarts.uk/%23bameover-the-statement [Accessed: October 31, 2020].

Introduction

Archer, M.S. (2010) "Introduction: The Reflexive Re-turn," in M.S. Archer (Ed.), *Conversations About Reflexivity* (Oxon: Routledge), pp. 1–14.

Dewey, J. (1933) *How We Think: A Restatement of the Relation of Reflective Thinking to the Educative Process* (Boston, MA: D.C. Heath & Co Publishers).

Lyons, N. (2010) "Reflection and Reflective Inquiry: Critical Issues, Evolving Conceptualizations, Contemporary Claims and Future Possibilities," in N. Lyons (Ed.), *Handbook of Reflection and Reflective Inquiry: Mapping a Way of Knowing for Professional Reflective Inquiry* (London: Springer), pp. 3–24.

Moon, J.A. (2004) *Reflection in Learning and Professional Development: Theory and Practice* (Oxon: RoutledgeFalmer).

Redmond, B. (2006) *Reflection in Action: Developing Reflective Practice in Health and Social Services* (Hampshire: Ashgate Publishing Limited).

Schön, D.A. (1983) *The Reflective Practitioner: How Professionals Think in Action* (USA: Basic Books).

Chapter 1

Abdi, M. (March 27, 2020) "Decolonising Higher Education," *Decolonising Education: Let's Talk About It!*, YouTube channel. Available at: https://www.youtube.com/watch?v=2Y0eBb0UuvQ&feature=youtu.be [Accessed: May 2, 2020].

AdvanceHE (2019) "Degree Attainment Gaps." Available at: https://www.advance-he.ac.uk/guidance/equality-diversity-and-inclusion/student-recruitment-retention-and-attainment/degree-attainment-gaps [Accessed: October 12, 2019].

Aljazeera (2020) "Remembering George Floyd: Devoted Father, 'Gentle Giant.'" Available at: https://www.aljazeera.com/news/2020/05/remembering-george-floyd-devoted-father-gentle-giant-200531070908430.html [Accessed: June 26, 2020].

Aratani, L. (May 29, 2020) "George Floyd Killing: What Sparked the Protests—And What Has Been the Response?," *The Guardian*. Available at: https://www.theguardian.com/us-news/2020/may/29/george-floyd-killing-protests-police-brutality [Accessed: June 26, 2020].

BBC News England (April 23, 2020) "Coronavirus: Academic's Concerns over BAME Deaths Data." Available at: https://www.bbc.co.uk/news/uk-england-leicestershire-52366390 [Accessed: April 27, 2020].

BBC News US and Canada (June 11, 2020) "Confederate and Columbus Statues Toppled by US Protesters." Available at: https://www.bbc.co.uk/news/world-us-canada-53005243 [Accessed: August 3, 2020].

Behari-Leak, K., L. Masehela, L. Marhaya, M. Tjabane, and N. Merckel (March 9, 2017) "Decolonising the Curriculum: It's in the Detail, Not Just in the Definition." Available at: https://theconversation.com/decolonising-the-curriculum-its-in-the-detail-not-just-in-the-definition-73772 [Accessed: January 17, 2020].

Black Lives Matter: About (2020). Available at: https://blacklivesmatter.com/about/ [Accessed: June 26, 2020].

Black Lives Matter: Her Story (2021) Available at: https://blacklivesmatter.com/herstory/ [Accessed: February 5, 2021].

Breen, P. (2018) *Developing Educators for the Digital Age: A Framework for Capturing Knowledge in Action* (London: University of Westminster Press).

Brooks, R. (February 14, 2017) "Renaming University Buildings with Racist Namesakes Is an Uphill Battle," *USA Today*. Available at: https://eu.usatoday.com/story/college/2017/02/14/renaming-university-buildings-with-racist-namesakes-is-an-uphill-battle/37427429/ [Accessed: October 12, 2019].

Brosi, G. and B. hooks (Fall 2012) "The Beloved Community: A Conversation Between bell hooks and George Brosi," *Appalachian Heritage*, 40:4, pp. 76–86.

Campbell, P.I. (April 15, 2020) "Coronavirus Is Hitting BAME Communities Hard on Every Front," *The Conversation*. Available at: https://theconversation.com/coronavirus-is-hitting-bame-communities-hard-on-every-front-136327 [Accessed: April 27, 2020].

Case, K.A. (2017) "Toward an Intersectional Pedagogy Model: Engaged Learning for Social Justice," in Kim A. Case (Ed.), *Intersectional Pedagogy: Complicating Identity and Social Justice* (Oxon: Routledge), pp. 1–24.

Cole, E.R. (2017) "Foreword: Teaching Intersectionality for Our Times," in Kim A. Case (Ed.), *Intersectional Pedagogy: Complicating Identity and Social Justice* (Oxon: Routledge), pp. ix–xii.

Cotton, D.R.E., M. Joyner, R. George, and P.A. Cotton (2016) "Understanding the Gender and Ethnicity Attainment Gap in UK Higher Education," *Innovations in Education and Teaching International*, 53:5, pp. 475–86.

Crenshaw, K. (1989) "Demarginalizing the Intersection of Race and Sex: A Black Feminist Critique of Antidiscrimination Doctrine, Feminist Theory and Antiracist

Politics," *University of Chicago Legal Forum*, 1:8. Available at: http://chicagounbound.uchicago.edu/uclf/vol1989/iss1/8 [Accessed: May 4, 2020].

Davies, C.B. (2003) "Introduction: Decolonizing the Academy: Advancing the Process," in C.B. Davies, M. Gadsby, C.F. Peterson, and H. Williams (Eds.), *Decolonizing the Academy: African Diaspora Studies* (Lawrenceville, NJ: Africa World Press, Inc), pp. ix–xvi.

De Montfort University (2019) "Decolonising DMU." Available at: https://decolonisingdmu.our.dmu.ac.uk/ [Accessed: April 25, 2020].

Decolonizing SOAS Working Group (2018) "Decolonizing SOAS Learning and Teaching Toolkit for Programme and Module Convenors." Available at: https://blogs.soas.ac.uk/decolonizingsoas/files/2018/10/Decolonizing-SOAS-Learning-and-Teaching-Toolkit-AB.pdf [Accessed: October 12, 2019].

Dei, G.J.S. (2016) "Decolonizing the University: The Challenges and Possibilities of Inclusive Education," *The Journal of the Society for Socialist Studies / Revue de la Société d'études socialistes*, 11:1, pp. 23–61.

Delgado, R. and J. Stefancic (2012) *Critical Race Theory: An Introduction*, second edition (New York: New York University Press).

Dennis, C.A. (2018) "Decolonising Education: A Pedagogic Intervention," in G.K. Bhambra, D. Gebrial, and K. Nişancıoğlu (Eds.), *Decolonizing the University* (London: Pluto Press), pp. 190–207.

DiAngelo, R. (2011) "White Fragility," *International Journal of Critical Pedagogy*, 3:3, pp. 54–70.

Dixson, A.D. (Ed.) (2014) *Researching Race in Education: Policy, Practice and Qualitative Research* (Charlotte, NC: Information Age Publishing Inc.).

Dixson, A.D. and C.R. Anderson (2018) "Where Are We? Critical Race Theory in Education 20 Years Later," *Peabody Journal of Education*, 93:1, pp. 121–31.

Dumbrill, G.V. and J. Green (2008) "Indigenous Knowledge in the Social Work Academy," *Social Work Education*, 27:5, pp. 489–503.

Equality Challenge Unit (2013) *Unconscious Bias and Higher Education*. Available at: https://www.ecu.ac.uk/wp-content/uploads/2014/07/unconscious-bias-and-higher-education.pdf [Accessed: May 10, 2019].

Fanon, F. (2005) *The Wretched of the Earth* (New York: Grove).

Felix, M. and J. Friedberg (April 8, 2019) "To Decolonise the Curriculum, We Have to Decolonise Ourselves," WONKHE. Available at: https://wonkhe.com/blogs/to-decolonise-the-curriculum-we-have-to-decolonise-ourselves/ [Accessed: October 12, 2019].

Ferguson, R., Coughlan, T., Egelandsdal, K., Gaved, M., Herodotou, C., Hillaire, G., Jones, D., Jowers, I., Kukulska-Hulme, A., McAndrew, P., Misiejuk, K., Ness, I.J., Rienties, B., Scanlon, E., Sharples, M., Wasson, B., Weller, M., and Whitelock, D. (2019) "Innovating Pedagogy 2019: Open University Innovation Report 7" (Milton Keynes: The Open University).

Fihlani, P. (April 30, 2019) "We Are Students Thanks to South Africa's #FeesMustFall protests," *BBC World News: Africa*. Available at: https://www.bbc.co.uk/news/world-africa-47952787 [Accessed: October 25, 2019].

Fomunyam, K.G. (2017) "Decolonising the Engineering Curriculum in a South African University of Technology," *International Journal of Applied Engineering Research*, 12:17, pp. 6797–805.

Frankenberg, R. (1993) *The Social Construction of Whiteness: White Women, Race Matters* (Minneapolis: University of Minnesota Press).

Gebrial, D. (2018) "Rhodes Must Fall: Oxford and Movements for Change," in G.K. Bhambra, D. Gebrial, and K. Nişancıoğlu (Eds.), *Decolonizing the University* (London: Pluto Press), pp. 19–36.

Gopal, P. (2017) "Yes, We Must Decolonise: Our Teaching Has to Go Beyond Elite White Men," *The Guardian*, October 27, 2017. Available at: https://www.theguardian.com/commentisfree/2017/oct/27/decolonise-elite-white-mendecolonising-cambridge-university-english-curriculum-literature [Accessed: October 31, 2018].

Guess, T.J. (2006) "The Social Construction of Whiteness: Racism by Intent, Racism by Consequence," *Critical Sociology*, 32:4, pp. 649–73.

Icaza, R. and R. Vázquez (2018) "Diversity or Decolonization? Researching Diversity at the University of Amsterdam," in G.K. Bhambra, D. Gebrial, and K. Nişancıoğlu (Eds.), *Decolonizing the University* (London: Pluto Press), pp. 108–28.

Haffner, D. (March 20, 2018) "Contesting Coloniality in International Relations' Reading Lists," The London School of Economics and Political Science: Department of International Relations blog. Available at: https://blogs.lse.ac.uk/internationalrelations/2018/03/20/contesting-coloniality-in-international-relations-reading-lists/ [Accessed: October 24, 2019].

Harris, C.I. (1995) "Whiteness as Property," in K. Crenshaw, K., N. Gotanda, G. Peller, and K. Thomas (Eds.), *Critical Race Theory: The Key Writings that Formed the Movement* (New York: New York Press), pp. 276–91.

Higher Education Policy Institute (July 23, 2020) "New Report Calls for the Decolonisation of Universities in Order Address a 'Silent Crisis.'" Available at: https://www.hepi.ac.uk/2020/07/23/new-report-calls-for-decolonisation-of-universities-in-order-address-the-silent-crisis-in-universities/ [Accessed: July 28, 2020].

hooks, B. (2003) *Teaching Community: A Pedagogy of Hope* (London: Routledge).

Joseph, D.T.R. (2010) "Decolonising the Curriculum; Transforming the University: A Discursive Perspective." Available at: https://www.dut.ac.za/wp-content/uploads/2017/03/T-JOSEPH.pdf [Accessed: October 26, 2019].

Keele University (2019) "Keele Decolonizing the Curriculum Network." Available at: https://www.keele.ac.uk/equalitydiversity/equalityawards/raceequalitycharter/keeledecolonizingthecurriculumnetwork/#keele-manifesto-for-decolonizing-the-curriculum [Accessed: October 12, 2019].

Khader, S.J. (2019) *Decolonizing Universalism: A Transnational Feminist Ethic* (New York: Oxford University Press).

Khan, O. (April 20, 2020) "Coronavirus Exposes How Riddled Britain Is with Racial Inequality," *The Guardian*. Available at: https://www.theguardian.com/commentisfree/2020/apr/20/coronavirus-racial-inequality-uk-housing-employment-health-bame-covid-19 [Accessed: April 27, 2020].

Ladson-Billings, G. and W.F. Tate IV (1995) "Toward a Critical Race Theory of Education," *Teachers College Record*, 97:1, pp. 47–68.

Lander, V. and N. Santoro (2017) "Invisible and Hypervisible Academics: The Experiences of Black and Minority Ethnic Teacher Educators," *Teaching in Higher Education*, 22:8, pp. 1008–21.

Lau, J. (March 23, 2020) "Coronavirus Sparks a Rising Tide of Xenophobia Worldwide," *Times Higher Education*. Available at: https://www.timeshighereducation.com/news/coronavirus-sparks-rising-tide-ofxenophobia-worldwide [Accessed: April 27, 2020].

Leeds University Union (2015) "Why Is My Curriculum White?; The Campaign So Far." Available at: https://www.luu.org.uk/news/archive/why-is-my-curriculum-white-the-campaign-so-far/ [Accessed: October 27, 2019].

Leonardo, Z. (2013) "The Story of Schooling: Critical Race Theory and the Educational Racial Contract," *Discourse: Studies in the Cultural Politics of Education*, 34:4, pp. 599–610, DOI: 10.1080/01596306.2013.822624.

Liyanage, M. (2020) "Miseducation: Decolonising Curricula, Culture and Pedagogy in UK Universities." Available at: https://www.hepi.ac.uk/wp-content/uploads/2020/07/HEPI_Miseducation_Debate-Paper-23_FINAL.pdf [Accessed: July 28, 2020].

Lorde, A. (1984) "Age, Race, Class and Sex: Women Redefining Difference," in *Sister Outsider: Essays and Speeches* (Freedom, CA: Crossing Press, 1984), pp. 114–23.

Lorde, A. (1984) "The Master's Tools Will Never Dismantle the Master's House," *Sister Outsider: Essays and Speeches* (Berkeley: Crossing Press), pp. 110–14. 2007. Print. Available at: https://theanarchistlibrary.org/library/audre-lorde-the-master-s-tools-will-never-dismantle-the-master-s-house.a4.pdf [Accessed: January 25, 2020].

Mahdawi, A. (June 6, 2020) "We Must Keep Fighting for Justice for Breonna Taylor. We Must Keep Saying Her Name," *The Guardian*. Available at: https://www.theguardian.com/commentisfree/2020/jun/06/we-must-keep-fighting-justice-breonna-taylor-say-her-name [Accessed: June 26, 2020].

Massey, N. and A. Makoni (April 21, 2020) "Coronavirus Disproportionately Affecting BAME Communities in UK, New Figures Show," Independent. Available at: https://www.independent.co.uk/news/uk/home-news/coronavirus-bame-communities-deaths-infections-uk-statistics-a9475406.html [Accessed: April 27, 2020].

Matebeni, Z. (February 19, 2018) "#RhodesMustFall—It Was Never Just About the Statue," *Heinrich Böll Stiftung Cape Town*. Available at: https://za.boell.org/2018/02/19/rhodesmustfall-it-was-never-just-about-statue [Accessed: October 12, 2019].

McKie, A. (May 7, 2020) "Chinese Students in UK 'Report Increased Racism and Discrimination,'" *Times Higher Education*. Available at: https://www.timeshighereducation.com/news/chinese-students-uk-report-increased-racism-and-discrimination [Accessed: June 27, 2020].

McLaughlin, J.M. and S.L. Whatman (2011) "The Potential of Critical Race Theory in Decolonizing University Curricula," *Asia Pacific Journal of Education*, 31:4, pp. 365–77.

Meda, L. (2019) "Decolonising the Curriculum: Students' Perspectives," *Africa Education Review*, DOI: 10.1080/18146627.2018.1519372.

Mgqwashu, E. (August 22, 2016) "Universities Can't Decolonise the Curriculum Without Defining It First," *The Conversation*. Available at: https://theconversation.com/universities-cant-decolonise-the-curriculum-without-defining-it-first-63948 [Accessed: October 8, 2019].

Miller, M. (April 2016) "The Ethnicity Attainment Gap: Literature Review," The University of Sheffield. Widening Participation Research and Evaluation Unit. Available at: https://www.sheffield.ac.uk/polopoly_fs/1.661523!/file/BME_Attainment_Gap_Literature_Review:EXTERNAL_-_Miriam_Miller.pdf [Accessed: October 12, 2019].

Morgan, H. and A.M. Houghton (2011), "Inclusive Curriculum Design in Higher Education: Considerations for Effective Practice across and within Subject Areas," The Higher Education Academy. Available at: https://s3.eu-west-2.amazonaws.com/assets.creode.advancehe-document-manager/documents/hea/private/resources/introduction_and_overview:1568037036.pdf [Accessed: October 8, 2019].

Namakkal, J. (June 26, 2015) "Re-Naming as Decolonization," *Counterpunch*. Available at: https://www.counterpunch.org/2015/06/26/re-naming-as-decolonization/ [Accessed: October 12, 2019].

Ndebele, N.S. (September 14, 2016) "They Are Burning Memory," 10th Annual Helen Joseph Lecture. Available at: http://www.crassh.cam.ac.uk/assets/general/Njabulo Ndebele_They_Are_Burning_Memory_HelenJoseph_Lecture_2016.pdf [Accessed: October 12, 2019].

Oladimeji, M. (2018) "Using Arts-Based Learning as a Site of Critical Resistance," in N.N. Wane and K.L. Todd (Eds.), *Decolonial Pedagogy: Examining Sites of Resistance, Resurgence, and Renewal* (Basingstoke, UK: Palgrave Macmillan), pp. 93–112.

Patel, A.D. (April 4, 2019) "UCT to Rename More Buildings," *Mail & Guardian*. Available at: https://mg.co.za/article/2019-04-04-uct-to-rename-more-buildings [Accessed: October 12, 2019].

Pete, S. (2018) "Meschachakanis, a Coyote Narrative: Decolonizing Higher Education," in G.K. Bhambra, D. Gebrial, and K. Nişancıoğlu (Eds.), *Decolonizing the University* (London: Pluto Press), pp. 173–89.

Pirbhai-Illich, F., S. Pete, and F. Martin (2017) "Part I 1: Culturally Responsive Pedagogy: Working Towards Decolonization, Indigeneity and Interculturalism," in F. Pirbhai-Illich, S. Pete, and F. Martin (Eds.), *Culturally Responsive Pedagogy: Working Towards Decolonization, Indigeneity and Interculturalism* (Switzerland: Palgrave Macmillan), pp. 3–28.

Quijano, A. (2000) "Coloniality of Power, Eurocentrism, and Latin America," *Nepantla: Views from South* 1.3. Available at: https://www.decolonialtranslation.com/english/quijano-coloniality-of-power.pdf [Accessed: November 3, 2019].

Rawlinson, K. (January 29, 2016), "Cecil Rhodes Statue to Remain at Oxford after 'Overwhelming Support'," *The Guardian*. Available at: https://www.theguardian.com/education/2016/jan/28/cecil-rhodes-statue-will-not-be-removed--oxford-university [Accessed: October 12, 2019].

Rea, N. (June 10, 2020) "Protests Targeting Colonial Statues in the UK and Belgium Have Ignited a Long-Brewing Reckoning Over Racist Monuments in Europe." Available at: https://news.artnet.com/art-world/monuments-uk-belgium-1883412 [Accessed: August 3, 2020].

Reality Check Team (June 3, 2020) "George Floyd Death: How Many Black People Die in Police Custody in England and Wales?," *BBC News*. Available at: https://www.bbc.co.uk/news/52890363 [Accessed: June 26, 2020].

Reilly, D., and D. Tran (2019), "Extending Conversations About What an Inclusive Curriculum Is," *Educational Developments*, SEDA, 20:4, pp. 23–5.

Rhodes, C. (1877) "Confession of Faith," in John E. Flint (1974), *Cecil Rhodes* (Little Brown, 1974), pp. 248–52 cited in "Cecil John Rhodes (1853–1902)," Oriel College University of Oxford. Available at: https://www.oriel.ox.ac.uk/cecil-john-rhodes-1853-1902 [Accessed: September 24, 2019].

Ridgwell, H. (June 15, 2020) "Oxford 'Rhodes Must Fall' Protests Reignited as Racial Tensions Rise in Britain," VOA. Available at: https://www.voanews.com/episode/oxford-rhodes-must-fall-protests-reignited-racial-tensions-rise-britain-4324731 [Accessed: June 26, 2020].

Rollock, N. and Gillborn, D. (2011) "Critical Race Theory (CRT)," *British Educational Research Association Online Resource*. Available at: https://www.bera.ac.uk/publication/critical-race-theory-crt [Accessed: October 28, 2019].

Shades of Noir. Available at: https://shadesofnoir.org.uk/about-shades-of-noir/ [Accessed: May 1, 2020].

Shay, S. (June 13, 2016) "Decolonising the Curriculum: It's Time for a Strategy," *The Conversation*. Available at: https://theconversation.com/decolonising-the-curriculum-its-time-for-a-strategy-60598 [Accessed: October 12, 2019].

Simpson, I. (April 18, 2017) "Georgetown University Renames Buildings to Atone for Slavery Ties," *Reuters*. Available at: https://www.reuters.com/article/us-washingtondc-georgetown-slavery/georgetown-university-renames-buildings-to-atone-for-slavery-ties-idUSKBN17K2AR [Accessed: October 12, 2019].

South African History Online (March 9, 2015), "Chumani Maxwele Ignites the #RhodesMustFall Movement at UCT." Available at: https://www.sahistory.org.za/dated-event/chumani-maxwele-ignites-rhodesmustfall-movement-uct [Accessed: October 12, 2019].

Stovall, D. (2005) "Critical Race Theory as Educational Protest," in W.H. Watkins (Ed.), *Black Protest Thought and Education* (Oxford: Peter Lang Publishing), pp. 197–212.

Students Union UCL, "Decolonise UCL." Created: November 29, 2017. Available at: http://studentsunionucl.org/make-change/what-were-working-on-0/decolonise-ucl [Accessed: October 26, 2019].

Tajudeen, B. (2016) "Is UAL Too White?," *Artefact*. Available: https://www.artefact magazine.com/2016/06/21/is-ual-too-white/ [Accessed: May 1, 2020].

Thomas, L. and H. May (2010) "Inclusive Learning and Teaching in Higher Education," *Advance HE*. Available at: https://s3.eu-west-2.amazonaws.com/assets.creode.advanc ehe-document-manager/documents/hea/private/inclusivelearningandteaching_fin alreport_1568036778.pdf [Accessed: October 12, 2019].

Tran, D. (2019) "Why We Shouldn't Shy Away from Discussions Around Decolonising Curricula," *Compass: Journal of Learning and Teaching*, 12:1. https://journals.gre.ac.u k/index.php/compass/article/view/882.

Tuck, E. and K.W. Yang (2012), "Decolonization Is Not a Metaphor," *Decolonization: Indigeneity, Education & Society*, 1:1, pp. 1–40.

UAL So White (2015) Twitter account. Available at: https://twitter.com/occupyual?lang =en-gb [Accessed: May 1, 2020].

University College London (November 11, 2014) "Why Is My Curriculum White?." Available at: https://www.youtube.com/watch?v=Dscx4h2l-Pk [Accessed: October 27, 2019].

University of Arts London: Arts Student Union and UAL Teaching, Learning and Employability Exchange co-production (2018) *Decolonising the Arts Curriculum: Perspectives on Higher Education*. Available at: https://decolonisingtheartscurriculum .myblog.arts.ac.uk/ [Accessed: April 4, 2020].

University of Arts London (2020) UAL Decolonising Arts Institute. Available at: https:// www.arts.ac.uk/ual-decolonising-arts-institute [Accessed: April 4, 2020].

University of Sussex Students' Union (2019) "Decolonize Sussex." Available at: https:// www.sussexstudent.com/campaigns/decolonize-education/ [Accessed: October 12, 2019].

Universities UK and National Union of Students (May 2019) "Black, Asian and Minority Ethnic Student Attainment at UK Universities: #Closingthegap." Available at: https://www.universitiesuk.ac.uk/policy-and-analysis/reports/Documents/2019 /bame-student-attainment-uk-universities-closing-the-gap.pdf [Accessed: October 12, 2019].

Wall, T. (June 14, 2020) "The Day Bristol Dumped Its Hated Slave Trader in the Docks and a Nation Began to Search Its Soul." Available at: https://www.theguardian.com/ uk-news/2020/jun/14/the-day-bristol-dumped-its-hated-slave-trader-in-the-docks -and-a-nation-began-to-search-its-soul [Accessed: August 3, 2020].

Warwick Open Education Series (March 3, 2015) "Why Is My Curriculum White?." Speakers: Adam Elliott-Cooper and Malia Bouattia. Available at: https://warwick.ac .uk/services/library/mrc/eventsandseries/openeducationseries/2015/curriculumw hite/ [Accessed: October 12, 2019].

Wen, J., J. Aston, X. Liu and T. Ying (2020) "Effects of Misleading Media Coverage on Public Health Crisis: A Case of the 2019 Novel Coronavirus Outbreak in China," *Anatolia*, pp. 1–6. Available at: https://doi.org/10.1080/13032917.2020.1730621 [Accessed: April 27, 2020].

WHO (27 April 020) "WHO Timeline—COVID-19." Available at: https://www.who.int/news-room/detail/27-04-2020-who-timeline---covid-19 [Accessed: April 27, 2020].

Wray, M. (2013) "Developing an Inclusive Culture in Higher Education: Final Report," *Advance HE*. Available at: https://s3.eu-west-2enga.amazonaws.com/assets.creode.advancehe-document-manager/documents/hea/private/inclusive_culture_report_0_1 568037054.pdf [Accessed: October 12, 2019].

Chapter 2

Ahmed, S. (2012) *On Being Included: Racism and Diversity in Institutional Life* (London: Duke University Press).

Andresen, L. (1995) "Accredited Courses in Teaching and Learning," in A. Brew (Ed.), *Directions in Staff Development* (Buckingham: The Society for Research into Higher Education and Open University Press), pp. 36–50.

Ashlee, A.A., B. Zamora, and S.N. Karikari (2017) "We Are Woke: A Collaborative Critical Autoethnography of Three 'Womxn' of Colour Graduate Students in Higher Education," *International Journal of Multicultural Education*, 19:1, pp. 89–104.

Blackwell, R. and P. Blackmore (2003a) "Preface," in R. Blackwell and P. Blackmore (Eds.), *Towards Strategic Staff Development in Higher Education* (Berkshire: SRHE and Open University Press), pp. xii–xv.

Blackwell, R., and P. Blackmore (2003b) "Academic Roles and Relationships," in R. Blackwell and P. Blackmore (Eds.), *Towards Strategic Staff Development in Higher Education* (Berkshire: SRHE and Open University Press), pp. 16–28.

Bovill, C., A. Cook-Sather, P. Felten, L. Millard, and N. Moore-Cherry (2016) "Addressing Potential Challenges in Co-creating Learning and Teaching: Overcoming Resistance, Navigating Institutional Norms and Ensuring Inclusivity in Student-Staff Partnerships," *High Education*, 71, pp. 195–208.

Currens, J.B. (2011) "How Might the Student Voice Affect Transformation in Higher Education," in G. Czerniawski and W. Kidd (Eds.), *The Student Voice Handbook: Bridging the Academic/Practitioner Divide* (Bingley: Emerald Group Publishing Limited), pp. 185–96.

Decolonizing SOAS Working Group (2018) "Decolonizing SOAS Learning and Teaching Toolkit for Programme and Module Convenors." Available at: https://blogs.soas.ac.uk/decolonizingsoas/files/2018/10/Decolonizing-SOAS-Learning-and-Teaching-Toolkit-AB.pdf [Accessed: October 12, 2019].

Doharty, N., M. Madriaga, and R. Joseph-Salisbury (2020) "The University Went to 'Decolonise' and All They Brought Back Was Lousy Diversity Double-Speak! Critical Race Counter-Stories from Faculty of Colour in 'Decolonial' Times," *Educational Philosophy and Theory*. DOI: 10.1080/00131857.2020.1769601.

Fung, D. and B. Carnell (2017) "Editor's Introduction, Developing the Higher Education Curriculum: Research-Based Education in Practice," in D. Fung and B. Carnell (Eds.), *Developing the Higher Education Curriculum: Research-Based Education in Practice* (London: UCL Press), pp. 1–12.

Grierson, J. (September 16, 2019) "Prevent Review Branded 'Superficial' as Past Decisions Overlooked," *The Guardian*. Available at: https://www.theguardian.com/uk-news/2019/sep/16/prevent-review-branded-superficial-as-past-decisions-overlooked [Accessed: June 26, 2020].

HEA (2013) "Fellowship of the Higher Education Academy: Code of Practice." Available at: https://www.heacademy.ac.uk/system/files/downloads/Code_Of_Practice_0.pdf [Accessed: April 20, 2020].

Johnston, L. (2019) "What Is Continuing Professional Development (CPD)?," jobs.ac.uk careers advice. Available at: https://career-advice.jobs.ac.uk/default/what-is-continuing-professional-development-cpd/ [Accessed: October 15, 2019].

Kupatadze, K. (2018) "Course Redesign with Student-Faculty Partnership: A Reflection on Opportunities and Vulnerabilities," *Teaching and Learning Together in Higher Education*, Issue 24. Available at: https://repository.brynmawr.edu/tlthe/vol1/iss24/2 [Accessed: May 15, 2020].

Le Grange, L. (2016) "Decolonising the University Curriculum," *South African Journal of Higher Education*, 30:2, pp. 1–12.

McGregor, H.E. (2012) "Decolonizing Pedagogies Teacher Reference Booklet," Service Project For: Aboriginal Focus School, Vancouver School Board. Available at: http://blogs.ubc.ca/edst591/files/2012/03/Decolonizing_Pedagogies_Booklet.pdf [Accessed: October 21, 2019].

Miller, M. (April 2016) "The Ethnicity Attainment Gap: Literature Review," The University of Sheffield. Widening Participation Research and Evaluation Unit. Available at: https://www.sheffield.ac.uk/polopoly_fs/1.661523!/file/BME_Attainment_Gap_Literature_Review:EXTERNAL_-_Miriam_Miller.pdf [Accessed: October 12, 2019].

Niculescu, I.O, S. Nagpal, and R. Rees (2020) "Creating Space for New Expertise: Considerations for Setting-Up Student-Staff Partnerships," in K. Gravett, N. Yakovchuk, and I.M. Kinchin (Eds.), *Enhancing Student-Centred Teaching in Higher Education: The Landscape of Student-Staff Research Partnerships* (Switzerland: Palgrave Macmillan), pp. 329–46.

Office for Students (2020) "Counter-Terrorism—The Prevent Duty." Available at: https://www.officeforstudents.org.uk/advice-and-guidance/student-wellbeing-and-protection/counter-terrorism-the-prevent-duty/ [Accessed: June 26, 2020].

O'Mahony, J. (July 9, 2019) "Building Inclusivity: Opportunities and Obstacles," Bridging the Inclusivity Gap, 9th Teaching and Learning Conference, Bloomsbury Institute.

Parsons, D., I. Hill, J. Holland, and D. Willis (2012) "Impact of Teaching Development Programmes in Higher Education," The Higher Education Academy. Available at:

https://s3.eu-west-2.amazonaws.com/assets.creode.advancehe-document-manager/documents/hea/private/resources/hea_impact_teaching_development_prog_15680 36615.pdf [Accessed: October 16, 2019].

Prevent Strategy (June 7, 2011) Policy Paper. Available at: https://www.gov.uk/government/publications/prevent-strategy-2011 [Accessed: June 26, 2020].

Prosser, M. and K. Trigwell (1999) *Understanding Learning and Teaching: The Experience in Higher Education* (The Society for Research into Higher Education and Open University Press: Buckingham).

Quinn, L. and J. Vorster (2017) "Connected Disciplinary Responses to the Call to Decolonise Curricula in South African Higher Education," in B. Carnell and D. Fung (Eds.), *Developing the Higher Education Curriculum: Research-Based Education in Practice* (London: UCL Press), pp. 131–44.

Ramaswamy, C. (2019) "The More the Word 'Woke' Is Used as a Slur and a Joke, the More We Need It," *The Guardian*. Available at: https://www.theguardian.com/lifeandstyle/2019/mar/04/chitra-ramaswamy-the-more-woke-is-used-as-a-joke-and-slur-the-more-we-need-it [Accessed: January 25, 2020].

Rogers, A. (1988) *Teaching Adults* (Milton Keynes: Open University Press).

Sisters of Resistance, Left of Brown, and Jenny Rodriguez (July 12, 2018) "Is Decolonizing the New Black?." Available at: https://sistersofresistance.wordpress.com/2018/07/12/is-decolonizing-the-new-black/ [Accessed: May 2, 2020].

Sociological Review Podcast (February 11, 2020) "Decolonising Methodologies, 20 Years On: An Interview with Professor Linda Tuhiwai Smith." Available at: https://www.thesociologicalreview.com/decolonising-methodologies-20-years-on-an-interview-with-professor-linda-tuhiwai-smith/ [Accessed: May 3, 2020].

Staples, L. (December 8, 2018) "Even for Young, Socially Aware Readers, There Is such a Thing as Too Woke," *Independent*. Available at: https://www.independent.co.uk/voices/wokeness-pc-minorities-left-wing-snowflake-campaign-brand-baby-its-cold-outside-ariana-grande-latest-a8673691.html [Accessed: January 25, 2020].

Stevenson, J., J. O'Mahony, O. Khan, F. Ghaffar, and B. Stiell (February 2019) "Understanding and Overcoming the Challenges of Targeting Students from Under-Represented and Disadvantaged Ethnic Backgrounds Guidance for Institutional Success: Access and Participation Practitioners," *The Office for Students*. Available at: https://www.officeforstudents.org.uk/media/0a6d56c9-9fe4-40af-a1f3-14fe5154 76d6/ethnicity-targeting-guidance-and-case-studies_.pdf [Accessed: October 12, 2019].

The CPD Certification Service (2019), CPD Explained. Available at: https://cpduk.co.uk/explained [Accessed: October 15, 2019].

Thomas, D. (2018) "Equality, Diversity, Inclusivity, Internationalisation: Institutional Inertia to Curriculum Decolonisation," Doing Diversity: "Decolonising" the Social Scientific Study of Religion, British Sociological Association Sociology of Religion Study Group (SocRel) Annual Response Day, November 21, 2018.

Thompson, F. (June 27, 2019) "Prevent: Government's Counterterrorism Programme Is 'Single Biggest Threat' to Free Speech at Universities, Report Finds," *Independent*. Available at: https://www.independent.co.uk/news/uk/home-news/prevent-free-speech-counter-terrorism-university-campus-hepi-home-office-a8976236.html [Accessed: June 26, 2020].

Trowell, M. (December 2019) "I Am Other: The Meeting of Two Cultures and a Widening Participation Perspective," in M. Moncrieffe, Y. Asare, R. Dunford, and H. Youssef (Eds.), *Decolonising the Curriculum: Teaching and Learning about Race Equality*, Issue 2, pp. 20–1.

Versi, M. (2015) Muslim Council of Britain, Meeting between David Anderson QC and the MCB, Concerns on Prevent. Available at: https://www.mcb.org.uk/wp-content/uploads/2015/10/20150803-Case-studies-about-Prevent.pdf [Accessed: June 26, 2020].

Bernadine Idowu-Onibokun's Contribution

Cureton, D. (2012) "Disparities in Student Attainment (DISA) Briefing Paper 6, The Power of the Teacher-Student Relationship," University of Wolverhampton and Higher Education Academy.

Griffiths, D.E. (2015) "What's 'Black' Got to Do with It: An Analysis of Low-Income Black Students and Educational Outcomes," CUNY Academic Works.

Healy, M., K.M. O'connor, and P. Broadfoot (2010) "Reflections on Engaging Students in the Process of Learning Teaching and Assessment: An Institutional Case Study," *International Journal for Academic Development*, 15:1, pp. 19–32.

Idowu-Onibokun, B. (2017) "Hidden Figures Is Just the Start—Here's How to Inspire More Black Scientists?" *The Guardian*. Available at: www.theguardian.com/commentisfree/2017/feb/24/hidden-figures-tommorrow-black-scientists-education [Accessed: April 28, 2020].

Idowu-Onibokun (March 7, 2018) "Who Can Save the Post-Brexit Economy? Black Professors," *The Guardian*. Available at: https://www.theguardian.com/commentisfree/2018/mar/07/brexit-economy-black-professors-minority-ethnic / [Accessed: April 28, 2020].

Idowu, B., M. Al-Adnani, P. O'Donnell, L. Yu, E. Odell, T. Diss, R.E. Gale, and A.M. Flanagan (2007), "A Sensitive Mutation-Specific Screening Technique for GNAS1 Mutations in Cases of Fibrous Dysplasia: The First Report of a Codon 227 Mutation in Bone," *Histopathology*, May 50:6, pp. 691–704.

Office for Students (2020). Available at: https://www.officeforstudents.org.uk/ [Accessed: April 28, 2020].

Oldham, S. and J. Dhillion (2012), "Disparities in Student Attainment DISA Briefing Paper 12," *Student Voices: Perceptions of Learning Assignments and Achievement*, University of Wolverhampton and Higher Education Academy.

Opara, E. (1997) "The Transformation of My Science Identity," in D. Gabriel and S.H. Tate (Eds.), *Inside the Ivory Tower: Narratives of Women of Colour Surviving and Thriving in British Academia* (London: Trenthem Books), pp. 124–35.

Peters, M.A. (2015) "Why Is My Curriculum White?," *Educational Philosophy and Theory*, 47:7, pp. 641–6.

Smith, J. (2017) "Exploring the Black and Minority Ethnic (BME) Student Attainment Gap: What Did It Tell Us? Actions to Address Home BME Undergraduate Students' Degree Attainment," *Journal of Perspectives in Applied Academic Practice*, 5:1, pp. 48–57.

The National Archives (2020) "UK Government Web Archive Timeline." Available at: https://webarchive.nationalarchives.gov.uk/*/http:/www.hefce.ac.uk/ [Accessed: April 27, 2020].

Wilson, M. (1997) "The Search for That Elusive Sense of Belonging, Respect and Visibility in Academia," in D. Gabriel and S.H. Tate (Eds.), *Inside the Ivory Tower: Narratives of Women of Colour Surviving and Thriving in British Academia* (London: Trenthem Books), pp. 108–23.

Chapter 3

Adams, R. (September 7, 2018) "UK Universities Making Slow Progress on Equality, Data Shows," *The Guardian*. Available at: https://www.theguardian.com/education/2018/sep/07/uk-university-professors-black-minority-ethnic [Accessed: November 4, 2019].

Akel, S. (October 2019) "Insider-Outsider: The Role of Race in Shaping the Experiences of Black and Minority Ethnic Students," Goldsmiths University of London. Available at: https://www.gold.ac.uk/media/docs/reports/Insider-Outsider-Report-191008.pdf [Accessed: November 8, 2019].

Balhara, Y.P.S. (2012) "Indexed Journal: What Does It Mean?," *Lung India*, April–June, 29:2, p. 193.

Bisht, P. (December 2017) "Decolonizing Futures: Exploring Storytelling as a Tool for Inclusion in Foresight," Submitted to OCAD University in partial fulfilment of the requirements for the degree of Master of Design in Strategic Foresight & Innovation Toronto, ON, Canada. Available at: http://openresearch.ocadu.ca/id/eprint/2129/1/Bisht_Pupul_2017_MDES_SFI_MRP.pdf [Accessed: January 16, 2020].

Cotton, D., J. Winter, and I. Bailey (2013) "Researching the Hidden Curriculum: Intentional and Unintended Messages," *Journal of Geography in Higher Education*, 37:2, pp. 192–203.

Chadderton, C. (2011) "Not Capturing Voices: A Poststructural Critique of the Privileging of Voice in Research," in G. Czerniawski and W. Kidd (Eds.), *The Student Voice Handbook: Bridging the Academic/Practitioner Divide* (Bingley: Emerald Group Publishing Limited), pp. 73–86.

Coughlan, S. (2018) "University Racism 'Complacency' Warning," *BBC News*. Available at: https://www.bbc.co.uk/news/education-44125777 [Accessed: November 4, 2019].

Dean, B., and R. Joldoshalieva (2007) "Key Strategies for Teachers New to Controversial Issues," in H. Claire and C. Holden (Eds.), *The Challenge of Teaching Controversial Issues* (Stoke on Trent: Trentham Books).

Decolonizing SOAS Working Group (2018) "Decolonizing SOAS Learning and Teaching Toolkit for Programme and Module Convenors." Available at: https://blogs.soas.ac.uk/decolonizingsoas/files/2018/10/Decolonizing-SOAS-Learning-and-Teaching-Toolkit-AB.pdf [Accessed: October 12, 2019].

Dennis, C.A. (2018) "Decolonising Education: A Pedagogic Intervention," in G.K. Bhambra, D. Gebrial, and K. Nişancıoğlu (Eds.), *Decolonizing the University* (London: Pluto Press), pp. 190–207.

Dhammi, I.K. and R.U. Haq (2016) "What Is Indexing" *Indian Journal of Orthopaedics*, March–April, 50:2, pp. 115–16.

Dumbrill, G.C. and J. Green (2008) "Indigenous Knowledge in the Social Work Academy," *Social Work Education*, 27:5, pp. 489–503.

Dunham, J., and D. Tran (May 2019) "The Forgotten Stage of Designing Curricula," SEDA blog: Supporting and Leading Educational Change Available at: https://thesedablog.wordpress.com/2019/05/16/danielletran-2/ [Accessed: November 10, 2019].

Fomunyam, K.G. (2017) "Decolonising the Engineering Curriculum in a South African University of Technology," *International Journal of Applied Engineering Research*, 12:17, pp. 6797–805.

Gebrial, D. (2018) "Rhodes Must Fall: Oxford and Movements for Change," in G.K. Bhambra, D. Gebrial, and K. Nişancıoğlu (Eds.), *Decolonizing the University* (London: Pluto Press), 19–36.

Harden, R.M. and J.M. Laidlaw (2012) *Essential Skills for a Medical Teacher E-Book: An Introduction to Teaching and Learning in Medicine* (London: Churchill Livingstone Elsevier).

Icaza, R. and R. Vázquez (2018) "Diversity or Decolonization? Researching Diversity at the University of Amsterdam," in G.K. Bhambra, D. Gebrial, and K. Nişancıoğlu (Eds.), *Decolonizing the University* (London: Pluto Press), pp. 108–28.

Istratii, R. and M. Hirmer (2020) "Decolonial Subversions." Available at: https://soas.hosted.panopto.com/Panopto/Pages/Viewer.aspx?id=fb415194-f702-4fb4-bde3-ab8a010f4179 [Accessed: May 16, 2020].

La Belle, T.J. and C.R. Ward (1994) *Multiculturalism and Education: Diversity and Its Impact on Schools and Society* (Albany: State University of New York Press).

Leibowitz, B. (2017) "Cognitive Justice and the Higher Education Curriculum," *Journal of Education*, issue 68, pp. 93–112.

Lusted, D. (September 1, 1986) "Why Pedagogy?," *Screen*, 27:5, pp. 2–16. Available at: https://doi.org/10.1093/screen/27.5.2 [Accessed: October 28, 2019].

Mbembe, A. (2015) "Decolonizing Knowledge and the Question of the Archive." Available at: https://wiser.wits.ac.za/system/files/Achille%20Mbembe%20-%20Decolonizing%20Knowledge%20and%20the%20Question%20of%20the%20Archive.pdf [Accessed: November 10, 2019].

Meda, L. (2019) "Decolonising the Curriculum: Students' Perspectives," *Africa Education Review*, DOI: 10.1080/18146627.2018.1519372.

Morreira, S. and K. Luckett (2018) "Questions Academics Can Ask to Decolonise Their Classrooms," *The Conversation*. Available at: https://theconversation.com/questions-academics-can-ask-to-decolonise-their-classrooms-103251 [Accessed: April 25, 2020].

Portelli, J.P. (1993) "Exposing the Hidden Curriculum," *Journal of Curriculum Studies*, 25:4, pp. 343–58.

Provenzo Jr., E.F. (2009) "Encyclopedia of the Social and Cultural Foundations of Education: Hidden and Null Curriculum," SAGE publications Inc. DOI: http://dx.doi.org/10.4135/9781412963992.n185 [Accessed: November 12, 2019].

Regan, P. (2010) *Unsettling the Settler Within: Indian Residential Schools, Truth Telling, and Reconciliation in Canada* (Vancouver: UBC Press).

Rehman, R. (March 24, 2019) "Universities Are Still Leaving BAME Students Behind—And the Problem Goes Beyond Oxbridge," *Independent*. Available at: https://www.independent.co.uk/voices/universities-bame-students-inequality-oxbridge-race-a8837771.html [Accessed: November 4, 2019].

Sabaratnam, M. (January 18, 2017) "Decolonising the Curriculum: What's All the Fuss About?," Decolonising SOAS. Available at: https://blogs.soas.ac.uk/decolonisingsoas/2017/01/18/decolonising-the-curriculum-whats-all-the-fuss-about/ [Accessed: April 25, 2020].

Sambell, K. and L. McDowell (1998) "The Construction of the Hidden Curriculum: Messages and Meanings in the Assessment of Student Learning," *Assessment & Evaluation in Higher Education*, 23:4, pp. 391–402.

Shilliam, R. (2018) "Black/Academia," in G.K. Bhambra, D. Gebrial, and K. Nişancıoğlu (Eds.), *Decolonizing the University* (London: Pluto Press), pp. 53–63.

Sium, A. and E. Ritskes (2013) "Speaking Truth to Power: Indigenous Storytelling as an Act of Living Resistance," *Decolonization: Indigeneity, Education & Society*, 2:1, pp. I–X.

Smith, L.T. (2012) *Decolonizing Methodologies: Research and Indigenous Peoples*, Second edition (London: Zed Books Ltd.).

Todd, K.L. and V. Robert (2018) "Reviving the Spirit by Making the Case for Decolonial Curricula," in N.N. Wane and K.L. Todd (Eds.), *Decolonial Pedagogy: Examining Sites of Resistance, Resurgence, and Renewal* (Switzerland: Palgrave Macmillan), pp. 57–72.

Trigwell, K. and M. Prosser (2004) "Development and Use of the Approaches to Teaching Inventory," *Educational Psychology Review*, Measuring Studying and Learning in Higher Education—Conceptual and Methodological Issues, 16: 4, pp. 409–24.

University and College Union (February 2016) "The Experiences of Black and Minority Ethnic Staff in Further and Higher Education." Available at: https://www.ucu.org.uk/media/7861/The-experiences-of-black-and-minority-ethnic-staff-in-further-and-higher-education-Feb-16/pdf/BME_survey_report_Feb161.pdf [Accessed: November 4, 2019].

Zembylas, M. (2017) "Re-contextualising Human Rights Education: Some Decolonial Strategies and Pedagogical/Curricular Possibilities," *Pedagogy, Culture & Society*, 25:4, pp. 487–99.

Chapter 4

AdvanceHE (September 9, 2019) "UK Professional Standards Framework (UKPSF)," Higher Education Academy. Available at: https://www.advance-he.ac.uk/knowledge-hub/uk-professional-standards-framework-ukpsf [Accessed: January 4, 2010].

Annala, J., J. Lindén, and M. Mäkinen (2016) "Curriculum in Higher Education Research," in J. Case and J. Huisman (Eds.), *Researching Higher Education: International Perspectives on Theory, Policy, and Practice* (SRHE Society for Research into Higher Education and Routledge), pp. 171–89.

Assemi, A. and M. Sheikhzade (2013) "Intended, Implemented and Experiential Null Curriculum," *Life Science Journal*, 10:1, pp. 82–5.

Barrier, J., O. Quéré, and R. Vanneuville (2019) "The Making of Curriculum in Higher Education: Power, Knowledge, and Teaching Practices," *Revue d'anthropologie des connaissances*, 13:1, pp. 33–60.

Basch, C.A (2012) "Student-Teacher Trust Relationships and Student Performance." Available at: https://fisherpub.sjfc.edu/cgi/viewcontent.cgi?article=1119&context=education_etd [Accessed: December 28, 2019].

Batchelor, K. (2009) *Decolonizing Translation Francophone African Novels in English Translation* (London: Routledge).

Biggs, J. (n.d.) "Aligning Teaching for Constructing Learning," The Higher Education Academy. Available at: https://www.heacademy.ac.uk/sites/default/files/resources/id477_aligning_teaching_for_constructing_learning.pdf [Accessed: January 4, 2020].

Bovill, C. and C. Woolmer (2019) "How Conceptualisations of Curriculum in Higher Education Influence Student-Staff Co-creation *In* and *of* the Curriculum," *Higher Education*, 78, pp. 407–22.

Brodie, K. (October 13 2016) "Yes, Mathematics Can Be Decolonised. Here's How to Begin." Available at: http://theconversation.com/yes-mathematics-can-be-decolonised-heres-how-to-begin-65963 [Accessed: January 27, 2020].

Crilly, J. (2019) "Decolonising the Library: A Theoretical Exploration," *Spark: UAL Creative Teaching and Learning Journal*, 4:1, pp. 6–15.

De Lissovoy, N. (2010) "Decolonial Pedagogy and the Ethics of the Global," *Discourse: Studies in the Cultural Politics of Education*, 31:3, pp. 279–293.

Donnelly, M. and S. Gamsu (2018), "Home and Away—Social, Ethnic and Spatial Inequalities in Student Mobility," The Sutton Trust, p. 11. Available at: https:// www.suttontrust.com/wp-content/uploads/2018/02/Home_and_away_ FINAL.pdf [Accessed: October 26, 2019].

Dunham, J. and D. Tran (2019) "The Forgotten Stage of Designing Curricula," Bridging the Inclusivity Gap, 9th Teaching and Learning Conference, July 9, 2019, Bloomsbury Institute, London.

Eizadirad, A. (2019) *Decolonizing Educational Assessment: Ontario Elementary Students and the EQAO* (Toronto: Palgrave Macmillan).

François, G. (2015) "The Economics of English in Europe," in T. Recento (Ed.), *Language Policy and Political Economy: English in a Global Context* (Oxford: Oxford University Press), pp. 119–44.

Fraser, S.P. and A.M. Bosanquet (2006) "The Curriculum? That's Just a Unit Outline, Isn't It?", *Studies in Higher Education*, 31:03, pp. 269–84.

Gibbs, P. (2017) "Higher Education: A Compassion Business or Edifying Experience?," in P. Gibbs (Ed.), *The Pedagogy of Compassion at the Heart of Higher Education* (London: Springer), pp. 1–18.

Goldsmiths University of London (2019) "Liberate Our Library." Available at: https://www.gold.ac.uk/library/about/liberate-our-library/ [Accessed: October 26, 2019].

Gorski, P.C. (2008) "Good Intentions Are Not Enough: A Decolonizing Intercultural Education," *Intercultural Education*, 19:6, pp. 515–25.

Lee, S.J. (2007) "The Relations Between the Student–Teacher Trust Relationship and School Success in the Case of Korean Middle Schools," *Educational Studies*, 33:2, pp. 209–216.

Macfarlane, B. (2009) "A Leap of Faith: The Role of Trust in Higher Education Teaching," pp. 221–38. Available at: http://www.cshe.nagoya-u.ac.jp/publications/journal/no9/14.pdf [Accessed: December 28, 2019].

Maguire, D. and D. Morris (December 13, 2018) "Homeward Bound: Defining, Understanding and Aiding 'Commuter Students,'" Higher Education Policy Institute. Available at: https://www.hepi.ac.uk/2018/12/13/homeward-bound-defining-understanding-aiding-commuter-students/ [Accessed: February 10, 2020].

Maloney, M.M. (2012) "Cultivating Community, Promoting Inclusivity: Collections as Fulcrum for Targeted Outreach," *New Library World*, 113: 5/6, pp. 281–9.

Meda, L. (2019) "Decolonising the Curriculum: Students' Perspectives," *Africa Education Review*, DOI: 10.1080/18146627.2018.1519372.

Olaleye, F. (November 18, 2019) "Keynote Addressing Barriers to Student Success—The Student Perspective," ABSS Conference, The Studio, Birmingham.

Osman, R. and D.J. Hornsby (2017) "Transforming Higher Education: Towards a Socially Just Pedagogy," in R. Osman and D.J. Hornsby (Eds.), *Transforming Teaching and Learning in Higher Education: Towards a Socially Just Pedagogy in a Global Context* (Palgrave Macmillan), pp. 1–14.

Pawlina, W., D.J.R. Evans, L. Ki Chan, K.G. Ruit, T.D. Wilson, and N. Lachman (2018) "Student-Teacher Trust and Journal-Reader Trust: Engines Driving Education and Research in Anatomical Sciences," *Anatomical Sciences Education*, January/February, 11, pp. 5–6.

Rumpus, A., J. Eland, and R. Shacklock (2011) "The Student Voice in Teacher Training and Professional Development," in G. Czerniawski and W. Kidd (Eds.), *The Student Voice Handbook: Bridging the Academic/Practitioner Divide* (Bingley: Emerald Group Publishing Limited), pp. 249–62.

Thomas, L. and R. Jones (2017), "Student Engagement in the Context of Commuter Students," The Student Engagement Partnership. Available at: https://www.liz thomasassociates.co.uk/projects/2018/Commuter%20student%20engagement.pdf [Accessed: October 26, 2019].

UT News (February 8, 2017) "A Trust Gap May Hinder Academic Success for Minorities." Available at: https://news.utexas.edu/2017/02/08/a-trust-gap-may-hind er-academic-success-for-minorities/ [Accessed: December 28, 2019].

Vandeyar, S. (2019) "Why Decolonising the South African University Curriculum Will Fail," *Teaching in Higher Education*. DOI: 10.1080/13562517.2019.1592149.

Vandeyar, S. and R. Swart (2016) "Educational Change: A Case for a Pedagogy of Compassion," *Education as Change*, 20: 3, pp. 141–59. DOI: http://dx.doi.org/10 .17159/1947-9417/2016/1362.

Waddington, K. (2018) "Editorial," *Journal of Perspectives in Applied Academic Practice*, 6:3, pp. 1–2. [Special Issue on Compassionate Pedagogy].

Woodfield, R. (2014) "Undergraduate Retention and Attainment across the Disciplines," Higher Education Academy. Available at: https://www.heacademy.ac.uk/knowle dge-hub/ undergraduate-retention-and-attainment-across-disciplines [Accessed: October 26, 2019].

Jason Arday's Contribution

Adams, R. (2017) *British Universities Employ No Black Academics in Top Roles, Figures Show*. Available at: https://www.theguardian.com/education/2017/jan/19/british-un iversities-employ-no-black-academics-in-top-roles-figures-show [Accessed: April 20, 2020].

Ahmed, S. (2012) *On Being Included: Racism and Diversity in institutional Life* (London: Duke University Press).

Alexander, C. and J. Arday (2015) *Aiming Higher Race, Inequality and Diversity in the Academy*. London: AHRC: Runnymede Trust (Runnymede Perspectives). London: Common Creative: Runnymede Trust (Runnymede Perspectives).

Andrews, K. (2016) *Black Studies University Course Long Overdue*. Available at: https ://www.theguardian.com/commentisfree/2016/may/20/black-studies-university-c ourse-long-overdue [Accessed: April 20, 2020].

Andrews, K. (2019) "Blackness, Empire and Migration: How Black Studies Transforms the Curriculum," *Area*, 10, pp. 1–7.

Arday, J. (2018) "Understanding Race and Educational Leadership in Higher Education: Exploring the Black and Ethnic Minority (BME) Experience," *Management in Education*, 32:4, pp. 192–200.

Arday, J. (2019) "Dismantling Power and Privilege through Reflexivity: Negotiating Normative Whiteness, the Eurocentric Curriculum and Racial Micro-Aggressions Within the Academy," *Whiteness and Education*, 3:2, pp. 141–61.

Bhopal, K. (2014) *The Experience of BME Academics in Higher Education: Aspirations in the Face of Inequality*, Stimulus Paper, London: Leadership Foundation for Higher Education.

Cotton, D.R.E., M. Joyner, R. George, and P.A. Cotton (2016) "Understanding the Gender and Ethnicity Attainment Gap in UK Higher Education," *Innovations in Education and Teaching International*, 53:5, pp. 475–86.

Dei, G.J.S., Karumanchery, L.L., and Karumanchery, N. (2004) *Playing the Race Card: Exposing White Power and Privilege* (USA: Peter Lang).

Delgado Bernal, D. and O. Villalpando (2016) "An Apartheid of Knowledge in Academia," in E. Taylor, D. Gillborn, and G. Ladson-Billings (Eds.), *Foundations of Critical Race Theory in Education, Second Edition* (New York: Routledge), pp. 72–92.

Equality Challenge Unit (Advance HE) (2018) *Equality in Higher Education: Statistical Report, Staff and Students*. Available at: http://www.ecu.ac.uk/publications/equality -higher-education-statistical-report-2018/ [Accessed: April 25, 2020].

Hamilton, C. (2016) *What's Wrong with a Euroecentric Curriculum*. Available at: https:/ /www.spiked-online.com/2016/09/27/whats-wrong-with-a-eurocentric-curriculum/ [Accessed: April 25, 2020].

Leonardo, Z. (2002) "The Souls of White Folk: Critical Pedagogy, Whiteness Studies, and Globalization Discourse." *Race Ethnicity & Education*, 5:1, pp. 29–50.

Leonardo, Z. (2016) "The Color of Supremacy," in E. Taylor, D. Gillborn, and G. Ladson-Billings (Eds.), *Foundations of Critical Race Theory in Education*, Second Edition (New York: Routledge), pp. 265–77.

Miller, P. (2016) "White Sanction," Institutional, Group and Individual Interaction in the Promotion and Progression of Black and Minority Ethnic Academics and Teachers in England, *Power and Education*, 8:3, pp. 205–21.

Molefe, T.O. (2016) "Oppression Must Fall: South Africa's Revolution in Theory," *World Policy Journal*, 33:1. Available at: http://dx.doi.org/10.1215/07402775-3545858, pp. 30–7 [Accessed: April 20, 2020].

Nwadeyi, L. (2016) "We All Have a Responsibility to Disrupt the Status Quo," *Mail & Guardian*. Available at: http://mg.co.za/article/2016-06-29-we-allhave-agency-and -we-must-use-it-to-disrupt-the-status-quo [Accessed: April 20, 2020].

Nwonka, C. (October 10, 2019) "Elite Universities Are Too Obsessed with Tradition to Tackle Racism Effectively," *The Guardian*. Available at: https://www.theguardian.com/education/2019/oct/10/elite-universities-are-too-obsessed-with-tradition-to-tackle-racism-effectively [Accessed: October 19, 2019].

Peters, M.A. (2015) "Why Is My Curriculum White?," *Educational Philosophy and Theory*, 47:7, pp. 641–6, DOI: 10.1080/00131857.2015.1037227.

Pilkington, A. (2013) "The Interacting Dynamics of Institutional Racism in Higher Education," *Race Ethnicity and Education*, 16:2, pp. 225–45.

Rollock, N. (2016) *How Much Does Your University Do for Racial Equality?* Available at: https://www.theguardian.com/higher-education-network/2016/jan/19/how-much-does-your-university-do-for-racial-equality/ [Accessed: April 25, 2020].

Sardar, Z. (2008) *"Foreword to the 2008 Edition. I Think It Would Be Good If Certain Things Were Said: Fanon and the Epidemiology of Oppression,"* in F. Fanon (1967), *Black Skins, White Masks*, 2008 edition (Pluto Books: London), pp. vi–xx.

Shay, S. (2016) "Decolonising the Curriculum: It's Time for a Strategy," *The Conversation*. Available at: https://theconversation.com/decolonisingthe-curriculum-its-time-for-a-strategy-60598

Shilliam, R. (2015) *Black Academia in Britain. The Disorder of Things*. Available at: https://thedisorderofthings.com/2014/07/28/black-academia-in-britain/ [Accessed: April 25, 2020].

Tate, S.A. and P. Bagguley (2017) "Building the Anti-racist University: Next Steps," *Race Ethnicity and Education*, 20:3, pp. 289–99.

Trigwell, K. and M. Prosser (2004) "Development and Use of the Approaches to Teaching Inventory," *Educational Psychology Review*, Measuring Studying and Learning in Higher Education—Conceptual and Methodological Issues, 16: 4, pp. 409–24.

Joanne Dunham's Contribution

American Library Association, "Cultural Competency for Academic Libraries." Available at: http://www.ala.org/acrl/standards/diversity [Accessed: January 16, 2020].

Bournemouth University. Available at: https://libguides.bournemouth.ac.uk/decolonising-the-curriculum [Accessed: January 30, 2020].

Charles, E. (2019) "Decolonising the Curriculum," *Insights*, 32:1. Available at: http://doi.org/10.1629/uksg.4752 [Accessed: January 30, 2020], p. 24.

Clarke, M. (2019) "Liberate Our Library: Social Justice and the Need for Change," UKSG eNews 488. https://www.uksg.org/newsletter/uksg-enews-438/liberate-our-library-social-justice-and-need-change [Accessed: January 30, 2020].

CILIP: Chartered Institute of Library and Information Professionals and the Archives and Records Association (ARA) (Ireland and UK) (2015). Available at: https://www.cilip.org.uk/page/Workforcesurvey/ [Accessed: July 20, 2020].

Damen, J. (2019) "How to Decolonise the Library." Available at: https://blogs.lse.ac.uk/africaatlse/2019/06/27/decolonize-the-library-academic/ [Accessed: January 30, 2020].

Goldsmiths University of London, "Liberate Our Library." Available at: https://www.gold.ac.uk/library/about/liberate-our-library/ [Accessed: January 30, 2020].

Foster, E. (2018) "Cultural Competence in Library Instruction: A Reflective Practice Approach," *Libraries and the Academy*, 18:3, pp. 575–93.

Hall, H., B. Ryan, R. Raeside, M. Dutton, and T. Chen (2015) *A Study of the UK Information Workforce* (Edinburgh: CILIP/ARA).

Hughes-Watkins, L. (March 2019) "Taking a Stand: Lae'l Hughes-Watkins University of Maryland College Park, " *Library Journal*, p. 41.

Ishaq, M. and A.M. Hussain (2019) *BAME Staff Experience of Academic and Research Libraries* (London: SCONUL).

Khan, Z. (November 25, 2019) Keynote: Decolonising Library Collections and Practices: From Understand to Actions, Cardiff.

Nwonka, C. (October 10, 2019) "Elite Universities Are Too Obsessed with Tradition to Tackle Racism Effectively," *Guardian Online*. Available at: https://www.theguardian.com/education/2019/oct/10/elite-universities-are-too-obsessed-with-tradition-to-tackle-racism-effectively [Accessed: January 16, 2020].

Shukla, N. (Ed.) (2016) *The Good Immigrant* (London: Unbound).

Chapter 5

Ashlee, A.A., B. Zamora, and S.N. Karikari (2017) "We Are Woke: A Collaborative Critical Autoethnography of Three 'Womxn' of Colour Graduate Students in Higher Education," *International Journal of Multicultural Education*, 19:1, pp. 89–104.

BBC (January 25, 2019) "Afrikaans Scrapped at South Africa's University of Pretoria." Available at: https://www.bbc.co.uk/news/world-africa-47001468 [Accessed: April 20, 2020].

Blackburn, M.V. and J.M. Smith (2010) "Moving Beyond the Inclusion of LGBT-Themed Literature in English Language Arts Classrooms: Interrogating Heteronormativity and Exploring Intersectionality," *Journal of Adolescent and Adult Literacy*, pp. 625–34.

Bothwell, E. (March 19, 2020) "Coronavirus Could Be 'Make or Break' for Universities" Finances," *Times Higher Education*. Available at: https://www.timeshighereducation.com/news/coronavirus-could-be-make-or-break-universities-finances [Accessed: April 30, 2020].

Caine, T.M. (2008) "Do You Speak Global?: The Spread of English and the Implications for English Language Teaching," *Canadian Journal for New Scholars in Education*, 1:1, pp. 1–11.

Clark, C. and P. Gorski (2001) "Multicultural Education and the Digital Divide: Focus on Race, Language, Socioeconomic Class, Sex, and Disability," *Multicultural Perspectives*, 3:3, pp. 39–44.

Cunningham, S. (2013) "Teaching a Diverse Student Body—A Proposed Tool for Lecturers to Self-Evaluate Their Approach to Inclusive Teaching," *Practice and Evidence of Scholarship of Teaching and Learning in Higher Education*, 8:1, pp. 3–27.

Dei, G.J.S. (2016) "Decolonizing the University: The Challenges and Possibilities of Inclusive Education," *The Journal of the Society for Socialist Studies / Revue de la Société d'études socialistes*, 11:1, pp. 23–61.

Duff, R.A. (2003) "Inclusion, Exclusion and the Criminal Law," *Policy Futures in Education*, 1:4, pp. 619–715.

Dumbrill, G.C. and J. Green (2008) "Indigenous Knowledge in the Social Work Academy," *Social Work Education*, *27*:5, pp. 489–503.

Gohlan, N. (December 2019) "Decolonising the Curriculum: Student Led Action," in M. Moncrieffe, Y. Asare, R. Dunford, and H. Youssef (Eds.), *Decolonising the Curriculum*: Teaching and Learning about Race Equality, Issue 2, p. 24.

Gomes, M. (2018) "Writing Assessment and Responsibility for Colonialism," in M. Poe, A.B. Inoue, and N. Elliot (Eds.), *Writing Assessment, Social Justice, and the Advancement of Opportunity* (Colorado: University Press of Colorado), pp. 201–26.

Gopnik, A. (January 9, 2017) "Montaigne on Trial: What Do We Really Know About the Philosopher Who Invented Liberalism?" *The New Yorker*. Available at: https://www.newyorker.com/magazine/2017/01/16/montaigne-on-trial [Accessed: April 25, 2020].

Grossmann, M. and E. Creamer (2017) "Assessing Diversity and Inclusivity within the Transition Movement: An Urban Case Study," *Environmental Politics*, 26:1, pp. 161–82.

Hodges, C., S. Moore, B. Lockee, T. Trust, and A. Bond (March 27, 2020) "The Difference Between Emergency Remote Teaching and Online Learning," *Educause*. Available at: https://er.educause.edu/articles/2020/3/the-difference-between-emergency-remote-teaching-and-online-learning [Accessed: May 30, 2020].

Institute for Policy Studies in Education, and London Metropolitan University (2011), Student Diversity and Success at Kingston University: An investigation of the progression and attainment of students from ethnic minority backgrounds to inform the development of teaching and learning strategy and practice. Available at: http://cdn.kingston.ac.uk/documents/aboutkingstonuniversity/equality-diversity-and-inclusion/documents/AD406a-BME-Full-Report.pdf [Accessed: April 25, 2020].

Johnson, A. (2020) "Throwing Our Bodies against the White Background of Academia," *Area*, 52, pp. 89–96. DOI: 10.1111/area.12568.

Kanu, Y. (2005) "Decolonizing Indigenons Education: Beyond Culturalism: Toward Post-cultural Strategies," *Canadian and International Education*, 32:2, article 2.

Karrim, A. and N. Seleka (October 10, 2019) "Constitutional Court Rules in Favour of Contentious Stellenbosch University Language Policy." Available at: https://www.new

s24.com/SouthAfrica/News/constitutional-court-to-rule-on-contentious-stellenbosch-university-language-policy-20191010 [Accessed: April 20, 2020].

Lempp, H. and C. Seale (2004) "The Hidden Curriculum in Undergraduate Medical Education: Qualitative Study of Medical Students' Perceptions of Teaching," *BMJ*, 329, pp. 770–703.

Louie, D.W., Y.P. Pratt, A.J. Hanson, and J. Ottmann (2017) "Applying Indigenizing Principles of Decolonizing Methodologies in University Classrooms," *Canadian Journal of Higher Education*, 47:3, pp. 16–33.

Mahtani, A. (December 2019) "Why Is My Curriculum White?—An International Students' Perspective," in M. Moncrieffe, Y. Asare, R. Dunford, and H. Youssef (Eds.), *Decolonising the Curriculum: Teaching and Learning about Race Equality*, Issue 2, p. 25.

Morreira, S. and K. Luckett (2018) "Questions Academics Can Ask to Decolonise Their Classrooms," *The Conversation*. Available at: https://theconversation.com/questions-academics-can-ask-to-decolonise-their-classrooms-103251 [Accessed: April 25, 2020].

Morris, S.M. and J. Stommel (2018) "Critical Digital Pedagogy: A Definition," in *An Urgency of Teachers: The Work of Critical Digital Pedagogy* (Hybrid Pedagogy Inc.), pp. 2–12. Available at: https://criticaldigitalpedagogy.pressbooks.com/chapter/chapter-1/ [Accessed: April 30, 2020].

Moy, R.G. (2000) "American Racism: The Null Curriculum in Religious Education," *Religious Education*, 95:2, pp. 119–33.

Ogden, J., S. Halford, L. Carr, and G. Earl (2015) "This Is for Everyone? Steps Towards Decolonizing the Web," ACM Web Science Conference, Oxford UK. Available at: https://eprints.soton.ac.uk/397709/1/jogden_decolonising_web.pdf [Accessed: May 2, 2020].

Orr, S., M. Yorke, and B. Blair (2014) "'The Answer Is Brought about from Within You': A Student Centred Perspective on Pedagogy in Art and Design," *International Journal of Art and Design Education*, 33:1, pp. 32–45.

O'Sullivan, S. (April 10, 2019) "Decolonizing the Classroom: A Conversation with Girish Daswani," Teaching Tools, *Fieldsights*. Available at: https://culanth.org/fieldsights/decolonizing-the-classroom-a-conversation-with-girish-daswani [Accessed: April 25, 2020].

Pohawpatchoko, C. (2015) "Cultural Constructionism: Indigenous Students' Experiences in an Interface Development Workshop," PhD diss., Computer Science Department, University of Colorado at Boulder.

Pohawpatchoko, C. Colwell, J. Powell, and J. Lassos (2017) "Developing a Native Digital Voice: Technology and Inclusivity in Museums," *Museum Anthropology*, 40: 1, pp. 52–64.

Richardson Jr., J.V. (2011) "The Digital Table: A Radical Proposal for Inclusivity," *Pakistan Journal of Library & Information Science*, 12, pp. 1–3.

Sanford, K, L. Williams, T. Hopper, and C. McGregor (2012) "Indigenous Principles Decolonizing Teacher Education: What We Have Learned," *INeducation*, 18:2.

Available at: https://ineducation.ca/ineducation/article/view/61/547 [Accessed: April 25, 2020].

Simpson, L. (2001) "Aboriginal Peoples and Knowledge: Decolonizing Our Processes," *The Canadian Journal of Native Studies*, XXI: 1, pp. 137–48.

Stommel, J. (2018) "What Is Hybrid Pedagogy," in *An Urgency of Teachers: the Work of Critical Digital Pedagogy* (Hybrid Pedagogy Inc.), pp. 2–12. Available at: https://criticaldigitalpedagogy.pressbooks.com/chapter/what-is-hybrid-pedagogy/ [Accessed: April 30, 2020].

Strayhorn, T.L. (2012) *College Students' Sense of Belonging: A Key to Educational Success for All Students* (Oxon: Routledge).

Truscott, A. and I. Malcolm (2010) "Closing the Policy-Practice Gap: Making Indigenous Language Policy More than Empty Rhetoric," in J. Hobson, K. Lowe, S. Poetsch and M. Walsh (Eds.), *Re-awakening Languages: Theory and Practice in the Revitalisation of Australia's Indigenous Languages* (Sydney: Sydney University Press), pp. 6–21.

Valdez, K. and D. Thurab-Nkhosi (2019) "Academic Developers as Disruptors: Reshaping the Instructional Design Process," in L. Quinn (Ed.), *Re-imagining Curriculum: Spaces for Disruption* (Stellenbosch, South Africa: SUN Press), pp. 193–216.

wa Thiong'o, N. (2009) *Something Torn and New: An African Renaissance* (New York: BasicCivitasBooks).

Zavala, M. (2013) "What Do We Mean by Decolonizing Research Strategies? Lessons from Decolonizing, Indigenous Research Projects in New Zealand and Latin America," *Decolonization: Indigeneity, Education & Society*, 2:1, pp. 55–71.

Chapter 6

AdvanceHE (2019) "Unconscious Bias." Available at: https://www.advance-he.ac.uk/guidance/equality-diversity-and-inclusion/employment-and-careers/unconscious-bias#publications [Accessed: January 15, 2020].

Ahmed, S. (2012) *On Being Included: Racism and Diversity in Institutional Life* (London: Duke University Press).

Atewologun, D., T. Cornish, and F. Tresh (2018) *Unconscious Bias Training: An Assessment of the Evidence for* Effectiveness, Equality and Human Rights Commission, Research Report 113. Available at: https://www.equalityhumanrights.com/en/publication-download/unconscious-bias-training-assessment-evidence-effectiveness [Accessed: January 15, 2020].

Bhopal, K., H. Brown, and J. Jackson (2018) "Should I Stay or Should I Go? BME Academics and the Decision to Leave UK Higher Education," in J. Arday and H. Safia Mirza (Eds.), *Dismantling Race in Higher Education: Racism, Whiteness and Decolonising the Academy* (London: Palgrave Macmillan), pp. 125–42.

Boler, M. and M. Zembylas (2003) "Discomforting Truths: The Emotional Terrain of Understanding Difference," in P.P. Trifonas (Ed.), *Pedagogies of Difference: Rethinking Education for Social Change* (London: Routledge Falmer), pp. 116–39.

Clay, S. (2018) "So You Want to Be an Academic? The Experiences of Black, Asian and Minority Ethnic Undergraduates in a UK Creative Arts University," in S. Billingham (Ed.), *Access to Success and Social Mobility through Higher Education: A Curate's Egg?* (Bingley: Emerald Publishing), pp. 99–114.

Eddo-Lodge, R. (May 30, 2017) "Why I'm No Longer Talking to White People About Race." Available at: https://www.theguardian.com/world/2017/may/30/why-im-no-longer-talking-to-white-people-about-race [Accessed: May 2, 2020].

Equality Challenge Unit (September 2013) "Unconscious Bias and Higher Education." Available at: https://www.advance-he.ac.uk/guidance/equality-diversity-and-inclusion/employment-and-careers/unconscious-bias#publications [Accessed: January 16, 2020].

Foucault, M. (1994) "For an Ethic of Discomfort," in J.D. Faubion (Ed.), *Essential Works of Foucault 1954–1984*, Vol. 3 (New York: The New Press), pp. 443–8.

HESA (January 24, 2019) "Higher Education Staff Statistics: UK, 2017/18." Available at: https://www.hesa.ac.uk/news/24-01-2019/sb253-higher-education-staff-statistics [Accessed: April 25, 2020].

Huber, L. and D. Solorzano (2015) "Racial Micro Aggressions as a Tool for Critical Research," *Race, Ethnicity and Education*, 18:3, pp. 297–320.

Ishaq, M. and A.M. Hussain (2019) "BAME Staff Experiences of Academic and Research Libraries," SCONUL. Available at: https://www.sconul.ac.uk/sites/default/files/documents/BAME%20staff%20experiences%20of%20academic%20and%20research%20libraries_0.pdf [Accessed: April 25, 2020].

Kernohan, D. (2020) "HESA Spring 2020: What Does the HESA Data about Black Senior Academics Really Mean?," *WONKHE*. Available at: https://wonkhe.com/blogs/hesa-spring-2020-what-does-the-hesa-data-about-black-senior-academics-really-mean/ [Accessed: January 27, 2020].

Khan, C. (November 16, 2017) "Do Universities Have a Problem with Promoting Their BAME Staff?," *The Guardian*. Available at: https://www.theguardian.com/higher-education-network/2017/nov/16/do-universities-have-a-problem-with-promoting-their-bame-staff [Accessed: April 25, 2020].

Lander, V., and N. Santoro (2017) "Invisible and Hypervisible Academics: The Experiences of Black and Minority Ethnic Teacher Educators," *Teaching in Higher Education*, 22:8, pp. 1008–21, DOI: 10.1080/13562517.2017.1332029.

Miller, P. (January 10, 2020) "Race/Ethnicity, Identity and Co-identification in Higher Education: Are We There Yet?," SHIFT 2020 conference keynote, University of Greenwich.

Phillips, J., S. Whatman, V. Hart, and G. Winslett (2005) Author version of article published as "Decolonising University Curricula—Reforming the Colonised Spaces Within Which We Operate," *Proceedings The Indigenous Knowledges Conference—*

Reconciling Academic Priorities with Indigenous Realities, Victoria University, Wellington, New Zealand. Available at: https://eprints.qut.edu.au/7331/ [Accessed: October 24, 2019].

Singh, G. (April 15, 2020) "Supporting Black, Asian Minority Ethnic (BAME) Students during the COVID-19 Crisis," *Shades of Noir*. Available at: https://shadesofnoir.org.uk/supporting-black-asian-minority-ethnic-bame-students-during-the-covid-19-crisis/ [Accessed: April 25, 2020].

Singh, G. and S. Masoca (2019) "Introduction," in *Anti-racist Social Work: International Perspectives* (London: Red Globe Press), pp. 1–12.

Vandeyar, S. (2019) "Why Decolonising the South African University Curriculum Will Fail," *Teaching in Higher Education: Critical Perspectives*, pp. 1–14. DOI: 10.1080/13562517.2019.1592149.

Zembylas, M. (2010) "Teachers' Emotional Experiences of Growing Diversity and Multiculturalism in Schools and the Prospects of an Ethic of Discomfort," *Teachers and Teaching: Theory and Practice*, 16:6, pp. 703–16.

Rahma Elmahdi's Contribution

Burke, P.J. and G. Crozier (2014) "Higher Education Pedagogies: Gendered Formations, Mis/recognition and Emotion," *Journal of Research in Gender Studies*, 4:2, pp. 52–67.

Dennis, C.A. (2018) "Decolonising Education: A Pedagogic Intervention," in G.K. Bhambra, D. Gebrial, and K. Nişancıoğlu (Eds.), *Decolonizing the University* (London: Pluto Press), pp. 190–207.

Dewey, J. (1933) *How We Think: A Restatement of the Relation of Reflective Thinking to the Educative Process* (Chicago: Henry Regnery).

Hobson, A. (Ed.) (2004) *The Oxford Dictionary of Difficult Words* (Oxford: Oxford University Press).

Rodgers, C.R. (2002) "Defining Reflection: Another Look at John Dewey and Reflective Thinking," *Teachers College Record*, 104:4, 842–66.

Schön, D. (1983) *The Reflective Practitioner* (New York: Basic Books).

Chapter 7

Anderson, R.S. and B.W. Speck (1998) "Oh What a Difference a Team Makes: Why Team Teaching Makes a Difference," *Teaching and Teacher Education*, 14:7, pp. 671–86.

Ball, S.J. (2013) *Foucault, Power, and Education* (London: Routledge).

Buckley, F.J. (2000) *Team Teaching: What, Why, and How?* (London: SAGE publications inc).

Coate, K. (2006) "Imagining Women in the Curriculum: The Transgressive Impossibility of Women's Studies," *Studies in Higher Education*, 31: 4, pp. 407–21.

Cushman, E. (2016) "Decolonizing Validity," *The Journal of Writing Assessment*, 9:1, pp. 1–6.

Domínguez, M. (2019) "Decolonial Innovation in Teacher Development: Praxis Beyond the Colonial Zero-Point," *Journal of Education for Teaching: International Research and Pedagogy*, 45:1, pp. 47–62.

Eizadirad, A. (2019) *Decolonizing Educational Assessment: Ontario Elementary Students and the EQAO* (Toronto: Palgrave Macmillan).

Gaytan, J. (2010) "Instructional Strategies to Accommodate a Team-Teaching Approach," *Business Communication Quarterly*, pp. 82–7. DOI: 10.1177/1080569909358097.

Hall, J. (December 2019) "Disrupting Value-Based Frameworks through Popular Culture Pedagogies: A Call for the Democratisation of Higher Education Curricula," in M. Moncrieffe, Y. Asare, R. Dunford, and H. Youssef (Eds.), *Decolonising the Curriculum: Teaching and Learning about Race Equality*, Issue 2, pp. 11–12.

Hook, D. (2007) *Foucault, Psychology and the Analytics of Power* (New York: Palgrave Macmillan).

Jalilipour, K. (January 31, 2017), "I U SHE: Pronouns, What's That All About?," *Queer Bodies*, Shades of Noir. Available at: https://issuu.com/shadesofnoir/docs/queer_bodies_online [Accessed: November 1, 2020].

Jones, C.J. (November 2019) "Race, Relational Trust, and Teacher Retention in Wisconsin Schools," University of Wisconsin Milwaukee, A Wisconsin Educator Effectiveness Research Partnership. Available at: https://uwm.edu/sreed/wp-content/uploads/sites/502/2019/11/WEERP-Brief-Nov-2019-Race-Relational-Trust-and-Teacher-Retention.pdf [Accessed: December 28, 2019].

Keval, H. (February 6, 2019) "Navigating the 'Decolonising' Process: Avoiding Pitfalls and Some Do's and Don't's." Available at: https://discoversociety.org/2019/02/06/navigating-the-decolonising-process-avoiding-pitfalls-and-some-dos-and-donts/ [Accessed: October 24, 2019].

Menegatti, M. and M. Rubini (2017) "Gender Bias and Sexism in Language," *Intergroup Communication*, DOI: 10.1093/acrefore/9780190228613.013.47 [Accessed: April 4, 2020], pp. 1–24.

Merriweather, L.R., T.C. Guy, and E. Manglitz (2019) "Creating the Conditions for Racial Dialogues," in S.D. Brookfield and Associates (Eds.), *Teaching Race: How to Help Students Unmask and Challenge Racism* (San Francisco, CA: Jossey-Bass), pp. 131–50.

Pauwels, A. and J. Winter (2006) "Gender Inclusivity or 'Grammar Rules OK?' Linguistic Prescriptivism vs Linguistic Discrimination in the Classroom," *Language and Education*, 20:2, pp. 128–40, DOI: 10.1080/09500780608668717.

Perry, B. and T. Stewart (2005) "Insights into Effective Partnership in Interdisciplinary Team Teaching," *System*, 33, pp. 563–73.

Prior, J. (March 1, 2017) "Teachers, What Is Gendered Language?" Available at: https://www.britishcouncil.org/voices-magazine/what-is-gendered-language [Accessed: April 4, 2020].

Schmidt, J. and T.E. Wartenberg (1994) "Foucault's Enlightenment: Critique, Revolution, and the Fashioning of the Self," in M. Kelly (Ed.), *Critique and Power: Recasting the Foucault/Habermas Debate* (London: MIT Press), pp. 283–314.

Tajino, A. and Y. Tajino (2000) "Native and Non-native: What Can They Offer? Lessons from Team-Teaching in Japan," *ELT Journal*, 54:1, pp. 3–11.

Vandeyar, S. (2019) "Why Decolonising the South African University Curriculum Will Fail," *Teaching in Higher Education*. DOI: 10.1080/13562517.2019.1592149.

Paul Breen's Contribution

Breen, P. (2018) *Developing Educators for the Digital Age—A Framework for Capturing Teacher Knowledge in Action* (London: Westminster University Press).

Chang, K.S. and M. Beaumont (2004) "Collaborative Learning in the Korean Secondary ELT classroom," Paper presented at the 2004 Korean Association of Teachers of English Conference in Seoul.

Ewing, S. and N. Reece (2019) *Decolonizing the EAP Curriculum*. Paper presented at BALEAP PIM: The Future of EAP at Goldsmiths, University of London BALEAP PIM.

Fink, L.D. (2007) "The Power of Course Design to Increase Student Engagement and Learning," *Peer Review*, 9:1, pp. 13–17.

Gimenez, J. (2020) Edulingualism: Linguistic Repertoires, Academic Tasks and Student Agency in an English-Dominant Urban University.

Gimenez, J. and P. Thomas (2015) "A Framework for Usable Pedagogy: Case Studies towards Accessibility, Criticality and Visibility," *Working with Academic Literacies: Case Studies towards Transformative Practice*, p. 29.

Hackett, S. (2017) *English for Academic Purposes (EAP): Enabling Non-1st English Language International Student Engagement in Higher Education*, Paper presented at HEA QQI Conference, December 11, 2017.

Hyland, K and L. Hamp-Lyons (2002) "EAP: Issues and Directions," *Journal of English for Academic Purposes* 1:1, pp. 1–12.

Icaza, R. and R. Vázquez (2018) "Diversity or Decolonization? Researching Diversity at the University of Amsterdam," in G.K. Bhambra, D. Gebrial, and K. Nişancıoğlu (Eds.), *Decolonizing the University* (London: Pluto Press), pp. 108–28.

Le Grange, L. (2016) "Decolonising the University Curriculum: Leading Article," *South African Journal of Higher Education*, 30:2, pp. 1–12.

Lea, M.R. and B.V. Street (1998), "Student Writing in Higher Education: An Academic Literacies Approach," *Studies in Higher Education*, 23:2, pp. 157–72.

Liao, W. (2019) "Journey to the West: Finding More Effective Ways of Addressing the Challenges Chinese Students Face in EAP Classes," Unpublished Master's thesis submitted for MA TESOL degree.

Pennycook, A. (1997) "Vulgar Pragmatism, Critical Pragmatism, and EAP," *English for Specific Purposes*, 16:4, pp. 253–69.

Tran, D. (2020) The TRAAC Model in *Decolonizing HE Teaching and Learning* (UK: Bloomsbury).

Vygotsky, L.S. (1978) *Mind in Society: The Development of Higher Psychological Processes* (A.R. Luria, M. Lopez-Morillas, and M. Cole [with J.V. Wertsch], Trans.) (Cambridge, MA: Harvard University Press) [Original manuscript, c.a. 1934].

Warschauer, M. (1996) "Computer-Assisted Language Learning: An Introduction," in S. Fotos (Ed.), *Multimedia Language Teaching* (Tokyo: Logos International). Available at: http://www.gse.uci.edu/faculty/markw/call.html], pp. 3–20. [Accessed: May 26, 2006].

Wiggins, G., G.P. Wiggins, and J. McTighe (2005) *Understanding by Design* (Ascd).

Anthony Cullen's Contribution

Brostoff, T. (2017) "Meditation for Law Students: Mindfulness Practice as Experiential Learning," *Law and Psychology Review*, 41, p. 157.

Cullen, A. and L. Kerin (2019) "Meditation in Legal Education: The Value Added Toward the Well-Being of Law Students," in C. Strevens and R. Field (Eds.), *Educating for Well-Being in Law: Positive Professional Identities and Practice* (London: Routledge, Taylor & Francis Group), pp. 158–71.

Doherty, M. (2018) *Public Law*, second edition (London: Routledge).

Fanon, F. (1986) *Black Skin, White Masks* (C.L. Markmann, Trans.) (London: Pluto Press).

Gandhi, M.K. (2001) *An Autobiography: The Story of My Experiments with Truth* (Mahadev Desai, Trans.) (London: Penguin).

Icaza, R. and R. Vázquez (2018) "Diversity or Decolonization? Researching Diversity at the University of Amsterdam," in G.K. Bhambra, D. Gebrial, and K. Nişancıoğlu (Eds.), *Decolonizing the University* (London: Pluto Press), pp. 108–28.

Keele University (2019) Keele Decolonizing the Curriculum Network. Available at: https://www.keele.ac.uk/equalitydiversity/equalityawards/raceequalitycharter/keeledecolonizingthecurriculumnetwork/#keele-manifesto-for-decolonizing-the-curriculum [Accessed: June 3, 2020].

Larcombe, W. (2016) "Towards an Integrated, Whole-School Approach to Promoting Law Student Wellbeing," in R. Field, J. Duffy, and C. James (Eds.), *Promoting Law Student and Lawyer Well-Being in Australia and Beyond* (Abingdon: Routledge), pp. 40–52.

Mandela, N. (2004) *Long Walk to Freedom* (London: Abacus).
Regan, P. (2010) *Unsettling the Settler Within: Indian Residential Schools, Truth Telling, and Reconciliation in Canada* (Vancouver: UBC Press).

Rahma Elmahdi's Contribution

Amineh, R.J. and H.D. Asl (2015) "Review of Constructivism and Social Constructivism," *Journal of Social Sciences, Literature and Languages*, 1:1, pp. 9–16.
Bell, A. and L.J. Santamaría (2018) *Understanding Experiences of First Generation University Students: Culturally Responsive and Sustaining Methodologies* (London: Bloomsbury Publishing).
Derry, S.J. (1999) "A Fish Called Peer Learning: Searching for Common Themes," *Cognitive Perspectives on Peer Learning*, pp. 197–211.
Di Vesta, F.J. (1987) "The Cognitive Movement and Education," in J.A. Golver and R.R. Ronning (Eds.), *Historical Foundations of Educational Psychology* (New York: Plenum Press), pp. 37–63.
Hobson, A. (Ed.) (2004) *The Oxford Dictionary of Difficult Words* (Oxford: Oxford University Press).
Keh, A. (Published October 12, 2019, Updated October 14, 2019), "Eliud Kipchoge Breaks Two-Hour Marathon Barrier," *The New York Times*. Available at: https://www.nytimes.com/2019/10/12/sports/eliud-kipchoge-marathon-record.html [Accessed: July 31, 2020].
Kim, B. (2001) "Social Constructivism," *Emerging Perspectives on Learning, Teaching, and Technology*, pp. 1–8.
Kukla, A. (2000) "Social Constructivism and the Philosophy of Science," (London: Routledge).
Leeds-Hurwitz, W. (2009) "Social Construction of Reality," *Encyclopedia of Communication Theory*, pp. 892–5.
McMahon, M. (1997) "Social Constructivism and the World Wide Web—A Paradigm for Learning," Paper presented at the ASCILITE conference: Perth, Australia.
Nagata, A. L. (2004) "Promoting Self-Reflexivity in Intercultural Education," *Journal of Intercultural Communications*, 8, pp. 139–67.
Piaget, J. (1970) *Structuralism* (New York: Basic Books).
Piaget, J. (1977) *The Development of Thought: Equilibration of Cognitive Structures* (A. Rosin, Trans). (New York: The Viking Press).
Van Meter, P. and R. Stevens (2000) "The Role of Theory in the Study of Peer Collaboration," *The Journal of Experimental Education*, 69:1, pp. 113–27.
Vygotsky, L.S. (1978) *Mind in Society* (Cambridge: Harvard University Press).

Peter Jones' Contribution

Ahmed, G. (2020) *Exploring Black African and South Asian Students' Experiences in Higher Education*. BA (Hons) Sociology Dissertation, University of Greenwich.

Akel, S. (2019) *Insider-Outsider. The Role of Race in Shaping the Experiences of Black and Minority Ethnic Students*. Goldsmiths, University of London. Available at: https://www.gold.ac.uk/media/docs/reports/Insider-Outsider-Report-191008.pdf [Accessed: April 30, 2020].

Barton, E. (1993) "Evidentials, Argumentation and Epistemological Stance," *College English*, 55:7, pp. 745–69.

Batty, D. (July 5, 2019) "UK Universities Condemned for Failure to Tackle Racism." *The Guardian*. Available at: https://www.theguardian.com/education/2019/jul/05/uk-universities-condemned-for-failure-to-tackle-racism [Accessed: April 30, 2020].

Bhambra, G. (2007) *Rethinking Modernity: Postcolonialism and the Sociological Imagination* (Basingstoke: Palgrave).

Block, D. (2008) *Multilingual Identities in a Global City: London Stories* (Hampshire: Palgrave Macmillan).

Chantiluke, R., B. Kwoba, and A. Nkopo (Eds.) (2018) *Rhodes Must Fall: The Struggle to Decolonise the Racist Heart of Empire* (London: Zed Books).

Clarke, P. and D. Beech (Eds.) (2018) *Reaching the Parts of Society Universities Have Missed: A Manifesto for the New Director of Fair Access and Participation*. HEPI Report 106 (Higher Education Policy Institute). Available at: https://www.hepi.ac.uk/wp-content/uploads/2018/05/HEPI-Brightside_WP-Manifesto-for-OfS_FINAL-Report-106.pdf [Accessed: April 30, 2020].

Davies, C. and M. Garrett (2012) "The BME Student Experience at a Small Northern University: An Examination of the Experiences of Minority Ethnic Students Undertaking Undergraduate Study Within a Small Northern University," *Compass: The Journal of Learning and Teaching at the University of Greenwich*, 3:5. Available at: https://journals.gre.ac.uk/index.php/compass/issue/view/5 [Accessed: April 30, 2020], pp. 1–10.

Equality and Human Rights Commission [EHRC] (2019) *Racial Harassment Inquiry: Survey of University Students*. Research Report No. 129. Available at: https://equalityhumanrights.com/sites/default/files/racial-harassment-inquiry-survey-of-university-students.pdf [Accessed: April 30, 2020].

Giddens, A. and P. Sutton (2017) *Sociology*, 8th edition (Cambridge: Polity Press).

Hall, S. (1992) "The West and the Rest: Discourse and Power," in S. Hall and B. Gieben (Eds.), *Formations of Modernity* (Cambridge: Polity Press), 275–331.

Leung, C. (2013) "The 'Social' in English Language Teaching: Abstracted Norms Versus Situated Enactments," *Journal of English as a Lingua Franca*, 2:2, pp. 283–313, DOI: 10.1515/jelf-2013-0016.

Metcalf, H. (2003) "Increasing Inequality in Higher Education: The Role of Term-Time Working," *Oxford Review of Education*, 29:3, pp. 315–29, DOI: 10.1080/0305498032000120274.

Moreau, M.-P. and C. Leathwood (2006) "Balancing Paid Work and Studies: Working (-Class) Students in Higher Education," *Studies in Higher Education*, 31:1, pp. 23–42, DOI: 10.1080/03075070500340135.

National Union of Students (2015) *Reaching Home: A Report on the Experiences of Students Living in the Parental Home During Study*. Available at: https://www.nus connect.org.uk/resources/reaching-home [Accessed: April 30, 2020].

Quality Assurance Agency for UK Higher Education [QAA] (2019) *Subject Benchmark Statement: Sociology*. Available at: https://www.qaa.ac.uk/quality-code/subject-be nchmark-statements# [Accessed: April 30, 2020].

Raju, C.K. (2018) "To Decolonise Math, Stand Up to Its False History," in R. Chantiluke, R., B. Kwoba, and A. Nkopo (Eds.), *Rhodes Must Fall: The Struggle to Decolonise the Racist Heart of Empire* (London: Zed Books), pp. 265–70

Said, E. (1978) *Orientalism: Western Conceptions of the Orient* (New York: Pantheon Books).

Rodney, W. (1972) *How Europe Underdeveloped Africa* (London: Bogle-L'Ouverture Publications).

Weale, S, D. Batty, and R. Obordo (July 5, 2019) "'A Demeaning Environment': Stories of Racism in UK Universities." *The Guardian*. Available at: https://www.theguardian .com/education/2019/jul/05/a-demeaning-environment-stories-of-racism-in-uk-un iversities [Accessed: April 30, 2020].

Womack, P. (1993) "What Are Essays For?," *English in Education*, 27:2, pp. 42–9. DOI: 10.1111/j.1754-8845.1993.tb01101.x.

Savvas Michael's Contribution

BBC (August 16, 2019) "How to Break into the Elite." Available at: https://www.bbc.co.u k/programmes/m000772n [Accessed: April 30, 2020].

Solicitor Regulation Authority (2017), "Ethnicity: How Diverse Are Law Firms?." Available at: https://www.sra.org.uk/sra/equality-diversity/archive/law-firms-2017/ [Accessed: April 30, 2020].

The University of Law, "The University of Law Access and Participation Plan 2019–20." Available at: https://www.law.ac.uk/globalassets/13.-media--doc-repo/08.-policies/ pdf_policies_access-and-participation-plan-2019-20.pdf [Accessed: April 30, 2020].

The University of Law (2020), "The University of Law Access and Participation Plan 2020–21." Available at: https://www.law.ac.uk/globalassets/13.-media--doc-repo/08. -policies/pdf_policies_access-and-participation-plan-2020-21.pdf [Accessed: April 30, 2020].

Smithers, R. (October 2, 2001) "Poor a Level Leads Family to Sue," *The Guardian*. Available at: https://www.theguardian.com/uk/2001/oct/02/schools.alevels2001 [Accessed: April 30, 2020].

Dawn Reilly's Contribution

Institute for Policy Studies in Education, and London Metropolitan University (2011), Student Diversity and Success at Kingston University: An investigation of the progression and attainment of students from ethnic minority backgrounds to inform the development of teaching and learning strategy and practice. Available at: http://cdn.kingston.ac.uk/documents/aboutkingstonuniversity/equality-diversity-and-inclusion/documents/AD406a-BME-Full-Report.pdf [Accessed: April 30, 2020].

Warren, E. and Reilly, D. (2019), "Addressing the Attainment Gap: Business Schools Can Lead the Way by Providing an Inclusive Approach to the Student Experience," *Chartered Association of Business Schools*. Available at: https://charteredabs.org/addressing-the-attainment-gap-business-schools-can-lead-the-way-by-providing-an-inclusive-approach-to-the-student-experience/ [Accessed: April 30, 2020].

Conclusion

Beaty, L. (1995) "Working Across the Hierarchy' in Teaching and Learning," in A. Brew (Ed.), *Directions in Staff Development* (Buckingham: The Society for Research into Higher Education and Open University Press), pp. 146–58.

Brew, A. (2013) "Understanding the Scope of Undergraduate Research: A Framework for Curricular and Pedagogical Decision-Making," *High Education*, 66, pp. 603–18.

Carr, P. (2007) "Educational Policy and the Social Justice Dilemma," in H. Claire and C. Holden (Eds.), *The Challenge of Teaching Controversial Issues* (Staffordshire: Trentham Books Limited), pp. 15–26.

Dowling, F. and A. Flintoff (2018) "A Whitewashed Curriculum? The Construction of Race in Contemporary PE Curriculum Policy," *Sport, Education and Society*, 23:1, pp. 1–13, DOI: 10.1080/13573322.2015.1122584.

Hayes, C.C. (May 2016) "How to Decolonize a Classroom," Capstone Collection. Available at: https://digitalcollections.sit.edu/capstones/2900 [Accessed: July 5, 2020].

Killick, D. (2017) *Internationalization and Diversity in Higher Education: Implications for Teaching, Learning and Assessment* (London: Palgrave).

McLoughlin, C. (2001) "Inclusivity and Alignment: Principles of Pedagogy, Task and Assessment Design for Effective Cross-Cultural Online Learning," *Distance Education*, 22:1, pp. 7–29.

Morrison, N. (January 16, 2017) "Inclusion Isn't Passive," *Change-Effect*. Available at: https://change-effect.com/2017/01/16/inclusion-isnt-passive/ [Accessed: January 4, 2020].

Quijano, A. (2000) "Coloniality of Power, Eurocentrism, and Latin America," *Nepantla: Views from South* 1.3. Available at: https://www.decolonialtranslation.com/english/quijano-coloniality-of-power.pdf [Accessed: November 3, 2019].

Ryan, A. and D. Tilbury (2013) "Flexible Pedagogies: New Pedagogical Ideas," The Higher Education Academy. Available at: https://www.advance-he.ac.uk/knowledge-hub/flexible-pedagogies-new-pedagogical-ideas [Accessed: November 10, 2019].

Sociological Review Podcast (February 11, 2020) "Decolonising Methodologies, 20 Years On: An Interview with Professor Linda Tuhiwai Smith." Available at: https://www.thesociologicalreview.com/decolonising-methodologies-20-years-on-an-interview-with-professor-linda-tuhiwai-smith/ [Accessed: May 3, 2020].

Smolicz, J.J. (2006) "Culture, Ethnicity and Education: Multiculturalism in a Plural Society," in J. Megarry, S. Nisbet, and E. Hoyle (Eds.), *World Yearbook of Education 1981: Education of Minorities* (London: Routledge) pp. 17–36.

Universities UK (May 2, 2019) "Universities Acting to Close BAME Student Attainment Gap." Available at: https://www.universitiesuk.ac.uk/news/Pages/Universities-acting-to-close-BAME-student-attainment-gap.aspx [Accessed: October 12, 2019].

wa Thiong'o, N. (2009) *Something Torn and New: An African Renaissance* (New York: BasicCivitasBooks).

Contributors

Jason Arday is an Assistant Professor in Sociology in the Department of Sociology at Durham University, UK and the deputy executive dean for people and culture in the Faculty of Social Science and Health. He is a visiting research fellow in the Office of Diversity and Inclusion at Ohio State University, USA, an adjunct professor at Nelson Mandela University in the Centre for Critical Studies in Higher Education Transformation, and a trustee of the Runnymede Trust, the UK's leading Race Equality Thinktank. Arday is also a trustee of the British Sociological Association (BSA) and a fellow of the Royal Society of Arts (RSA). He sits on the Centre for Labour and Social Studies (CLASS) National Advisory Panel and is a school governor at Shaftesbury Park Primary School in London, UK.

Paul Breen is a Senior Lecturer in the University of Westminster's Centre for Education, Teaching and Innovation, UK. Originally from Ireland, he has worked in higher educational contexts in both Britain and overseas with a particular recent focus on language teaching and cultural exchange in China. His research interests are in the areas of educational development, English for Academic Purposes, and the integration of technologies into higher educational teaching. He is the author of several published works, including *Developing Educators for the Digital Age* (2018).

Ryan Carty is a Post 16-19 Football Academy Education tutor at Bromley Football Club, UK. Carty was formerly a sport development officer at De Montfort University (DMU), UK, where he used his university experiences to empower student leaders to make positive changes and create more inclusive environments within DMU Sport sports clubs. Carty studied at the University of Bolton, UK, and during his time there, he had a number of different roles in paid and volunteering capacities, including Sports Council Chair, Football Activator, Chairman, and First Team Captain. During his time as a student, these roles allowed Carty to make positive changes to the holistic sporting culture at the University of Bolton. These efforts were recognized with Carty receiving the Platinum Award for the volunteering program at Bolton and a Governor's Award for exemplary conduct in representing students' views to enhance the student experience.

Anthony Cullen is a Senior Lecturer of Law in the School of Law at Middlesex University, London, UK. He currently teaches Public Law, international criminal law, and international humanitarian law. In addition to his position at Middlesex University, Cullen is also a Visiting Professor at the University of Bordeaux, France, and an external examiner at the University of Exeter, UK. His research focuses on the areas of international humanitarian law, international human rights law, the use of contemplative methods in higher education, decolonization, and student well-being.

Joanne Dunham is the Associate Director of Resources and Information in the Division of Library, Learning and Information Services, University of Leicester, UK. Having worked for nearly thirty years in academic libraries, she now heads up the teams acquiring, describing, making discoverable, managing, and developing collections including copyright and licensing. Dunham manages the Division of Library, Learning and Information Services' budget and is responsible for the digital environment. She is part of strategic planning and development, including decolonizing and making inclusive collections, supporting teaching and research, diversifying workforce, and raising staff awareness of equality, diversity, and inclusion.

Rahma Elmahdi is a junior doctor and postdoctoral student currently working at Statens Serum Institut, Denmark. Her research interests are in infectious and autoimmune disease epidemiology. She has published in HIV epidemiology and teaches global health to medical and public health students.

Emilie Fairnington is a sport project coordinator at Participation at De Montfort University, UK, where she has had significant impact on creating inclusive environments in Sport at DMU. Fairnington previously studied at De Montfort University, UK and during her time there, she has had a number of different volunteer sport roles, including Basketball Ambassador, First Team Captain, Basketball Club Secretary, Health and Safety Welfare Officer, and Club Social Secretary. This allowed her to increase her awareness of different cultural backgrounds and fuel an ever-growing passion for creating inclusive environments. After graduation she was employed as a graduate sport development assistant at DMU Sport. Fairnington has gained recognition for her hard work and won the 2019 De Montfort University Inspirational Women Award.

Bernadine Idowu-Onibokun is a Senior Lecturer and course leader on the new Biomedical Science degree within the new school of Biomedical Science at the University of West London, UK. She is also a Visiting Lecturer on the Intercalated Regenerative Medical BSc degree at the Centre for Oral Clinical and Translational Sciences, King's College London, UK. She is an award-winning scientist, having been a recipient of the Roger Cotton *Histopathology* Prize. She is a diversity and inclusion champion supporting BME students at various universities, and founder and director of the BME Early Career Researcher Conference. She freelances for *The Guardian* newspaper. Bernadine is a principal fellow of the Higher Education Academy.

Peter Jones is a Principal Lecturer in Social Sciences at the University of Greenwich, London, UK. His background is in sociology and human geography, and most of his teaching and scholarship have been at the interface of these two disciplines—for example, global migrations and "race," environmental risk, global inequalities, and globalization (including the "populist" reaction). Jones currently teaches mainly in sociology, where the rich diversity of students inspires, challenges, and motivates him to develop curricula and pedagogies that respond to their experiences and meet their needs.

Nelly Kibirige is the first two-term president at London South Bank University Students' Union, UK, where her innovative ideas have changed the culture of the organization. She is highly engaged in student activism and defending the rights of students, from petitions, campaigns, to rallying students to sit in on parliamentary debates. In 2019, Kibirige started a petition that has led to an agreed All-Party Parliamentary Group meeting on student funding and cowritten a Wonkhe published article on student loans. Having taken a nontraditional route to education, she has dedicated her time to ensuring access for all is key in all decision making.

Savvas Michael is a Lecturer and Master of Laws (LLM) course head at the University of Law, UK. His main areas of research and expertise are public, European Union, and international law. He has previously held teaching roles at University College London, UK, London Southbank University, UK, and University of Cambridge, UK (where he completed his law degree in 2012). Prior to moving into academia, Michael worked in the public legal sector in London for five years, at the Bank of England and Financial Ombudsman Service, UK.

Dawn Reilly is a Principal Lecturer in accounting and leads the undergraduate accounting degrees at the University of Greenwich, UK. Before becoming a university lecturer, Reilly taught professional accountancy qualifications at a college of further education. This early experience sparked her interest in widening participation, and the impact of program design and academic support on student performance. Reilly's current research interests are mainly in the area of business education, including how to close attainment gaps, formative feedback, and employability support within the curriculum.

D. Tran is interim dean of Learning, Teaching, and Enhancement at the University of the Arts London, UK. She previously held the role of Associate Dean: Academic Enhancement at UAL. Prior to joining UAL, Tran was an Associate Professor of Higher Education Learning and Teaching at the University of Greenwich, UK. Tran has worked at various UK HE institutions across different roles and areas. Her research interests include decolonizing teaching and learning, belonging, and reflective practice.

Index

Abdi, M.   11
Aboriginal people   90
Academic Committees   80
academic essay   96
Access and Participation Plan
    (2019–20)   152, 153
additional optional support   59
Addressing Barriers to Student Success
    conference   71
#AfrikaansMustFall campaign
    92
ahistoricism   19, 20
Ahmed, Gulnaz   148
Ahmed, S.   27, 105
Akel, S.   57, 148
American Library Association
    (ALA)   82, 83
Anderson, C. R.   18, 19
Andresen, L.   25
Annala, J.   64
Archer, M. S.   3
Archives and Records Association
    (ARA)   81
Arday, Jason   4, 29, 63, 71, 84, 85,
    122
Ashlee, A. A.   27
Assemi, A.   68
Atewologun, D.   102
attainment gap   17, 76, 77, 152, 158
authenticity   30, 31
awarding gap   1, 6, 17–20, 22, 70, 152,
    168

Ball, S. J.   125, 132
Bannister, Roger   143
Beaty, L.   165
Beaumont, M.   138
Behari-Leak, K.   10
belief system   5, 50, 103
bell hooks   12
Bhambra, Gurminder   150
Biggs's model   65

Black, Asian, and Minority Ethnic
    (BAME) communities   1, 6, 16,
    17, 20, 22, 45, 72, 81, 143
    role models   57
    solicitors   153–5
    staff   57, 81, 102, 106, 107, 122, 162
Black Americans   16
Blackburn, M. V.   89
Black Civil Rights Movement   16, 118,
    157
Black Lives Matter Foundation, Inc   17
Blackmore, P.   25
Blackwell, R.   25
Black women   42
BME Early Career Researcher (ECR)
    41
"BME Early Career Researcher (ECR)-
    How to Stay in Academia in
    2017"   41
Boler, M.   104
Bosanquet, A. M.   64
Bovill, C.   29, 65
Breen, Paul   5, 92, 129, 135, 136, 167
British University and Colleges Sport
    (BUCS)   111, 112
Brodie, K.   70
Brostoff, Teresa   142
Byrne, Ed   41

Caine, T. M.   92
Carnell, B.   28
Carr, P.   167
Carty, Ryan   5, 34, 107–13, 121, 122, 132,
    164
censorious parochialism   151
Chadderton, C.   58
Chang, K. S.   138
Chartered Institute of Library and
    Information Professionals
    (CILIP)   81
Chauvin, Derek   16
Clarke, Marilyn   78

classroom(s)   5, 20, 30, 32, 33, 50–4, 57, 59, 70, 87, 95, 105, 141
   decolonized   113–16, 143–6
   dynamics   65
   interactions   4, 68
   participation   38, 39, 43, 95
   responses   104
Coate, K.   132
colonial history   7, 20, 102, 149, 166
colonialism/colonization   9, 12, 17, 22, 26, 73, 93, 142, 150, 163
coloniality   7, 126, 163
colonial legacies   2, 6, 8, 11, 14, 20
compassion   67–8
continuing professional development (CPD)   23–5
Cotton, D. R. E.   62
Covid-19 pandemic   15–16, 130
CPD Certification Service   23
Creamer, E.   87
Crenshaw, Kimberlé   21, 37
critical race theory (CRT)   2, 7, 18–21, 50
critical thinking   49, 70, 99, 105
Cullen, Anthony   5, 135, 139, 166
Cullors, Patrisse   16
culture
   of assessment   87, 95–8
   awareness   82
   competence   79, 82
   constructionism   95
   imperialism   94
   practices   20
   relativism   36, 156
   Western   20, 60
Cunningham, S.   99
curriculum   2, 4, 11–13, 15, 18, 26, 28, 30, 40, 46, 49, 58, 60, 63–8, 71, 73, 98, 162, 167, 168
   content   89
   decolonized   4, 15, 49, 63, 68–71, 77–8, 96
   design   3, 4, 29, 38, 50, 75, 85, 168
   engineering   57
   Eurocentric   74–6
   formal   62
   hidden   62
   inclusive   13, 71, 75, 77
   rise of   7–10
Cushman, E.   132

Daswani, Girish   96
decoloniality   10, 18, 66, 126
"Decolonise UCL" campaign   8
Decolonising DMU   9
Decolonising the Arts Curriculum Zine   9
Decolonising the Arts Institute   9
Decolonising the Curriculum Movement campaign   72
"Decolonize Sussex" campaign   9
decolonizing movement   2, 12, 163, 164, 168
Decolonizing SOAS Working Group   9
Dei, G. J. S.   13
Delgado, R.   18
De Lissovoy, N.   64, 65
"Demarginalizing the Intersection of Race and Sex: A Black Feminist Critique of Antidiscrimination Doctrine, Feminist Theory and Antiracist Politics" (Crenshaw)   21
de Montaigne, Michel   96
De Montfort University (DMU)   9, 111, 112
Dennis, C. A.   22, 113
Derry, S. J.   145
developing and decolonizing   26–8
developmental activity   2, 56
developmental dialogue   28–35, 46
Dewey, J.   3, 116
Dewey Decimal   83
Dhillion, J.   39
digital tools   93
discussion   1–4, 6, 7, 12, 14, 15, 19, 20, 22, 23, 25, 27, 28, 31, 32, 54, 59, 81
diversity   6, 56, 57, 105–7, 141, 147–52
Diversity Book Display Initiative   69
Di Vesta, F. J.   144
Dixson, A. D.   18, 19, 21
Doharty, N.   27
Domínguez, M.   55
Dowling, F.   165
Dumbrill, G. C.   21, 91
Dunham, Joanne   4, 63, 66, 69, 71, 84

Eddo-Lodge, R.   122
education   12, 52, 73, 76
   anti-racist   72
   contemporary   151
   intercultural   70
   multicultural   94

race and 7, 15–22
relationship 54
system 8, 11
technology and 95
Education Excellence Programme 78, 82
"Edulingualism" 136, 139
Eizadirad, A. 70
electronic portfolios 97
Elmahdi, Rahma 5, 113–17, 121, 122, 135, 143, 164
embedded support 59
employability skills 70
English as primary language 4, 92, 93
English for Academic Purposes (EAP) 129, 136–9
English Language Teachers (ELT) 92, 138, 139
epistemology 73
Equality Act (2010) 17, 157
Equality Challenge Unit 15, 106
Equality Diversity and Inclusion (EDI) 44, 81
equality/inequality 5, 8, 9, 15, 16, 19, 21, 25, 32, 37, 44, 50, 72, 75, 76, 117–22, 125, 143
Eurocentrism/Eurocentricity 22, 38, 51, 56, 71, 77, 94, 113, 114, 146, 147, 149, 164
European Convention of Human Rights 157
European industrialization 150
European Union (EU) Law 156, 157
exam-based assessment strategies 97

Fairnington, Emilie 5, 117–22
Fanon, Frantz 140
#FeesMustFall protests 8
Felix, M. 14
Fellows of the Higher Education Academy 24
feminist linguistic activism 131
feminist theory 12
Ferguson, R. 12
Flintoff, A. 165
Floyd, George 16
focused discussion groups 59
Fomunyam, K. G. 11, 57
formal review processes 3, 62
Foster, Elizabeth 82
Foucault, M. 104

Frankenberg, R. 20
Fraser, S. P. 64
Friedberg, J. 14
Fung, D. 28
Futsal World Cup 120

Gandhi, Mahatma 140
Garza, Alicia 16
Gebrial, D. 10, 60
gender
  bias 36, 131
  identities 131
  language 131
Gibbs, P. 67
Gimenez, J. 136, 139
globalization 60
Gohlan, N. 89
Goldsmiths College 57, 61
Goldsmith University 69
Goldsmith University Library 78
Gomes, M. 93
good development 2, 23–6
Good Immigrant (Shukla) 80
Gopal, P. 15
Gorski, P. C. 70
Green, J. 21, 91
Griffiths, D. E. 37
Grossmann, M. 87
Guardian, The 15, 38, 122
Guy, T. C. 126

Hadlow College 108
Haffner, D. 13
Hall, J. 132
Hall, Stuart 150
Hamp-Lyons, L. 137
Harris, C. I. 19
Hayes, C. C. 163
hegemony 6, 10, 22, 28, 51, 92, 101, 165
HE Sport 112, 117, 120
heteronormativity 89–90
higher education (HE) 1, 2, 5, 7, 13, 14, 17–19, 23, 47, 52, 60, 63, 65, 70, 72, 87, 93, 96, 103, 104, 105, 107, 127, 136, 140, 158, 163, 168
  Eurocentric curriculum in 74–6
  institutions 3, 4, 9, 74
  issues 6
  professional development in 24
  studies 52, 67, 96

Higher Education Policy Institute
    (HEPI)   14
Higher Education Statistics Agency
    (HESA)   147
Hornsby, D. J.   70
Houghton, A. M.   13
"How to Break into the Elite" (2019)   154
Huber, L.   122
Hughes-Watkins, L'ael   78, 83
human rights   142, 143, 156
Human Rights Law   156, 157
hybrid pedagogy   94
Hyland, K.   137

Icaza, R.   51, 141
Idowu-Onibokun, Bernadine   2, 23,
    35–40, 46, 47, 133
Imperial College London   41, 114
Inclusive Curriculum Stream   78
inclusivity   1, 6, 7, 18, 35, 39–40, 46, 54,
    110, 164
    vs. decolonizing   13–15
    passive   4, 87–91
Indian Civil Service   151
informal formative assessments   59
information exchange   94
information literacy skills   77–9, 82
Institute for Policy Studies in
    Education   97, 159
interactive learning process   65
International Law   156, 157
intersectionality   19, 21, 46, 147
Is Our Curriculum White? campaign   78

Jalilipour, Katayoun   131
Johnson, A.   90
Johnston, L.   23
Jones, Peter   5, 6, 96, 135
Joseph-Salisbury, R.   27
journal indexing   60–1

Keele University   9
Kernohan, D.   105
Kibirige, Nelly   2, 23, 35, 42, 46, 47, 131,
    132
Killick, D.   165
King's College London (KCL)   41
Kipchoge, Eluid   146
knowledge   74, 144
    indigenous   13

production   51, 52, 58, 60, 61, 65,
    131–3
types   72
Western   13, 84
Kukla, A.   145
Kupatadze, K.   29

La Belle, T. J.   60
Ladson-Billings, G.   18
Lander, V.   13
language choices   92, 93
Lau, J.   16
learning   2–6, 7, 9–14, 19, 22, 26, 66, 88.
    See also teaching
    activity   59, 110
    environment   7, 9, 18, 26, 43, 44, 46,
      51, 55, 57, 64, 108–10, 128, 131,
      159, 168
    online   81, 93–5, 141
    styles   43, 80, 144, 145
Leeds University Union   8
Left of Brown   27
Le Grange, L.   10, 11
Leibowitz, B.   49
Leonardo, Z.   18
lesbian, gays, bisexuals and transsexuals
    (LGBT)   58
Leung, Constant   151
liaison activities   78, 80, 82, 83
Liao, W.   138
"Liberate our Curriculum" initiative   69
"Liberate our degrees" initiative   69
Liberate our Library, Goldsmiths   78
librarians   77, 80, 82
libraries   4, 63, 69
    academic   77–8, 80, 82, 83
    role in decolonizing curricula   78–9
    TRAAC in   79–84
Library of Congress   83
lived experiences   35, 61, 63, 68, 75–7,
    81, 107, 161, 166
Liyanage, Mia   14
London Metropolitan University   97, 159
London South Bank University   2, 42
London University   149
Lorde, A.   12, 19
Louie, D. W.   98
Luckett, K.   95
Lusted, D.   51
Lyons, N.   3

Macfarlane, B.   127
McGregor, H. E.   26, 28
McLaughlin, J. M.   18
Madriaga, M.   27
Mahtani, A.   88–9
Malcolm, I.   92
Maloney, M. M.   69
Mandela, Nelson   140
Manglitz, E.   126
marginalization   58, 73–5
marginalized groups   58, 89, 165
Martin, F.   10
Masoca, S.   122
mass protests   17
Maxwele, Chumani   7, 8
Mbembe, A.   54
Meda, L.   13, 58, 68
Menegatti, M.   131
Merriweather, L. R.   126
Mgqwashu, E.   11
Michael, Savvas   5, 6, 92, 93, 135
microaggressions   76, 114, 122–3
Middlesex University   140
Miller, P.   17, 106
"Miseducation: decolonising curricula, culture and pedagogy in UK universities" (Liyanage)   14
modernity/modernization   149, 150
module choice   39
morality   36
Morgan, H.   13
Morgan, Winston   38
Morreira, S.   95
Morris, S. M.   94
Morrison, N.   164
Moy, R. G.   89, 90
multiculturalism   56, 60, 72, 77, 104
multicultural society   44, 72–4, 105, 168
Muslim community   30
Muslim Council of Britain (MCB)   30

Nagpal, S.   29
National Union of Students   17, 18, 61
Native American Museum and Technology Workshop   95
Nego True   118
New School of Biomedical Sciences   41
Niculescu, I. O   29
nondiscrimination   142, 143
non-European societies   149

Norfolk, Kate   154
NUS Black Students conference   9
Nwadeyi, L.   73

Office for Students   37
Officers of the Students Union   80
Ogden, J.   94
Oladimeji, M.   13
Olaleye, F.   71
Oldham, S.   39
O'Mahony, J.   32
oppression   8, 19–21, 27
Osman, R.   70
O'Sullivan, S.   96

"parallel boundaries"   18, 19
Pauwels, A.   131
pedagogy   2, 7, 9, 12, 26, 28, 29, 43, 50, 51, 60, 65–8, 70, 73, 75–7, 80, 98, 104, 125, 164, 168
peer-assisted learning activities   59
Pennycook, A.
people of color   27, 74, 75
Perry, B.   129
personal development   5, 25, 121
Pete, S.   10
Peters, M. A.   40, 76
Phillips, J.   102
Piaget, J.   144
Pirbhai-Illich, F.   10
Pohawpatchoko, C.   95
police brutality   16
Portelli, J. P.   62
Postgraduate Certificate in Higher Education (PGCert in HE) program   24, 55
power dynamics   10, 42–3, 51–4, 90, 97, 116, 117, 166
   in classroom   125–8, 133, 134, 165
   as product of teaching approaches   129–31
Prevent Strategy   30
Prince Ea   118
problem solving   70
professional development   2, 24, 25, 121
professional trust   127–8
Prosser, M.   29, 52, 64

quality review processes   30
"Queer Bodies" (Jalilipour)   131

race   32, 57
  divisions   11
  inequity   18, 19, 21
  privilege   20
"Race, Relational Trust, and Teacher Retention in Wisconsin Schools"   127
Race Equality Charter Mark   41
Race Relations (Amendment) Act (2000)   17
racism   9, 10, 27, 72, 75, 76, 122, 149, 154
Ragavan, Anjana   10
Raju, C. K.   150
Ramaswamy, C.   28
Read@Leicester campaign   80
Rees, R.   29
reflection and reflexivity   3–5, 31, 113–17, 121
reflective practice   55, 82, 116, 121, 165
Regan, P.   53, 143
Reilly, Dawn   5, 6, 97, 135, 158, 166
"Represent" campaign   80
Rhodes, Cecil   7, 8
Rhodes Must Fall campaign   8, 17, 78, 149, 163
Richards, Aisha   9
Richardson, J. V., Jr.   94
Robert, V.   53
Rodney, Walter   150
Rodriguez, Jenny   27
Rogers, A.   25
Rubini, M.   131

Said, Edward   37, 150
Sanford, K.   97
Santoro, N.   13
scholarship   1, 18, 27, 50, 88, 149
Schön, D. A.   3, 116
School of Oriental and African Studies (SOAS)   9, 61, 149
school system   40, 53
self-reflection and self-reflexivity   113–17
seminars   24, 52, 141
Shades of Noir (SoN)   9, 131
Shay, S.   12
Sheikhzade, M.   68
Shilliam, R.   49
Shukla, Nikesh   80

Simpson, L.   90, 91
Singh, G.   121, 122
Sisters of Resistance   27
slavery   17, 150
Smith, J. M.   89
Smith, L. T.   31, 60
Smolicz, J. J.   165
social constructivism   5, 143–6
social justice   9, 27, 142
social media   9, 27, 34, 84, 145
Society of College, National and University Libraries (SCONUL)   81
Sociology   149, 150, 152
Solicitor Regulation Authority   153
Solorzano, D.   122
South Africa   7, 8, 57, 68, 92
South African History Online   7
Spoken Word   118
staff. *See also* student(s)
  development   165
  perceptions   4, 101–23
Staples, L.   27
'stay woke'   27–8
Stefancic, J.   18
Stellenbosch University   92
stereotypes   21, 36, 56, 73, 74, 76, 104, 125
Stevenson, J.   28
Stewart, T.   129
St. Mary's Medical School   144
Stommel, J.   94
storytelling   54–5
Stovall, D.   22
Strayhorn, T. L.   91
Student Ambassadors   33
student-centered approach   52
Student Champions   80, 81
student(s)
  Aboriginal   92
  activists   8
  BAME   17, 19, 22, 29, 35–40, 42, 57, 61, 67, 70, 74–7, 97, 101, 106, 112, 121, 122, 147, 148, 150, 152–9, 162
  belonging   2, 4, 5, 14, 26, 30, 46, 55, 57, 69, 87, 89, 91–3, 101, 131, 132, 165
  Chinese   129, 137, 138

commuter 67, 158, 160
engagement 2, 4, 46, 57, 71, 95, 129
experience 4–6, 14, 26, 29, 35, 46, 57, 61, 63, 64, 88, 102, 110, 140, 167, 168
feedback 34, 95, 125
led campaigns 9
medical 5
perceptions 5, 29, 44, 57, 65, 87, 101–23, 131
protest 8, 29
role models for 101
roles 29
shared connections 43–4, 55, 57, 107, 116
voices 3, 4, 9, 29, 30, 32, 34–8, 46, 53, 63, 68–71, 85, 95, 111–12
White 6, 17, 22, 67, 70, 74, 106, 122, 148, 150, 152
working with 28–35
Student Staff Committees 80
student-staff partnership 29, 67
Students Union 8–9, 33, 35, 42, 57, 78, 80
Subject Benchmark Statement for Sociology 150
subjugation 8, 125
Suli Breaks 118
Swart, R. 67
system-based approach 65
systemic racism 16, 73

Tajino, A. 129
Tajino, Y. 129
Tate IV, W. F. 18
Taylor, Breonna 16
teacher-centered approach 52, 97
teacher(s) 32, 33, 99, 107
  education 55
  training courses 30, 65
  White 127
teaching 2–3, 6, 7, 9–14, 19, 22, 26. *See also* learning
  activities 39–40, 82
  approaches 42–3, 51–4, 63, 79–80, 129–31, 133, 140, 154, 159
  decolonizing essentials 113–17
  face-to-face 5
  inclusive 78

online 129, 130
practices 4, 87, 167
team 129–30
Teaching, Relationship, Activity and Assessment, and Content (TRAAC) model 1–6, 26, 35, 42–7, 63, 85, 101, 112–13, 115, 117, 121, 135, 144, 147, 157, 162, 167, 169
  in Academic English context 136–9
  in accounting module 158–61
  activity and assessment 35–40, 45–6, 58–9, 82, 141–2, 155, 159–60
  content 45, 59–62, 83–4, 142–3, 156, 160
  in field of law 152–7
  in library context 79–84
  overview 49–51
  Public Law teaching 139–43
  relationship 54–7, 80–1, 107, 112, 125, 140–1, 161
  teaching approach 51–4, 79–80, 125, 140, 159
Teaching and Learning Centre, Rhodes University 31
technology 4, 87, 93–5
The Library, Leicester 78, 81
Thomas, P. 136
Thurab-Nkhosi, D. 95
Tilbury, D. 164
Todd, K. L. 53
Tometi, Opal 16
Traditional Ecological Knowledge (TEK) 90
Tran, D. 66, 137
Transition Town Tooting (TTT) initiative 87–8
Trigwell, K. 29, 52, 64
Trowell, M. 33
Truscott, A. 92
Tuck, E. 10

'UAL so White' campaign 9
unconscious bias 4, 5, 15, 44, 46, 50, 55, 56, 68, 81, 115, 116, 121, 123, 137, 155, 165, 166
  impact on teaching and learning 102–5

learning environment and   108–10
   relationships and   101–2
unconscious bias training (UBT)   102, 104, 105, 123
United Kingdom (UK)   4, 7, 8, 13, 14, 17, 72–4, 78, 81, 87, 93, 104, 141–3, 156, 157, 160
United Kingdom Professional Standards Framework (UKPSF)   70
United Nations (UN)   156
United States   16, 18, 92
Universal Declaration of Human Rights (UDHR, 1948)   156
universities   6, 9, 13, 15, 18, 19, 22, 28, 31, 76, 169. *See also individual entries*
   campaigns   7, 8
   degree programs   77
   mass participation   147
   teachers   29, 107
   UK   14, 17, 57, 158
University College London (UCL)   8
University of Bolton (UoB)   110, 111
University of Cambridge   155
University of Cape Town (UCT)   7, 8
University of Law   152, 153, 157
University of Oxford   8, 17
University of Pretoria   92
University of Sussex   8
University of the Arts London (UAL)   9
University of West London   41
University of Wolverhampton   39

Valdez, K.   95
Vandeyar, S.   67, 103

Vázquez, R.   51, 141
virtual learning   91
Vygotsky, L. S.   138, 145, 146

Waddington, K.   68
Ward, C. R.   60
Warwick Open Education Series   8
wa Thiong'o, N.   92, 163
Weale, Sally   148
Wen, J.   16
Western-centrism   11, 20, 85, 137
Whatman, S. L.   18
whiteness   8, 13, 15, 19–20, 27, 71, 72, 75, 76, 147
White supremacy   8, 17, 73
WHO   16
"Why Is My Curriculum White?" (Peters)   40
"Why Is My Curriculum White?" (WIMCW) campaign   8, 72, 74
Why Isn't My Professor Black? campaign   74
Winter, J.   131
Womack, Peter   151
Woolmer, C.   65
workshops   24, 28, 52, 59, 80–2
Wuhan Municipal Health Commission   16

xenophobic attacks   16

Yang, K. W.   10
Yeager, David   126

Zavala, M.   90
Zembylas, M.   51, 104

www.ingramcontent.com/pod-product-compliance
Lightning Source LLC
Chambersburg PA
CBHW062221300426
44115CB00012BA/2168